A Friend in the Kitchen
Old Australian Cookery Books

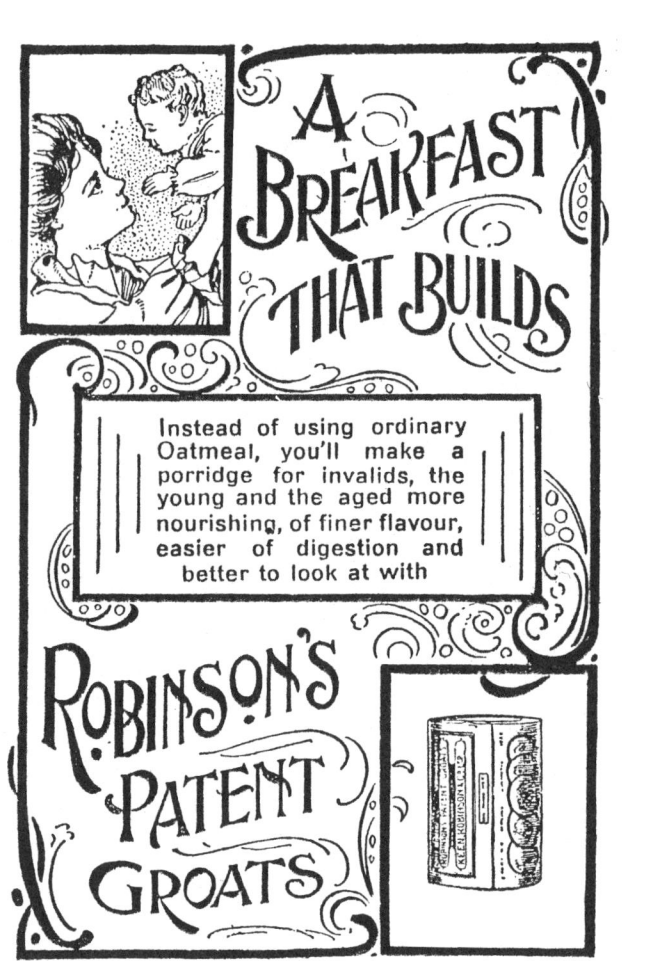

A Friend
in the
Kitchen
Old Australian Cookery Books

Colin Bannerman

Kangaroo Press

FOR LYN

companion in the gentle passion

Recipes and text from The Schauer Cookery book *are reproduced with permission of the copyright owners, Lansdowne Publishing Pty Ltd.*

Designed by Wing Ping Tong

© Colin Bannerman 1996

Published in 1996 by Kangaroo Press Pty Ltd
3 Whitehall Road Kenthurst NSW 2156 Australia
PO Box 6125 Dural Delivery Centre NSW 2158
Printed in Malaysia by SNP Offset (M) Sdn Bhd

ISBN 0 86417 805 0

Contents

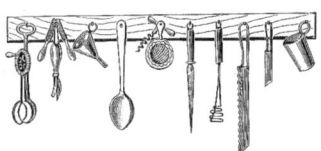

Explanations		6
Pre-prandial: The gentle passion		8
1	In search of Federation cookery	11
2	The Reformer	28
3	The Teachers	39
4	The Contributors	61
5	The Country Cooks	80
6	The Smart Cook	96
7	The Hotel Keeper	113
8	The Gas Cooker	123
9	The Advertisers	132
10	Festivities	137
11	Practicalities	152
12	The Awful Truth	173
13	Entrée or Breakfast?	184
14	Dining Federation-style	191
15	Sweeping up the Crumbs	206
Appendix 1 Who's Who		219
Appendix 2 What's What		221
Notes		234
References		242
Index		247

Explanations

Selected recipes have been reproduced to illustrate the style of dishes Federation cooks were aiming for and the instructions they had for arriving at them. They are therefore given in their original form (and without conversion to metric measurements), even though in some cases a few changes to quantities, cooking times or methods would be justified in modern kitchens. Experienced cooks who wish to try some of the recipes will have little difficulty in adapting them to their own requirements – after all, that is precisely what Federation cooks would have done.

Federation recipes routinely included salt amongst their ingredients for all savoury dishes. To avoid the tedium of repetition, references to it have been omitted from narrative descriptions except where an understanding of the dish demands otherwise. Salt should therefore be taken for granted. Pepper has been treated similarly, though many cooks were shy of it.

As a general practice the names of dishes have been given in *italics*, except where the reference is to a class of dishes, such as plum puddings, or to a standard culinary preparation, such as roux. Federation cooks were fond of naming dishes in French or a combination of French and English, but were not always careful with accents. To avoid drawing attention to their errors too often, accents have generally been restored except in quoted passages. Spelling and grammar have been left alone.

For the sake of authenticity, weights and measures have been kept in their original forms. They can be converted to modern expressions as follows:

1 oz	1 ounce	28.3 g
1 lb	1 pound	454 g
1 fl oz	1 fluid ounce	28.4 ml
1 gill	5 fl oz	142 ml
1 pt	1 pint	568 ml
1 qt	1 quart	1.14 litre
1 gal	1 gallon	4.55 litre

1 in	1 inch	25.4 mm
1 ft	1 foot	30.5 cm
1 mile	1.61 kilometres	

Federation currency can be converted to decimal as follows (though it should be remembered that actual purchasing power has diminished considerably):

£1	1 pound	2 dollars
1s or 1/-	1 shilling (12 pence)	10 cents
1d	1 penny	5/6 cent
1 guinea	21 shillings	

Temperatures given in degrees Fahrenheit may be converted to Celsius by subtracting 32 and multiplying by 5/9.

PRE-PRANDIAL

The Gentle Passion

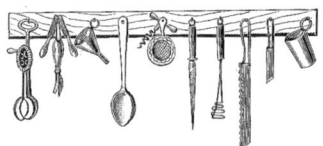

The gentle passion for lining one's walls with books which others have discarded – that harmless and agreeable disease known as *antiquarian bibliomania* – opens up a wealth of possibilities for learning about early Australian cooking.[1]

The gentle passion that converts the most reasonable and restrained personality into an unashamed fossicker, whose map of the world is a directory of second-hand bookshops; who searches even among the *quality antiquarians*, dealers in ancient leather, to whom 'old cookbooks' are *infra dignitatem*. 'I believe we might have a Mrs Beeton, but would be all.' (And the Mrs Beeton is hardly ever *really* old.)

The gentle passion that turns the head unconsciously to any shop that might hold possibilities, now or in the future, and adds it to the map. That revels in the musty nose of old books, is not put off by a torn page or worn endpapers, and finds marginal annotations positively *interesting*.

The gentle passion that is cheerfully tolerant of the book recyclers to whom 1970 is *old*, that is undeterred by the dusty chaos of junk shops (at least for as long as it takes to rummage through the boxes of old books in the corner), that carries always its list of books acquired and books wanted and seeks out not only the first edition (while rarely finding it) but later editions that might cast light on how a book developed with the years.

The gentle passion that sheds all reason and restraint when the *Australian Aristologist* at last comes up for sale.[2]

This passion, more interested in contents than in bindings, places one not within the worshipful company of book collectors but just beyond its fringe. For old cookery books were utilitarian things; they were used, used up and thrown away. Their covers were plain; their typesetting untidy. They were not works of art: their illustrations were of cuts of beef or of how to truss a chicken. They were not works of literature, but instruction manuals; yet even here lovers of language can find a charming turn of phrase, a gentle witticism, an amusing malapropism or an engaging piece of down-to-earth advice on some matter whose importance has long since passed.

In these old books we find what people thought they *should* be cooking, what they thought they should be *seen* to be cooking and what they were *actually* cooking. Here we find how they were taught to cook and how they actually cooked. We find how the various dishes were supposed to be made and how they were actually made. We see British migrant cooks trying to preserve their past and to make a new future at the same time, for these old books are not about Australian cookery so much as about the translation of British cookery to Australia. Behind them all were colonists clinging to the food and culture of their homeland, trying to make a little England in this foreign place – it was a losing battle, though nearly a hundred years passed before that seems to have been widely understood.

The seasons were upside-down, but that was no serious inconvenience except at Christmastide, when summer heat challenged heavy feasting. Cities and towns grew quickly and were well supplied with English food. Meat was so cheap that many chose to eat it three times a day. In the country, where the proper ingredients were not always 'to hand', they accepted the limitation of their diet or became adaptors and improvisers.

Native foods could have relieved the dreadful monotony of salt meat, flour, sugar and tea and made them less reliant on supplies, yet very little attention was ever given to native resources and Aboriginal know-how, except for the possibilities of native game.

On the whole, our forebears seemed determined to ignore the riches around them and to implant a familiar but unsuitable cookery. In much the same way, town and city dwellers bought their vegetables from John Chinaman, but made no attempt to learn his own ways with them.

By the end of Australia's first century of Federation Australians had turned away from most things British, yet as handbooks of British cookery in Australia the early books are full of interest. There were plenty of ideas for good eating. There was also plain cookery, some of it very plain indeed, the victim of convenience. There were ideas on exotic cookery (which often came down to ostentatious displays of expensive ingredients or elaborately decorated plainer food). There were tides of fashion driven by the same endless search for novelty that shapes the dishes appearing in modern restaurants and magazines. There were ideas on 'foreign' foods, always adapted and usually misunderstood.

For the modern browser there is the challenge of understanding the unexplained, for writers of cookery books usually assumed that their readers understood the common terms and methods of the day. And there are insights into how households were run, what domestic products were marketed and how they were marketed. In short, there is much these old books can teach us about what domestic life was like as Australia faced the twentieth century.

This book is an unashamedly self-indulgent browse through these treasures of Australian history.

It is not a cookery book, but a book *about* cookery books – those which might have been found in the kitchens of Australia around the time of Federation. Its purpose is to open up an area of Australian social history that is too often glossed over by the historians with a few easy generalisations and quotes, and by the nostalgia merchants with charming little collections of old recipes and photographs or illustrations. It is intended for people who have an interest in social history and who enjoy their food.

I have taken the Federation period as beginning in 1888, when Australia celebrated its first centenary. This is arbitrary, but justified, since the wave of nationalistic sentiment stirred up by those celebrations must have been one of the driving forces towards federation of the colonies. I have taken it as ending formally in 1914 when Australia first went to war as a nation. This date was also a turning point for national identity, though its significance here lies mainly in the changes which wartime economy brought into households, kitchens and cookery. Those changes were clear enough to mark the end of a culinary era.

The setting is Britain's emergence from the conservative preoccupations of its Victorian age towards the brief splendour of Edwardianism, the flowering elegance of *art nouveau* and Australia's adoption of the form (in advance of the substance) of national unity. These developments have been well documented by others.

My aim is to describe the coming out of Australian cookery from its colonial kitchens and its shaky and somewhat unconvincing assertion of independence. For it was in this same period that Australians, faced with the odd contradictions between the English pretensions of the cities and the inevitable coarseness of bush manners, came to some reluctant conclusions. They began to accept that much of the British household domestic order was unsuitable for Australian conditions and should give way to a specifically Australian order – in short, that *Mrs Beeton* would not do here. Australian cookery books were needed and the period that marked Federation also founded the tradition of writing and buying our own.

CHAPTER 1

IN SEARCH OF FEDERATION COOKERY

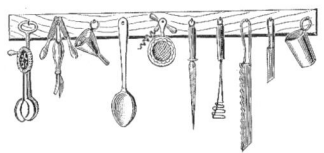

It is well to establish from the outset what Federation cookery was all about. Mrs Lance Rawson went to the heart of the matter when she said in 1895:

> Man must be cooked for. He'll do without his shirt-buttons, and he'll do without his slippers, but he will not do without his dinner, nor is he inclined to accept excuses as regards under- or over-done meals after the first week or so of the honeymoon. If there be any young girls reading these pages who are contemplating marriage in the near future, take an old wife's advice and learn to cook, for only by feeding him well will you succeed in gaining your husband's respect and keeping his affection. The husband is a creature of appetite, believe me, and not to be approached upon any important matter, such as a new bonnet or a silk dress, on an empty stomach.[1]

One may cringe at the accepted sexism in these words, but there is no escaping the fact that Australian home life was dominated by considerations of practicality and the comfort of the husband. Housekeeping, also known as 'domestic duties', was the sole employment of most women at the end of the nineteenth century.

The woman's duties were largely defined by her husband's station in life. Wives of working-class men could expect to spend their lives washing, sewing, cleaning, cooking, bearing babies and caring for children. In the country there would be additional chores: tending poultry, the household dairy, gathering and preserving fruits and vegetables for winter use, salting meat, curing hams, and so on. Middle class households would engage what domestic help they could, from casual female labour to live-in nurse, maid and cook. While adding a task of supervision, this lightened the burden of physical work and generally enabled the women of such households to engage in limited social activities and practical charity work according to their rank. In wealthy households housekeeping was entirely a matter of organising staff to do the work; the ladies were expected to pass their time in artistic pursuits, letter-writing, making social calls and supporting charitable causes – but their chief duty was to arrange for the comfort of their husbands.

In the beginning, the household order in Australia was essentially that brought from England. *Warne's Model Cookery*, one of the many British books that served as early models for Australian colonists, included among its hints to housekeepers this stern warning:

> On the Lady of the house devolves the task of providing food for her household; it should be her care that no waste or ignorant misuse shall squander the property of her husband – most frequently the bread-winner for the family – and that nothing is lost by carelessness or bad cookery. She is to take care that there is no lack through fault of hers, nor any drawback to domestic comfort through injudicious rule; no neglect caused by the love of idle pleasure.[2]

Mixed reports

The British order was soon adapted to conditions in the new country, and by the end of the nineteenth century some patterns of household management, food and eating were markedly different from those in Britain. Many migrants and visitors to the colonies recorded their observations of these differences, and of the Australian way of life generally, for the benefit of the folks back home.

The Reverend James Morison was said to be the first Presbyterian clergyman to settle in the New England area of New South Wales. After 13 years in the interior he recorded his observations of the country and the colonial way of life in his 1867 book *Australia as it is* (and in it offered the startling insight that Australia, in its physical outlines and configuration, could be likened to the 'dropping from a cow').[3] He observed that 'the consumption of animal food is very great in the Australian colonies. Beef or mutton is the principal dietary in the three meals a day, and every individual is estimated to consume a bullock in the year.' He described a number of native fruits, including something he called 'manna' from the peppermint tree. 'There are strawberries, currants, an uneatable orange, and pears, with varieties of small berries in the scrubs, but all are of little account. The native currants, perhaps, claim some importance from being seen in great quantities in Sydney markets for sale. They are sent there in a green state, and are used in making tarts. The only really valuable wild fruit is the raspberry – more properly, the bramble – found in cold districts, and largely used by the settlers in making preserves. One seldom hears complaints of the want of fruit.'

Morison continued with a discussion of the propagation of imported fruit and suggestions as to where to grow all the varieties of fruit enjoyed back home. He noted that in times of drought the want of vegetables was often severely felt. Wealthy stock-owners were usually well provided in their stores with pickles and preserved potatoes, but these articles of consumption were too expensive for the working people. Along the coast, and on the dividing ranges, pumpkins, all the varieties of melons, English vegetables and fruit, such as peaches and apricots, were grown plentifully. 'In the interior, however, and where hot scorching winds prevail in summer, the fruit is roasted on the trees, and no succulent vegetable of any kind is able to stand the withering heat.'

Mrs George Cross arrived from England in 1870 and lived in Victoria as the wife of an Anglican clergyman. To supplement the household income she published many books under the name Ada Cambridge. In 1903 she wrote for her readers at home:

> Living, *i.e.*, feeding, in Australia is proverbially good, although the cooking is often unworthy of the material. Few in the land are, perhaps I should say were, they who do (or did) not sit down to a meat meal three times a day. Fruit that in England was nursed in orchard-houses and counted on south walls we could batten on now; a few pence would heap the sideboard with grapes or apricots, but all was so plentiful that it generally cost us nothing. Wine was not what it is now, and we could not at once break ourselves of our English beer; but it was not long before we learned to prefer the product of the local vineyards, to which we shall remain faithful to our lives' end. We got it, as we do still, in large stone jars, at less than the price of Bass or Guinness. With a poultry yard and a cow, and John Chinaman's vegetables, even a poor parson could live like a prince...[4]

The reference to John Chinaman was a recognition of the contribution of the Chinese immigrants, who came primarily to work the gold fields and then turned to market gardening.

Nat Gould was a journalist who arrived in Australia from England in 1884. He worked for newspapers and sporting journals in Brisbane, Sydney and Bathurst. In 1896 he wrote:

> Fruit is very cheap in the colonies – and what luscious fruit it is! A fruiterer's window in Sydney or Melbourne is a glorious sight in the season.
>
> Luscious grapes from three-halfpence up to sixpence a pound, as good as anyone could wish for. Peaches – and such peaches! – at a fraction

of the cost they are in London; a dozen peaches could often be bought in Sydney for the price of one decent-sized peach in London. Bananas at twopence a dozen when plentiful, apricots, melons, passion-fruit, guavas, Cape gooseberries, custard-apples, mangoes, pears, apples, walnuts, filberts, oranges – and such oranges! not half dead and leathery – tamarinds, pineapples, figs, strawberries (dear), damsons, lemons, plums, citrons, etc. These are fruits named at random as I think of a shop-window in Sydney. In Brisbane I have bought good juicy pineapples at threepence a dozen, and I have no doubt a cartload could be had for half the price a respectable English pineapple costs. Fruit-growers around Sydney complain that it hardly pays expenses to send the fruit to market. At Ryde, or near it, I have seen bushels of fruit rotting on the ground because of a glut in the market.[5]

Parrot pie

The 1892 *Mrs Beeton's Cookery Book* included a section on Australian cookery that had some of the character of a report from the colonies. It was not a supplement for Australian users of the book, but one of several sections on international cookery included for British readers who enjoyed novelty. It commented:

> The only difference in provisions in Australia may be said to be that the supply is so far more abundant there than here. Almost everything we consume can be found there cheaper and more plentiful, and many of the luxuries of English food are within the reach of the poorest of the colonists.

The book defended Australian canned meat against the prejudice that was said still to exist amongst the poorer classes, and noted that in Australian towns fresh meat was much like English meat in quality, and very cheap. 'In up-country stations, where beasts are not stall fed,' the meat was not so good, but cheaper than in the towns; 'only the best parts are eaten, the inferior ones being wasted or going to feed the dogs'. Fish was plentiful, except that sole, a favourite of the English, was absent. Freshwater cod was considered superior to the English equivalent. Oysters were plentiful and cheap, and not considered a luxury. Fruit and vegetables were easy to grow and were therefore to be had in abundance.

The same book gave a selection of Australian recipes: oyster soup, kangaroo tail soup, parrot pie, roast wallaby, broiled cod steaks, pumpkin pie, preserved water melon rind (a round variety, not the large oval type now popular) and a moulded dessert of creamed rice with poached apricots. It was said that 'neither roast wallaby, which might be compared to our hares, nor parrot pie, not unlike one made of pigeons, would be found at the dinner-table in the hotels, but up country they are esteemed as very nice dishes.' This list illustrates the difficulties of summing up a body of cookery in a few dishes, even with the acknowledged bias toward novelty.

Oyster soup could be found in any respectable Federation cookery book. Recipes for pumpkin pie or tart and for kangaroo tail soup were not common, but given in a few books. A thorough search would also turn up roast wallaby, preserved melon and parrot pie. I never found a recipe for broiled cod steaks.

Class distinctions

Many of the 'lower orders' who came to escape the grinding poverty they had endured in Ireland, Scotland or parts of England found their prospects much improved, but from a base so low that any account of what they cooked and ate is bound to leave a poor opinion of Australian cookery. Richard Twopenny, commenting on the scarcity of good domestic servants in the 1880s, illustrated the point well:

> Your Irish immigrant at eight and ten shillings a week has as often as not never been inside any other household than her native hovel, and stares in astonishment to find that you don't keep a pig on your drawing-room sofa. On entering your house, she gapes in awe of what she considers the grandeur around her, and the whole of her first day's work consists of ejaculating 'Lor' and 'Goodness!'[6]

Twopenny had left England as a child when his father was appointed Archdeacon of Flinders in 1865. From his position of relative comfort he also described the food in Australia and compared it with that back home. He considered that generally Australian food, while cheaper and more plentiful, was poorer in quality than that in England. The 'working-man', for whom cheapness and availability were more important than quality, was therefore immeasurably better off than in England.

> Up-country the meat is excellent; but in the towns it is not, as a rule, so good as in England, as the sheep and cattle have often to be driven long distances before they are slaughtered... Neither vegetables nor fruit, as sold in the markets and shops, are as good as those you buy in England. The inferior quality is due to the grow-as-you-please manner in which the fruit is cultivated, pruning and even the most ordinary care being neglected; but you *can* get as fine-flavoured fruit here as

anywhere, and to taste grapes in perfection you must certainly go to Adelaide.

Of course meat is the staple of Australian life. A working-man whose family did not eat meat three times a day would indeed be a phenomenon. High and low rich and poor, all eat meat to an incredible extent, even in the hottest weather. Not that they know how to prepare it in any delicate way, for to the working and middle, as well as to most of the wealthy classes, cooking is an unknown art. The meat is roast or boiled, hot or cold, sometimes fried or hashed. It is not helped in mere slices, but in good substantial hunks. In everything the colonist likes quantity.

Thus Twopenny's opinions of 'up-country' meat as compared with town meat and of the quality of fruit and vegetables as compared with those sold in England were the exact opposites of those in the Beeton book.

Tea was the national beverage. A large majority of the population drank it with every meal, even, Twopenny observed, in the metropolitan middle classes. Beer – either English or 'colonial' – ranked next in popularity but was taken at public houses rather than at meals. ('There is no trade at which more fortunes have been made here than the publican's.') Champagne was a social necessity for parties among the wealthy. The top French houses seem

to have done good trade with Australia – labels such as Moët and Roëderer were mentioned – but 'most champagnes, like all other wines, [were] "specially prepared for the Australian market," and you know what that means.'

The upper classes suffered by comparison with their counterparts in the old country. It seemed to Twopenny that poor quality of food supplies, a general shortage of competent cooks and a hundred years of making-do had blunted their sensibilities.

> If it be true that, while the French eat, the English only feed, we may fairly add that the Australians 'grub'... how can you expect a man who – for the greater part of his life – has been eating mutton and damper, and drinking parboiled tea three times a day, to understand the art of good living?

One suspects that either Twopenny had been tempted to exaggerate a little for the sake of attracting his readers' attention, or his childhood memories of food and dining in England were rosier than they deserved to be. However that may be, one does get a sense more generally throughout the early Australian literature on food and wine, of an upper crust which had a fond collective memory of fine dining in the old country and a determination to maintain that standard, while often falling just short of it. The collective memory may, of course, have been flavoured with a drop or two of nostalgia essence, improving the legend of Victorian English dining beyond the reality of it. Perhaps, too, there was a tendency to take as the standard of English cookery the finest meal enjoyed or heard of rather than the average (they would not have taken the worst). A similar problem stands in the way of any retrospective appreciation of food and eating habits: did they really eat as well (or badly) as that, every day?

The kitchen door

The hardships suffered by the upper classes are not the main concern of this book. Dwelling at the tables of the very rich, with their hare soup, salmon, roast turkey with truffles, and cabinet puddings – however badly all these may have been made by poorly trained cooks – will lead to little understanding of Federation cookery in general. At the other end of the scale there is little to be said of the mutton, bread and tea of the lower orders. It was the mass in the middle, the extended middle class in employment or private enterprise, with income somewhere between nearly adequate and distinctly comfortable, who did most to shape the character of Federation cookery. To find out what it was we must search for what middle class families ate and how it was cooked.

Mrs Rawson gave us a clue to set us on the search: look behind their kitchen doors.

> I saw an excellent idea in a friend's kitchen some little time ago. For the benefit of her servants she had written out all the recipes for their favourite puddings, cakes, etc., and a few special dishes of meat, and these were tacked up behind the door. And in another place she had the days of the week, with the duties for each day. It struck me as a capital idea for the housewife doing her own work. In the first case of the recipes, one often is puzzled for a moment to know what to make, and would perhaps not recall to mind some recipes till it was too late, whereas if it were there handy one would be grateful; and as regards the daily duties, the list would act as a good reminder very often.

How is it made? A Friend in the Kitchen will tell. (Anna Colcord's 1898 book)

A friend in the kitchen

What seemed a capital idea to Mina Rawson provides little help to anyone now trying to understand Australian Federation cooking and its common repertoire. Whatever was pinned behind the kitchen door in 1895 has long since disappeared; we can only guess at how many people may have taken up the idea. Some mistresses kept kitchen or household scrap-books. Queen Victoria herself kept one; it was later turned into a book by Elizabeth Craig.

A few Australian scrap-books have survived and some of them make interesting reading. However, as sources of history they leave much to be desired. Great-grandma's scrap-book is evidence that she knew of a dish, not (unless the page is annotated or heavily stained) that she made it regularly, or indeed at all. It is the evidence of one; how many other great-grandmas included a recipe for the same dish in their scrap-books? To build up a general understanding of Australian food and eating habits we would need perhaps thousands of great-grandmas' scrap-books.

Newspapers are favourite sources of information for researchers, but they present the same problems as scrap-books. Publication of a recipe is not evidence that a dish was commonly made: was it published in response to popular demand or as an item of novelty or passing interest, which may or may not be taken up by readers? We need to remember that newspaper or magazine food columnists rarely take it on themselves to provide systematic or basic instruction; items of novelty, curiosity or fashion attract better reader support. A glance at food columns in modern newspapers should be enough to show that what is published there may have little relevance to what people commonly cook and eat.

Oral history – what people can talk about from memory – is of little use in a search for Federation cookery. Too many generations have applied their own filters to memories of what was once popular: forgetting dishes that have lost their appeal, reinterpreting old recipes, adding new favourites. Besides, most people's understanding of traditional food is based on what they were fed as children, not on what came out of their great-grandmother's kitchen. Oral history is more useful in learning about more recent customs in cooking and eating.

The problems of drawing on informal and anecdotal sources for recipes are well illustrated by the many *nostalgia books* that have been published in recent years. Their theme is familiar: a few snippets of history, some old photographs or charming pen-and-ink drawings, a small collection of recipes (usually unsourced) and some household hints. Perhaps the recipes are drawn from family tradition (handed down by great-grandma orally or in her scrap-book), from old newspaper cuttings or even from an old cookery book or two. The basis for selecting them is rarely, if ever, explained, but it usually seems to boil down to whatever attracts the attention of the compiler – 'granny food' and curiosity dishes have always been popular, even if they were not particular favourites in their day.

Old cookery books

Old cookery books, especially those whose writers have made some attempt to provide systematic and comprehensive collections, are perhaps the richest source. The best of the household lore and the most popular of the scrap-books and newspaper recipes usually found their way into published works. However, even they have their limitations.

Some dishes were probably thought to be so simple or common that hardly anyone bothered to include them in a book (or, for that matter, in a newspaper column or personal scrap-book). Although, for example, one can find recipes for boiled egg, toast, tea and coffee, it is certain that they do not appear in the books as often as they appeared on the table. At first glance one may gain little appreciation from old cookery books of the dominance at daily meals of beef and mutton, plain roast or boiled. Few directions were given. However, the evidence is there in the many recipes for variations on the theme, to be called upon when the family is tired of the same old thing, and for dishes which use up left-overs.

Other dishes were probably included for the sake of completeness or to lend a touch of class, with no great expectation that they would often be made. As long as writers or compilers had differing ideas of what was classy, no such dishes would occur frequently enough to be reckoned in the main body of cookery. But if it were commonly thought that any good book of recipes should tell you how to roast a pheasant, though few people expected ever to have one, or how to braise a calf's head, though few people might ever have wanted one, then the frequency of such dishes in print would certainly be misleading.

When looking to old cookery books for the light they can shed on the eating habits and fashions of their time it is important to consider why they were written and who was intended to use them. There are four main groups: *documentary, educational, personal* and *contributory*.

The gatherers

In the first group are *documentary* collections, each of which aims to lay out a representative sample of the food of a region or nation. The food of provincial France, for example, has inspired a host of such books and there must be few national cuisines left that cannot boast at least one. Documentary collections of this sort can be enormously interesting, adding to our knowledge of cultures and of lifestyles with which we have little daily contact, and stimulating our interest in different foods and approaches to cooking. We may try some of the recipes out of interest and even take a few of them into our cooking repertoire.

Producing a worthwhile documentary collection is a daunting task. Even if the search is confined to a small geographic area, the work of identifying every local dish is formidable in all but the simplest of cultures. But the real problem is to select the dishes to be included in such a way as to produce a book which is comprehensive and representative. To collect only the most common and easily found dishes may be to leave out those which are important on special occasions but are not made every day. To pay too much attention to unusual or interesting dishes may exaggerate their importance (while nevertheless enhancing the general appeal of the book and sparing the writer some drudgery – little wonder that most documentaries are samplers rather than systematic collections). Not all the documentaries are what they pretend to be: some of the glossy 'Australian cookery' books of the 1980s and 1990s owe more to imagination in a test kitchen than to field research.

The shortcomings of such books need not bother us overmuch; Federation cookery escaped the gatherers.

The teachers

A second group is more plainly educational in purpose. Many books, such as Anna Colcord's *A Friend in the Kitchen* or *What to cook and how to cook it* have been written to teach how common dishes are properly made or to provide instruction for beginners in the general principles and techniques of cookery, basic preparations and the simplest dishes. Some include a wider range of everyday dishes, and even a few advanced ones, in order to provide in one handy volume everything a developing cook would need to know. The *Commonsense Cookery Book* was compiled by the Public School Cookery Teachers' Association of New South Wales for use in primary schools.[7] Countless thousands of young women, faced with the task of putting their cookery studies into practice, have turned instinctively to this little textbook which told them everything from how to make porridge and buttered toast to how to reheat roast beef and to make salmon cakes, stuffed tomatoes and *date roly-poly*. And at Christmas they turned to it for the Christmas pudding and Christmas cake. These books are useful as a source of history because their very purpose was to present the common core of cookery: the dishes that every competent cook of the day needed to be able to make.

Many other educational books are written not as primers, but as more general reference manuals of cookery. They may include instructions on basic techniques and preparations or assume that these have been mastered and that only a general reference is needed.[8] They are the books to which more experienced cooks could turn to find directions for a wide range of dishes which they might be expected to be able to make, if not every day. They would be indispensable to inexperienced cooks thoroughly familiar with only a few dishes and uncertain about how best to make many others. They could be a ready help to more experienced cooks seeking ideas for new or different dishes. Many early Australian cookery books were of this kind.

The first full-scale British cookery book appeared in 1660. *The Accomplisht Cook or the Art and Mystery of Cookery* was written by Robert May, a Paris-trained cook to the households of a number of members of the English Catholic nobility. It seems that England has never since been without at least one contemporary reference manual. Another important work was Charles Carter's *Complete Practical Cook: Or, a New System of the Whole Art and Mystery of Cookery* which was published in London in 1730. The most famous, whether deservedly or not, was Isabella Beeton's *Book of Household Management*. It was published in monthly supplements to Sam Beeton's *Englishwoman's Domestic Magazine* and then in one volume in 1861. Isabella Beeton died almost as soon as her great work was completed, but ever since then Britain and most other English-speaking countries have been supplied with a steady stream of new cookery books produced in her name.

Taken individually, reference books on cookery do not tell us much about what people commonly cooked because their purpose was to go well beyond what was commonplace. They tell us what dishes were *known*. From an encyclopaedic collection such as Mrs Beeton's it would be nearly impossible to identify the popular dishes of the period.

There is yet another group of books which might be classed as broadly educational: those written to promote change in some way or to teach about new or uncommon dishes or methods. Not general how-to-cook manuals, they are driven by some particular interest or concern of the writer. Vegetarian cooking, cooking with gas, cooking with some commercial product or even *cooking something different* are examples.[9] Most are not complete cookery manuals. An interesting example was a tiny volume of about 1915 called the *Milky Way Housewife's Book*, promoting Nestlé milk products. It contained recipes for puddings and cakes, a few household hints, advice on etiquette, a generous seasoning of proverbs and 'an amusing extract from a seventeenth-century work' on table etiquette. The book appears to have been adapted for Australia from a British original. Another was produced by a Sydney grocer, James Kidman in 1890 to promote his business. It gave a wide selection of recipes, laced with many product recommendations and accompanying advertisements. It claimed to be Australian and to provide 'a collection of practical recipes from the most eminent cooks of Australia', but the number of recipes for fresh salmon, cod, eels and sprats makes one wonder. The advice that fresh cod is at its best in the winter months around Christmas puts the real origin of the book beyond doubt. Anna Colcord's small book *A Friend in the Kitchen* promised 'to furnish in an inexpensive and convenient form, plain directions on healthful cookery'. Nothing was said of it being vegetarian.

Other promotional books were quite comprehensive, though as sources of information on food and eating habits they would still have to be treated with caution. Some of their recipes may have been unknown at the time of publication and passed into common use only later. A book on vegetarian cooking is likely to contain many new or unfamiliar recipes. On the other hand, early books on gas cooking may well have concentrated on dishes in common use, their promotional character being limited to showing people how to make them with a gas cooker instead of a wood-burning stove. A book on cooking with commercial products would be likely to offer both adaptations of old dishes and recipes for new ones. Of course, not all recipes which mention branded products are intended as promotions, though one may fairly suspect them to have been copied from a manufacturer's pamphlet. A book on *something different* would tell us just that: what dishes were not common.

Frontispiece of the first Australian cookery book.

Ma cuisine

There are also personal collections. Whether to seek a place in history or simply to share their art with others, professional cooks like to publish books of their favourite recipes, their own versions of known dishes and recipes for a few of their own creation. In the 1970s and 1980s it seemed that just about every chef with a reputation or an aspiration to one had gone to print and that every public identity with gastronomic pretensions had done the same. Australia's contribution to this exploding body of literature even included an entry by a State Premier.[10] Such books, however interesting or inspired some of them were, are not places to go for evidence of food and eating habits. The more they fulfil their purpose of presenting the culinary art or vision of their creators, the less they are likely to reflect prevailing food habits and attitudes. However, some writers have managed to convey a lively sense of their own culinary art from within a more general manual which is accepted into popular use. Such a writer was Hannah Maclurcan, whose book included recipes using seafoods and tropical fruit which seemed to go beyond what might have been expected of North Queensland cookery at that time.

Contributors

Last, but most revealing, are the contributory books of recipes solicited from individuals or common-interest groups. The many small, short-lived collections put together by local associations to help their fund-raising efforts are of little value to us. Some of them were good; a few, such as the *War Chest Cookery Book*[11] and those published in aid of the Disabled Men's Association of Australia1[12] are of historical significance; but most are of passing interest only. They were driven more by a need to raise money than to preserve or improve the body of cookery.

Popular teachers and writers on cookery often attracted or solicited from pupils or readers contributions of favourite recipes and included some of them in their books. In the preface of her sixth edition, Hannah Maclurcan found it necessary to say, '...so as to clear up any doubt there might be on the subject, that the great majority of the recipes in this book are my own invention, a few more were bought by me, and are, consequently, my own property, and a few have been given to me by friends.'

Quite a few quite comprehensive collections of recipes were compiled by associations from members' contributions. These were also put together as fund-raisers, but often met other needs as well, providing activities of great common interest in which all members could participate and from which all could benefit. In each case the result was supposed to be a recipe collection especially relevant to the needs of the group.

The Presbyterian Church, through the Women's Missionary Association of New South Wales and the Women's Missionary Union of Victoria, and later the Country Women's Associations[13] provided excellent examples. They were carefully compiled, with every attempt to keep out unreliable or useless recipes (at least as far as local politics would allow) and maintained, with unpopular or unworkable recipes dropped from subsequent editions and new ones added. They showed remarkable energy and dedication on the part of their compilers.

Although contributory collections are probably the best of the available sources of information on popular cookery, some caution is yet needed in trying to draw conclusions from them. When asked to contribute a recipe to a local collection does the cook submit the 'meat and two veg' that may be the daily fare, or a favourite dish made less often – perhaps the one that earns most compliments at the parish supper? Or does one put in a rarely made but more exotic dish so as not to be thought common?

An Australian book

In the early decades of white settlement food and cookery had been dominated by considerations of survival: securing regular supplies from overseas, coaxing crops to grow in an unfamiliar environment and exploring the possibilities of native game. By the late nineteenth century the raw need for survival had largely given way to longer term requirements of colonisation – establishing independence in food supplies, developing social structures and promoting trade.

The emerging differences between food here and 'at home', on which Mrs Cross and others had remarked, led to a growing belief that the cookery books of England, though widely sold, were not entirely suitable. Mrs Beeton, Eliza Acton and the others called for too many ingredients that were hard to come by, or for cookery methods or equipment that were too advanced for Australia's primitive conditions, or gave too little attention to the problems of preparing and preserving food in a hot climate. A book suitable for local conditions was wanted.

Many of the early Australian works attempted to address these problems, though rarely to the extent claimed by their authors. The recipes were nearly all copied or adapted from British books, whether the upper-class *Mrs Marshall*, the middle class *Mrs Beeton* or the working-class 'shilling' books. Some of the ingredients for high-class cookery were not always readily to hand, but this did not have as great an influence on the selection of recipes as one might have expected. Hare, snipe, teal and – at the most pretentious – truffles were all called for.

The earliest known Australian cookery book was published in 1864. It was written by Edward Abbott (1801-1869) at Bellerive in Tasmania under the pen name 'an Australian aristologist' (one who is skilled in aristology, the art of fine dining) with an equally pretentious title: *The English and Australian Cookery Book: Cookery for the many, as well as for the "upper ten thousand"*. His father, also Edward, had arrived in 1790 to take up a commission in the New South Wales Corps. He served at Norfolk Island, Hawkesbury, Parramatta, where he was appointed a magistrate, and Sydney, where he supported the removal of Governor Bligh but shrewdly avoided direct involvement in the matter. He was later appointed deputy-judge-advocate in Tasmania and 'despite his small knowledge of law and his large concern for the welfare of his own family' was very successful.[14] Success included the acquisition or promise of large grants of land.

Edward junior took over his father's land and prospered as a pastoralist. He showed much the same vigour as his father in pursuing his material interests. A small part of the grant originally promised to his father had been disallowed by the Colonial Office and when W. C. Wentworth later claimed it Abbott brought an action against the Crown – unsuccessfully. He entered the Tasmanian Legislative Assembly in 1856, created a disturbance by accusing four fellow members of having robbed him by owing him money, and moved to the Legislative Council about the time his book appeared.

The book was no working kitchen manual. It was more like a scrap-book, the diverting amusement of a comfortable gentleman, than an organised body of instruction. He was a bower bird with a lively interest in food, literature and current affairs. The bulk of his material was drawn from Britain, but he also tried to embrace the emerging body of Australian cookery. He included a listing of known Australian fish and described a number of native game animals – though more as curiosities than as items of common consumption. They included emu ('a very unctuous sort of food... much resembles coarse beef in flavour'); goat ('very good eating') if it can be considered game; mutton bird ('salted, but we can't say we should like them... the eggs are good, and largely used'); ortolan ('the most delicate mouths can masticate the bones'); peacock (stuffed, roasted and reconstituted with feathers and claws); black swan ('when young they are tender, and if properly roasted, with good sauce, they are eatable; and that is all we can say'); venison ('unless [it] is very tender and fat, a haunch of good mutton... is preferable'); wattle bird ('very fine eating') and wombat ('some persons like its flavour, others, again, decry it').[15] He also gave a few recipes for what was even then recognised as bush cookery. His recipes for kangaroo suggest that it was widely accepted both as survival food and as meat for a well-served table.

By the 1890s other Australian authors had followed Abbott's lead and those who felt the need for an Australian cookery book no longer had to make do with Mrs Beeton.

ROBERT MAY'S MEAT PIE

[The following is a recipe 'To make minced Pies of Beef', and is arguably one of the ancestors of the modern Australian meat pie. Note that it could be made with or without fruit; the fruity version eventually became the fruit mince pie of Christmas.]

Take of the buttock of beef, cleanse it from the skins, and cut it into small pieces, then take half as much more beef-suet as the beef, mince them together very small, and season them with pepper, cloves, mace, nutmeg, and salt; then have half as much fruit as meat, three pound of raisins, four pound of currants, two pound of prunes, &c. or plain without fruit, but only seasoned with the same spices.

CHAPTER 2

THE REFORMER

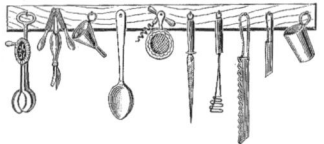

Dr Philip Muskett lived and practiced his profession in Elizabeth Street, Hyde Park, Sydney, just round the corner from Market Street. He was unmarried, and shared house with his sister Alice, a noted artist and author.

Australian born (in Fitzroy, Melbourne), of English parents, Muskett had books in his blood. His father had been a bookseller until his early death; his mother, herself the daughter of a printer and bookseller, carried on the business.[1] In his turn Philip became an avid reader and book collector, obtaining much of his material from the bookshop owned by Messrs David Angus and George Robertson in Sydney.[2]

About 1890 he began compiling a book with the bold aim of reforming Australian ways of living. The book, entitled *The Art of Living in Australia (together with three hundred Australian cookery recipes and accessory kitchen information by Mrs H. Wicken, Lecturer on Cookery to the Technical College, Sydney*, was completed in 1893 and published in London the following year.[3] Bred of the collector's passion and the reformer's zeal, it anticipated by nearly one hundred years the widespread acceptance of Mediterranean influences into Australian food and eating habits. The title page carried the slogan 'Australia is practically Southern Europe'.

Philip Muskett's theme was that Australia's geography and resources were quite unsuited for the prevailing diet of beef, mutton, bread, potatoes, cabbage and tea, but ideally suited for the lighter diet of Southern Europe,

28

with much less of butcher's meat and more emphasis on seafood, salads and a wide range of fresh vegetables. His stated purpose was 'to bring about some improvement in the extraordinary food-habits at present in vogue'.

According to one account, Muskett was not a patient man. Recalling his days as a young hand at Angus and Robertson's Market Street book store, James Tyrrell, who became an important figure in the Sydney book trade in the early part of the twentieth century, wrote of Philip Muskett:

> However the word got to him, he was always first at the shop for the opening of the cases of new books from Edinburgh or London, per P. and O. ship. Fred or I would be pulling the nails out with the shop's "Yankee opener" while the doctor stamped impatiently round and round like a caged panther – all in vain, for it was almost a certainty that he would be joined by other ardent collectors whose noses for newly arrived books were just as keen . . . [4]

Muskett's book does not project an image of a moderate and patient man. Instead, one can imagine a tireless worker and ceaseless thinker. He saw a task to be done and gathered a stream of information from many sources on problems besetting the colonies – the condition of patients who consulted him, public health, streetlife, the markets, social customs, current affairs, even industry. Working on it all, he began to draw in opinions and consider possibilities – from medical writings, social commentary, Government reports, public debate – earnestly working, forming ideas, adding more facts and opinions, enlarging his proposals. Visions of possibility swelled to a passion for reform and he finally burst forth in a torrent of fact and speculation, rhetoric and reason, reproach and demand. Chapter after chapter he poured it out until, seemingly exhausted, he handed the pen to Harriet Wicken to add some recipes.

In a preface to their work, he began with thinly disguised restraint. 'For years past the fact that our people live in direct opposition to their semi-tropical environment has been constantly before me.' But he was not content with a brief statement of the book's purpose and scope and an acknowledgment of Mrs Wicken's work, as would suit most people. He went through it all again, in a second rising tide of impatience for reform. Not a person to mince words, he wrote:

> ...the consumption of butcher's meat and of tea is enormously in excess of any common sense requirements, and is paralleled nowhere else in the world. On the other hand, there has been no real attempt to develop our deep-sea fisheries; market gardening is deplorably neglected, only a few of the more ordinary varieties being cultivated; salads, which

are easily within the daily reach of every home, are conspicuous by their absence; and Australian wine, which should be the national beverage of every-day life, is at table – almost a curiosity.

He went on to assert that 'the manners and customs of Australians are a perpetual challenge to the range of temperature in which they live' and that 'the form of food they indulge in proves incontestably that they have never yet realized their semi-tropical environment.'

Between completion of the book and penning the preface Dr Muskett had not been idle. He now took the opportunity to include a few observations on the reddening effect of sunshine on the blood, the unresolved question of acclimatisation (would future Australians show biological differences from their ancestors as a result of prolonged exposure to this climate?) and on how the semi-tropical climate might shape the future lifestyles of Australians.

The alphabetical pentagon

The first half of the book contained twelve chapters on health and diet, beginning with a general description of the climate of Australia to prove his contention that ours is semi-tropical. Dr Muskett then set forth his advice on what he saw as the five essentials of health and diet using as an *aide memoir* the 'Alphabetical Pentagon of health for Australia': Ablution; Bedroom ventilation; Clothing; Diet; and Exercise.

His comments on ablution covered the structure and functions of skin, perspiration and skin oils, the merits of a cold bath as a preventive of disease and aid to the maintenance of health, the use of a warm cleansing bath (and the beneficial effect of adding salt at the end of it) and care of the nails, teeth and hair, including 'excellent applications for promoting the growth of the hair'.

He then set out the desirable qualities of a bedroom and the importance of fresh air in both summer and winter, followed by advice on such aspects of clothing as the 'varying powers of clothing to detain air in its meshes', the 'transmission of the body heat to the clothes' and the properties of cotton, linen, silk and wool ('one of the best materials to wear next the skin').

Turning to diet, he began with a plea for more attention to be given to breakfast and for something more original to be dished up than the 'eternal trio' of chops, steak and sausages ('it is a matter of deep conjecture as to what most people would do if a prohibition were placed upon [them] for breakfast'). In a later chapter he repeated the plea, this time mocking the trio as 'the faith, hope, and charity' of domestic life.

He was highly critical of the customary Australian mid-day meal:

> Strange to say, all through the hot season, as well as the rest of the year, this consists in most cases of a heavy repast always comprising meat. Why, even in the cooler months, a ponderous meal of this kind is not required! My own views are that meat in the middle of the day is quite unnecessary, and, indeed, during the hot months actually prejudicial. Most people in Australia, after a fair trial, will find that a lunch of some warm soup, with a course perhaps of some fish, and vegetables, or salad, or whatever it may be to follow, will not only be ample, but will give them a sensation of buoyancy in the afternoon they never before experienced... The heavier meal should certainly be towards the evening after the sun-heat of the day is over, at which time it is more enjoyed and better digested.

He lamented that 'if the potato and the cabbage were taken away, Australia would be almost bereft of vegetables' and that:

> For years and years [the tomato] struggled desperately, but unsuccessfully, for a place, and the attempt to bring it into use was on the point of being abandoned in consequence. But at last its undeniable merits were acknowledged, and today it is in universal request.

He complained that the value of salads in a semi-tropical climate was not widely appreciated:

> ...if there is one desirable form of food which we should expect to find in daily use by the whole community, it is surely the salad. More than this, it deserves to meet with favour as a national dish. It takes pre-eminent rank in Southern Europe, and is certainly entitled to occupy a similar high position in the Australian food list . . . the strange neglect of salads can only be expressed by the term 'incomprehensible'. It is a waste-saving dish; it is wholesome, in that it is purifying to the blood; it is full of infinite variety; and its low price brings it within easy everyday reach even of the humblest dwelling. But, as things are, even the salad plants themselves are represented by a meagre list, and are confined to only a few varieties. And as far as salad herbs are concerned, they are literally unknown.

He described the difference between the English and the French methods of making a salad, gave detailed instructions for the preparation of a French salad, decried the poor display of greengrocery in Australia as compared with the show of meat, gave a list of salad plants and herbs which ought to be cultivated here and threw in for good measure recipes for 'the famous Mayonnaise sauce' and a herring salad.

His list of plants and herbs was lettuce ('cabbage' and 'cos'), endive ('broad-leaved' and 'curly'), chicory, lamb's lettuce ('corn salad'), celery, radish and mustard, salad and watercress – though he acknowledged that Australia was already fairly well off with celery and radish and that watercress might be obtained from 'John Chinaman'. He recommended that burnet, chervil, chives and tarragon be added to our salad herbs.

Dr Muskett praised the abundance and quality of fruit in Australia and urged that more should be taken at meals, particularly at breakfast, mentioning the old proverb that 'fruit is gold in the morning, silver at noon, and lead at night'. (This proverb can indeed be found in English cookery books of the period.) He discussed the value of fruit in the prevention of scurvy and the virtues of olives, noting that the terms 'French' and 'Spanish' indicated the state of ripeness at which they were picked rather than their country of origin.

He denounced the excessive consumption of tea which, he said, 'causes severe functional derangement of the digestive organs, and prejudicially affects the nervous system'. He was especially concerned about its over-use by women:

> The gentler sex are greatly driven to extravagant tea-drinking, exceeding all bounds of moderation in this respect. Many of them, moreover, live absolutely on nothing else but tea and bread and butter. What wonder, then, that they grow pale and bloodless; that their muscles turn soft and flabby; that their nervous system becomes shattered; and that they suffer the agonies of indigestion?

He was much kinder to coffee, which he thought occupied 'a very high position as a beverage'. He described its 'exhilarating and agreeable properties', among which he found those of 'relieving the feeling of fatigue or exhaustion, whether this be produced by brain work or bodily labour' and of enabling the system 'to bear up under an empty stomach'. He gave several ways of making coffee.

Contemporary medical opinion was divided over the good and bad effects of iced drinks. Muskett criticised the popularity of ice in America but cited several authorities who believed that, when used in moderation, iced drinks and soda water greatly relieved thirst and were not generally injurious.

He stressed the importance of exercise to bodily health. Men under 60 should walk six or eight miles a day in cooler months (or half the distance in summer). He gave no specific advice for women and drew no connection between lack of exercise and the pale flabbiness he had associated with excessive tea drinking.

Further reforms

Having completed his alphabetical pentagon, Dr Muskett turned his attention to the teaching of cookery, its influence on the Australian daily life, and his main theme. Australia was 'inhabited by a people largely carnivorous and addicted to tea. Surely not one person in a thousand would advocate such a diet under any circumstances.' He attributed the unsuitability of Australians' meat-laden diet to the reluctance of Anglo-Saxons to adjust their eating habits to their climatic conditions. 'It will be the same, too, when the British restaurant-keeper begins business in Equatorial Africa. For an absolute certainty his bill-of-fare for the delectation of the unfortunate colonist will consist of roast beef, Yorkshire pudding, plum pudding, and the old familiar throng.'

He lamented the unrelieved tedium of Australian cooking, seen in the treatment of vegetables and the lack of concern for breaking 'the conventional chain of joints, roasted or boiled, and the inevitable grill or fry.' And took another swipe at breakfast.

He reproached Australia for not having any national dish and hoped that when such a dish was devised and approved of by the nation it would be 'a *macédoine* of vegetables, or a vegetable curry, or some well-concocted salad'. As we shall see, several writers were to try to attach the Australian label to their dishes.

The key to change from this generally unfortunate state of affairs, said Muskett, was a thorough and systematic teaching of cookery and domestic management to girls in school. In this he was aligning himself with a small, but vocal movement of the times. He argued that the benefits would not be confined to the improvement of diet and household management. Cookery required accuracy, attention to detail, cleanliness, punctuality and wise economy. Acquisition of these virtues through the study of cookery was character forming. Moreover, cookery 'is in reality an art; indeed it is a master art. At the same time, also, it is a science – the science of applied chemistry. There are no other elements of education which thus blend within themselves these two factors – the practical and the scientific.' If only the education system would instil in girls a love of cookery and domestic management, as alternatives to getting into business as a dressmaker, milliner, saleswoman or employee in a large establishment, a disastrous trend in Australian family life could be averted. His foresight in dietary matters does not appear to have extended to social change.

Muskett complained that fish were comparatively scarce and 'outrageously expensive', that the lack of development of deep sea fishery was inexplicable in a colony drawn from maritime stock and that local oyster supplies to New South Wales and Victoria were falling seriously behind demand. He had much to say on the improvement of Australia's fishing industry and on its distribution and marketing arrangements.

On the subject of oysters he became almost lyrical:

> . . . it would be a difficult matter indeed to say too much in favour of the oyster. It is as highly appreciated at the present day as it was by the Romans hundreds of years ago, and it is certain that in centuries to come it will be found occupying a similar unrivalled position. At the same time, it must not be forgotten that it is not every person who cares for the oyster, showing that there are various forms of affliction; and we find, accordingly, that there is no half-heartedness about the like or dislike for the oyster – it is either held in the loftiest admiration, or looked upon almost with repugnance. It is both food for the sick-room and food for the strong man. It is one of the most valuable forms of nourishment for the growing child, and it gives strength to those in declining years. It is specially appropriate for the brain worker, and yet it is deservedly in great repute with the muscle user – whether athlete or artisan. It is the opening ceremony at our feasts, while it reigns supreme at supper.

Wine was a subject dear to Muskett's heart and his comments showed considerable foresight. He devoted many pages to viticulture and wine-making in Australia and to discussion of European wines. He was enthusiastic about the potential for Australia to supply the world with large quantities of excellent wine – and to become, in time, 'the vineyard of the world'.

The first obstacle to this international success was Australians' lack of acceptance of their own product; wine should be the national beverage. He criticised the erratic, unreliable and unattractive labelling, high alcoholic strength and coarseness of many of the wines. He thought that lower alcohol wines were more appropriate for consumption in Australia than the wines of greater strength favoured in cooler climates and that better handling, rather than high alcohol, was the key to safe transportation to Britain. He advocated the establishment of viticultural colleges and a federal Australian Wine-Growers' Association.

A glimpse of the future

The most striking feature of Muskett's book is its contemporary relevance. So many of the themes on which he held forth were still current 80 or 100 years later, with writers complaining of Australia's neglect of its abundant seafood resources, of the immense wealth and variety of fresh fruit and vegetables that were unknown to most households, of the potential for Australia to become a major wine-exporting nation, of the need for uniformity and consistency in wine labelling, and so on. The revolution in Australia's food and wine habits – at least the better part of it, not the rising popularity of 'fast food' and the many compromises tolerated for the sake of it – may have had its origins firmly in the nineteenth century in people such as Philip Muskett.

THE KITCHEN

The second part of the book was written by Harriet Wicken and was intended to be a collection of recipes purely for Australian use and of a 'strictly economical order'. It began with a few short chapters of 'accessory kitchen information'. Now the stridently critical, lecturing tone of the first part gave way to something altogether more practical; it was the voice of the teacher-demonstrator rather than the haranguer.

First she laid out a suitable kitchen, recommending deal boards for flooring, kept well scrubbed or covered with linoleum that must only be 'rubbed with a damp cloth first and then with a piece of flannel dipped in oil soda', a dresser with cupboards underneath and a deal table which 'must be kept white with constant scrubbing'. Recommended kitchen equipment included wooden and iron cooking spoons, a conical strainer, 'agate iron' mixing bowls, saucepans and frying pans, a small sausage machine, a pestle and mortar, wire and hair sieves, wire and tin dish-covers, and a French (deep) fryer. That most important piece of equipment, the stove, could be fuelled by gas, wood or coal; there seemed to be no preference, providing it was well maintained and understood. After an exhortation to cleanliness and neatness in the kitchen Harriet Wicken offered this vision of the future:

> How cosy and delightful everything seems in a kitchen like this, and what visions can we not see of home-made bread and cakes, well-cooked joints, succulent vegetables, delicious puddings, dainty dishes of all kinds concocted with skilful fingers! And why should not these visions turn into substantial realities? They will do so if women will consider it a pleasure, instead of a degradation, to 'look well to the ways of her household', and establish a system of order and neatness

from cellar to garret. When this happy time comes she will be 'emancipated' from many cares and have more leisure to cultivate her intellect than she has now.

Three short chapters praised the ice chest, the stock pot and that 'splendid restorative', soup. She admitted that 'soup is often disliked because it is greasy and served lukewarm'; these objections could be overcome by carrying out her directions for removing the fat and by boiling up just before serving.

Australian cookery recipes

The final six chapters presented her 50 'Australian Cookery Recipes' each for soups, fish, meat dishes, vegetables, salads and sauces, and sweets.

The emphasis on economy is obvious: most dishes were costed. The average costs were soup 6d, fish dish 1s, meat dish 8½d, vegetables 4½d, sauce 2½d, salad 7½d, pudding 5d, cake 5d. The most expensive dishes were soup: 1s 7d for *water souchet* (a soup of small fish and vegetables); fish dish: 1s 8½d for *collared eels* (moulded in aspic); meat dish: 1s 8d for *pressed beef*; vegetables: 9½d for *curried tomatoes*; sauce: 4½d for *mayonnaise*; pudding: 9d for her *Kingswood pudding* (a suet pudding with dried fruit and apples, boiled in a basin – a less elaborate recipe than had already appeared in her own *Kingswood Cookery Book*)[5] and cake: 8d for *banbury cakes*. On the other end of the scale, for a mere penny or two one could have *vermicelli or tapioca soup*, a baked loin chop, *cauliflower fritters*, or a sweet dish of *potato fritters*. For 2½d the possibilities included a dish of mutton or ham bone boiled with onion

---

KINGSWOOD PUDDING

½ lb. Bread Crumbs, 4 ozs. Flour, ½ lb. Brown Sugar, 3 Large Apples, 4 ozs. Raisins, 2 ozs. Sultanas, 2 ozs. Currants. 2 ozs. Candied Peel, 6 ozs. Suet.

Put the bread crumbs, flour, and sugar into a basin; chop the suet and apples finely, and add them with the currants and sultanas, well cleaned, and the raisins stoned and cut in half, the candied peel cut into small pieces; mix all this well together until it becomes like paste; no egg or moisture is required; press very firmly into a well-buttered basin or mould; tie over a cloth dipped in boiling water and boil for 7 hours; hang in a dry place, and boil again for 3 or 4 hours the day it is required. This is an excellent pudding.[6]

and potato ('a very homely dish, but a very savoury and economical one'); vegetable dishes such as sautéed turnips, stewed leeks or *potatoes à la maître d'hôtel*; and an imitation omelette (an omelette soufflé extended with milk and flour, baked in a saucer with jam).

For no additional cost a soup could be made of the bones and trimmings from roasted or boiled meat. *Pot boilings* (the liquid in which meat or fish has been boiled) were also recommended as 'an excellent foundation for many soups and sauces which might otherwise have to be made with water'. Even the boilings from corned beef or salt pork had their uses; although the liquid was too salty for stock, the fat on top could be rescued and used for pastry or 'an excellent and wholesome substitute for butter in cooking'.

In keeping with the theme of economy the recipes presented by Mrs Wicken were quite plain, some painfully so. For example, the recipe for *Jersey Soup* required white stock, milk, one leek, an ounce of sago (it actually said 'sage'; the cook presumably knew better), herbs, peppercorns and salt. In her own book, Mrs Wicken gave a better version with 'best white stock', turnip, leek, celery, cream and, of course, 'sago'. A few of the plainer dishes, such as *mutton broth* were intended for invalids and convalescents, and appear to have assumed that the sufferers had little interest in food.

The meat dishes included many of the nineteenth century English standards such as *steak and kidney pudding, stewed steak and pickled walnuts, Scotch collops, breast of mutton and peas, beef olives* and *tripe and onions*. There were few interpretations of foreign dishes. *Kebobs* were made by skewering rolled pieces of steak spread with a mixture of curry powder, Worcester sauce, vinegar, flour and chutney and simmering them in stock for one and a half hours. They were served with boiled rice and their gravy. Mrs Wicken explained that the 'skewers should be made from a very small splint of wood, just large enough to hold one or at most two of the rolls'. *Köttbullar* were meatballs made from minced beef, unsweetened egg custard and soda biscuit crumbs. They were fried in dripping. *Roman ragoût* was a stew of gravy beef, bacon, onion and tomatoes served with a very fair attempt at baked *gnocchi di semolina*. It would need little adaptation to appeal to modern lovers of homely Italian-style food.

In recognition of Dr Muskett's health theories, vegetables were very well represented, though in rather less variety than found in some other books at the time. Given the lack of popular interest in vegetables, the emphasis was on extending their use rather than their range; the only real novelties were green bananas stewed, with brown sauce. Her standard methods of cooking vegetables were boiling or stewing with butter or a plain white or butter sauce. *Beetroot and onion stew* was made with milk and served in a border of mashed potatoes; the same dish was repeated under a different name eight pages later. There was a pie of sliced potatoes and tomatoes under short crust pastry. Jerusalem artichokes were boiled and served with white sauce. A vegetable marrow was stuffed with *veal forcemeat*, boiled and served with a melted butter sauce (the veal forcemeat was a mixture of beef suet, bread crumbs, herbs and lemon rind bound with egg; it was used for stuffing veal and just about anything else). Lentils, both stewed and curried, were offered – 100 years before they became popular in Australia.

Mrs Wicken gave various salads, including a *breakfast salad* of tomatoes, cucumbers, spring onion and lettuce; a salad of boiled macaroni, cheese, celery and lettuce; a turnip salad; a *bread salad* (presumably an adaptation of the Tuscan *panzanella*); an economical *soup meat salad* using meat which had been boiled down for soup; and a sweet *banana and orange salad*.

Finally, she offered some puddings and cakes, including a *banana soufflé* (actually banana in egg custard, topped with meringue), a *Bedford pudding* which looks rather like the better known *queen of puddings* and was more economical than the version in her own book, a rhubarb and sago mould with which 'a little boiled custard is a great improvement' and, of course, a selection of boiled puddings.

On Muskett's own account, one would not expect the 'Australian Cookery Recipes' to be typical of colonial eating habits. One might look for a range of new dishes borrowed from the Mediterranean. They were in fact not Mediterranean but, on the whole, very English. Nor were they novel. On the contrary, in proportion to its size the book contained more recipes that were typical[7] of the day than did any of the other important Federation cookery books. Certainly he, like other reformers, used the tricks of rhetoric – including plenty of exaggeration and generalisation – to attract attention to his message. And perhaps poor eating habits were not entirely due to ignorance. But in the area of cookery his intention was more to urge upon his readers the potential for variety and wholesomeness in the existing body of culinary knowledge than to introduce a new or foreign cuisine.

The Art of Living was neither the beginning nor the end of Philip Muskett's reform efforts. Altogether, he wrote nine books on health and diet, a number of monographs on the same subjects and many articles for journals and newspapers. He was an energetic lecturer and a keen debater. For a time he was President and Chairman of the Sydney School of Arts Debating Club and he founded the New South Wales Literary and Debating Societies' Union. His recreations were given as 'mental relaxation in writing, physical in walking'. If he walked as vigorously as he debated, few would have been able to keep up with him. Like a candle that splutters and burns too brightly and is consumed too quickly, Muskett blazed with reformist zeal, suffered a 'nervous breakdown' and died in August 1909. He was 52 years old.[8]

CHAPTER 3

The Teachers

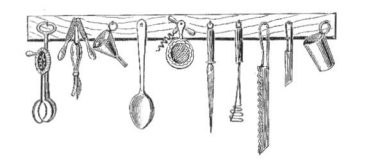

A Model School

In 1850 the old military hospital erected in 1815 at Fort Phillip (later known as Observatory Hill), Sydney, was converted to a school. This was a time when education in New South Wales was still suffering from poor organisation, makeshift classrooms and a severe shortage of competent teachers. The intention was to make it a 'model school' along the lines of the Irish national system – a working school, but one in which teachers themselves were trained in school organisation, instruction and discipline.

William Wilkins, then 24, arrived from England in 1851 to become headmaster of the new Fort Street Model School. He was not quite what the Education Board had wanted, for he was trained in England rather than under the chosen Irish system. However, he soon turned Fort Street into a model in the largest sense and earned the respect of the Board. Wilkins was there until 1854, then became Inspector and Superintendent of National Schools and rose through the growing education hierarchy to become Under-Secretary of the Department of Education by the time he retired in 1884.[1]

From 1854 Fort Street offered the 'higher branches of learning' in addition to the primary curriculum, beginning its important role of later years in secondary education. The old military hospital was able to accommodate 300 pupils, but it soon became crowded and a new building, able to accommodate another 300, was added in 1856. Other additions followed. By the turn of the century enrolment had reached 2000, including infants.

Competent teachers in the colony were in very short supply. The preferred method of recruitment was the pupil-teacher system in which students as young as 13 were employed to spend four years teaching children and being instructed themselves by a qualified teacher after school hours. Pupil-teachers who had completed their apprenticeships, and adults who were recruited to teaching, attended a short full-time course at Fort Street before they were appointed to schools. A small teacher-training school for this purpose was attached to the Fort Street model school. The course was extended to three months in 1867, six months in 1873 and 12 months for some in 1876.

The pupil-teacher system was expedient and cheap, but it took many years to produce adequate numbers of at best partially trained teachers. By the mid 1880s it had become the dominant method of entry to teaching, though only small numbers were able to complete their preparation at the teacher-training school and many teachers appointed to small schools received only nominal training in local public schools.

In 1883 teacher training capacity was expanded with the establishment of a residential training school for women at Hurlstone Estate near Ashfield, leaving Fort Street for the men. In 1889 the training school course was further extended to two years and included attendance at university lectures. By the turn of the century the pupil-teacher system was under serious criticism for producing teachers who were in the main poorly educated and inadequately prepared. No new pupil-teachers were taken on after about 1905. The Fort Street and Hurlstone Training Schools were amalgamated to form the Sydney Teachers College which was eventually located in the grounds of the University of Sydney. The Hurlstone site became Trinity Grammar School.

As early as 1868 domestic economy was included in the training program for all new women teachers, though it does not seem to have amounted to much and the subject was not included in the curriculum for government schools. After some years of public advocacy an attempt was made in the early 1880s to organise cookery lectures and demonstrations for the older girls attending city schools in Sydney. Classes began in May, 1882 at 127 Macquarie Street with Miss Ramsay Whiteside, holder of a first class diploma from Liverpool College, England and former private school teacher. Attendance was voluntary and cost ten shillings for 10 lessons. The scheme was doomed from the start. As early as 1883 the fee was abolished in an effort to attract more girls, but this only hastened the school's downfall, since the Department of Public Instruction then found the course too expensive. An 1884 report of inspectors recommended that the gas stoves which, at that time, were still a novelty in kitchens, be removed.[2] The school was closed at the end of 1895. Ramsay Whiteside returned to England for a year, then became cookery teacher at a high school for ladies.

According to Philip Muskett's short account of the introduction of cookery teaching in New South Wales schools, Annie Fawcett Story, 'who had previously taught Cookery successfully in connection with the Sydney Technical College', was engaged early in 1886 to train cookery instructors for schools. However, it was not until 1889 that cookery was formally included in the curriculum as part of an effort to provide systematic instruction in 'technical' subjects and to broaden the emphasis from basic literacy and book learning. In that year Mrs Fawcett Story established a cookery school at Fort Street Public School and quickly developed a scheme for extending classes as widely as possible at low cost. She proposed the use of 'portable kitchens', as used in Leeds, to avoid the cost of permanent facilities that would see only limited use. The portable kitchens, each comprising sink, stove with ovens and fireplace, cupboard doors that served as tables when placed on trestles, and a collection of utensils, could be transferred from school to school as required. The cost of supplies was reduced by having the pupils serve meals to staff and students.

Cookery teaching began to spread to suburban schools and major country centres, beginning with Bathurst and Goulburn. Muskett recorded that by 1891 the number under instruction had reached 757. Classes were aimed at fifth year girls in the primary schools, but were extended to high schools, on a limited basis, from 1893. By that time Annie Fawcett Story had become 'Directress of Cookery' in the Department of Public Instruction. She was still responsible for teacher training at Fort Street, but also for the public school classes there and for the expansion to other schools. She resigned in 1895 and moved to the Department of Education in Victoria, where she became Directress of Cookery in 1898.

The 1897 program of lessons in New South Wales is an excellent summary of everyday Federation cookery.

Although the New South Wales school system had flourished during the 1880s, caught up in a wave of idealistic public commitment to education, progress came to an abrupt halt when the colony was hit by severe depression at the end of 1891 and funds for education were seriously reduced. Cookery enrolments declined from a peak of nearly 1500 in 1894 to less than 900 in 1899. Not until the turn of the century was an adequate flow of funds restored, enabling 'technical' subjects such as cookery to be established in most schools.

Cookery Classes for Public School Pupils, N.S.W.

A course of twenty-one lessons in plain cookery (1897)

1. Practical cleaning.
2. Roasting and baking meat, Yorkshire pudding, clarified fat and caramel.
3. Grilling: Chop and steak. Boiling: Mutton, corn beef.
4. Vegetables: Potatoes, cabbage, peas, beans, cauliflower, &c.
5. Stewing: Tripe and onions, Irish stew, stewed steak, stewed ox-tail.
6. Puddings: Urney, currant, rice, boiled fruit, steak and kidney.
7. Pastry: Meat and fruit pies, turnovers, jam tart, Cornish pasties.
8. Soups: Stock, vegetable soup, pea soup, cottage broth.
9. Tea, coffee, porridge, toast, boiled eggs, poached eggs, eggs and bacon, steak and onions.
10. Cakes: Plain, sponge, currant cakes, scones, milk loaves.
11. Fish: Boiled, baked, fried and stewed fish.
12. Mutton broth, beef tea, gruel, arrowroot, rice water, toast and water.
13. Liver and bacon, pancakes, cutlets (piquant sauce), fritters.
14. Blanc mange, custard, apple dumplings, stewed fruit-custard.
15. Tomato, onion, ox-tail soups.
16. Gingerbread, seed cake, jam roll, buns, Yorkshire tea cakes.
17. Boiled fowl, egg sauce, roast fowl, bread and celery sauce, grilled chicken.
18. Date, lemon, bread and butter, plum puddings.
19. Braised steak, rissoles, brawn.
20. Salads: Mixed, potato, tomato, chicken, fruit.
21. Bottled fruits, tomato sauce, pickles.[3]

The College near Ultimo House

The spreading network of country and suburban technical colleges had also played an important role from the late nineteenth century in teaching young women to cook and, increasingly, in training cookery teachers. In 1884 the Sydney Technical College established a Department of Domestic Economy in rooms at the Royal Arcade, Pitt Street with Annie Fawcett Story as Instructress. One-year classes were given in Cookery and 'High Class Cookery', with average weekly attendances in the first year of 4.1 and 17.5 respectively.[4] Advanced Cookery was introduced in 1885.

Mrs Fawcett Story prescribed as a textbook for her 'high class' cookery course the *South Kensington Official Handbook of Cookery*. This was the text used by the National Training School for Cookery, London which had been established in 1874 to train teachers. In its 1886 handbook it offered a 'full' cookery course of twenty weeks and a recently introduced 'plain cookery' course of 14 weeks.[5] The full course included a series of six lessons on the use of 'Australian meat', each lesson based on a recipe. The first was *mulligatawny* made with tinned calf's head and tinned mutton. *Sausage rolls* were made with a tin of 'Australian mince meat'. *Meat pie* was made with a tin of mutton or beef and a small tin of kidneys. *Rissoles* used unspecified Australian tinned meat; *savoury hash* used tinned mutton; and *mince* (served with mashed potatoes) used – you guessed it – Australian tinned mince. It would be interesting to know if these lessons were ever given at the Sydney College.

After Annie Fawcett Story departed for Fort Street, Mary Gill took over, then Harriet Wicken, who boasted a diploma from the London School and had started her Australian career in Melbourne and also visited Warrnambool (1888) and Hobart (1890) to give cookery lessons.[6] Like Mrs Fawcett Story, she was something of a pioneer in cookery teaching and is credited with having been one of the first to attempt to educate Sydney women in the use of gas cookers. She was promoted Lecturer-in-charge of the expanded Department of Domestic Economy when the college moved to its permanent location at Ultimo. She remained in the position until 1896, then moved to Western Australia as lecturer to the Perth High School and was succeeded in Ultimo by Mrs Fawcett Story's daughter, Fanny, who produced her own cookery text. Fanny remained in her position only until 1902, then moved to Cape Town, where she was joined by her mother two years later.

FEDERATION PUDDING
(*Fanny Fawcett Story*)

1 sponge sandwich, 2 oz. raisins, 3 oz. sugar, 1 doz. white small meringues, ½ doz. apples, 1 oz. almonds, 2 tablespoons apricot jam, 1½ oz. butter.

Slice the apples and stone the raisins, chop the almonds; put all in a stewpan with the sugar, butter and half-gill water, stew till tender; cut the middle out of a flat round sandwich, fill the centre with the stewed apple, spread the jam on top and decorate with very small white meringues, with small pieces of cherries and angelica on the top of each one.

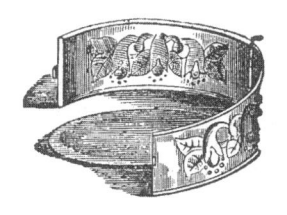

By 1909 Amie Monro, herself apparently a former student of Harriet Wicken and compiler of another fine cookery book, was in charge of the domestic economy department.[7] The Sydney Technical College now boasted three well-appointed kitchens, a fine lecture room, a large dining room, a laundry and a model room for instruction in housewifery. These newly completed facilities were already taxed to their limit and there was a waiting list of prospective students.

Among the courses offered was 'plain cookery':

> This course also is theoretical and practical. It includes instruction in scullery work, the management of stoves, of the kitchen, and of the pantry; Rules for roasting, baking, boiling, braising, frying, soup-making, vegetable cookery, pastry and cake making, puddings, sauces (sweet and savoury), cold-meat cookery, breakfast cookery, salad making, and invalid cookery.
>
> This course includes all dishes used in ordinary cottage cookery, and may be completed in one year.

An advanced cookery course included:

> ...instruction in the preparation and service of dishes in the higher branches of cookery, such as:– Hors d'Œuvres, Soups, Stocks, Consommées, Purées; Dressed Fish and Fish entrées; Sauces (savoury meat, fish, sweet, and stock); Entrées; Game and Poultry: trussing, boning, larding and cooking of poultry; Entremets, sweet and savoury; Sweets, soufflees [sic], omelettes, jellies, creams; Pastry, puff pastry; Dressed Vegetables and Salads, Supper dishes and savouries; Garnishes, Farces, &c.; Fancy cakes, large cakes and icing.[8]

Shorter courses were available for students wishing to qualify for positions as cook. For this purpose a formal qualification was usually unnecessary; they needed attend classes only until they, their teachers and prospective employers were satisfied. A course in invalid cookery was provided for trainee nurses. Special practical lessons and short courses were also offered from time to time in subjects such as garnishes, ornamental icing, confectionery, preserving, jam and pickle making, menu preparation, table arrangement and service. Practical training was given with both gas stoves and wood and coal ranges.

Students who had completed the 'full course' – elementary, advanced, theoretical and practical – could sit an examination for entry to the Training School for Teachers of Cookery and Domestic Science.

To relieve growing pressure on the Fort Street Training School, from 1907 trainee teachers and practising teachers wishing to qualify for teaching adult classes were sent to the Technical College for the advanced cookery course. In 1910 Amie Monro was appointed Supervisor of public school cookery classes, a position she held together with her senior teaching position at the Technical college. It is hardly surprising that in the following year the College took over all cookery and domestic science teacher training on behalf of the public school system.

THE KINGSWOOD COOKERY BOOK

In 1885 Harriet Wicken of Kingswood published a modest little book to accompany her cookery demonstrations and dedicated it to the 'Women of England'. After moving to Melbourne, she re-wrote it because she 'found that English Cookery Books were not suitable for the climate and conditions of life here'.[9] She discarded more than a quarter of the original recipes, altered most of the others and added nearly 400 new ones. One might therefore expect a comparison of the original English and re-written Australian books to give an insight into how a cookery teacher of the time thought those differences in climate and conditions should affect food and cooking. Unfortunately it is not so. Apart from a few recipes for sole, eel and partridge, those she dropped were as 'suitable' as those she kept and many were replaced by different recipes for similar dishes. Some of her alterations might have been prompted by local conditions – here and there a shallot became a 'shred of onion', fewer eggs were called for or more gelatine was suggested – but most seem to have been no more than minor revisions made in the light of experience and show no consistent changes in style or method. Nor did the many 'new' recipes Australianise the book. All were thoroughly in the English mould and, except for a handful of local adaptations such as *colonial goose*, *Melbourne pudding*, *Sydney relish* and an *Australian drink* of port and ginger beer, they were for dishes that could have been expected in her first edition.

That the Australian *Kingswood* was intended to be used as a textbook for her classes is clear from the beginning: 'The first subject upon which I wish to speak to the student in cookery is …'. One of the firms which subscribed advertisements in the 1891 edition claimed to be 'Purveyors to the School of Cookery under care of Mrs. Wicken' and, for the benefit of the many people who asked where the various things mentioned in her recipes could be obtained, she advised her readers of three firms which would supply and send into the country any goods used in her classes.

It is interesting to compare the recipes with those she produced for *The Art of Living*. At first glance, some 90 dishes seem to be the same. However, she was careful not to copy any recipes across exactly. A third of them would produce almost identical dishes; of the remaining 60 or so the *Art of Living* versions were almost all plainer and more economical. Few cooks having both books on the shelf would reach for Muskett unless driven by economy. For example, both books gave *mulligatawny soup* – the thick sort with stock, apple, onion, carrot, curry powder, butter, flour and lemon juice. The *Kingswood* version added a rabbit or wild duck, bacon, mulligatawny paste and peppercorns. Both were sent to table in traditional fashion, with boiled rice. Neither version has much contemporary appeal, but most diners, if forced to choose, might be expected to go for the one with the meaty bits, providing they did not find the idea of bacon in curry unattractive.

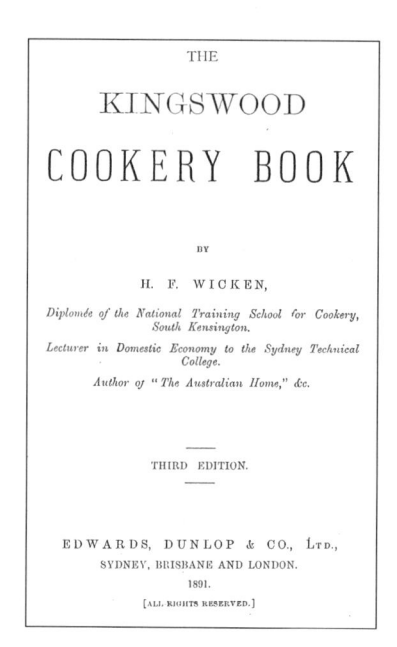

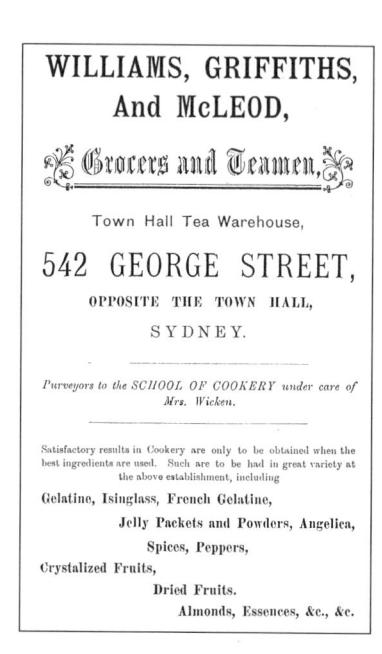

Fish à la crème was a simple dish of boiled fish in white sauce. There was little to choose between the two recipes other than a *faggot of herbs*. However, there was a real difference in the garnish: *Kingswood* called for a sprinkling of parsley and lobster coral, while the other took a parsimonious approach, suggesting parsley and red bread crumbs.

Harriet Wicken commenced her book as she meant to continue, with some forthright, teacherly advice: 'I do not think that in ordinary English and Colonial households importance enough is attached to soup as food.' She praised both its stimulation to digestion and appetite, and its economy. 'Now, in an ordinary way, expensive soups are not necessary, and when two or three joints are cooked in the course of the week, soup sufficient for three or four persons every day may easily be made without buying soup meat.' And it deserved greater popularity. 'Nothing is more disagreeable than lukewarm soup. The reason why soup is not so popular with us as it is in

France and other countries is because it is so often served nearly cold and greasy.' Does this remind you of the *Art of Living*?

She did not instruct her readers systematically in basic cookery methods, as might have been expected in a textbook, but left that to her household manual, *The Australian Home*. Instead she was content with a scatter of explanations, hints and warnings and the advice to novice cooks that many dishes reputed to be difficult or troublesome were really simple if the directions were carried out faithfully. A few of the highlights will serve to illustrate the kind of cookery she taught.

For frying fish she recommended the deep-fry (French) method, though her economy in oil was disconcerting. 'The same fat can be used for weeks if a little fresh dripping or lard be added from time to time. When it looks very black, and bubbles up like soap suds, it has lost its virtue and must be thrown away.' Few would argue with that.

She explained the methods of boiling, stewing and braising meat, but her comments on roasting meat were confined to how to do it in a gas oven – in her enthusiasm for the new medium ignoring, for the moment, the needs of many of her students who would have to do without it and find some way of cooking meat nicely with a wood- or coal-fired range. She said nothing of the other methods of cooking meat, such as grilling or pan-frying, but gave a few hints on how to use up the remains of a cold joint. Her advice on gravies – that they 'should be carefully and nicely seasoned, but depend upon plenty of fresh vegetables for flavouring' – is still sound.

All this advice was presented in 1888 and she apparently saw no reason to revise it. It was not so with vegetables. In 1888 she had been content with giving general directions for boiling potatoes and a few other vegetables, and a handful of made-dishes.

SAVOURY CABBAGE
(Kingswood Cookery Book)

1 Cabbage; 3 ozs. Cheese; 1 oz. Butter; 2 ozs. Bread Crumbs; Pepper and Salt.

Boil a cabbage until soft; drain and squeeze very dry; put half of it in a hot dish, and sprinkle over half the grated cheese; season with pepper and salt and a few small pieces of butter; then put in the rest of the cabbage; strew on the remaining cheese and butter in small pieces, and cover the top well with bread crumbs; bake in an oven 20 minutes. This is a delicious dish, and a nice change from plain cabbage.

But she hinted at things to come:

> Vegetable, especially in the summer time, should form a very important item in our diet; they contain a great deal of potash, which is very beneficial to the blood. Nature herself teaches us this in the abundant supply which she gives us in hot weather. Well-cooked vegetables and fruit should be seen on our tables at every meal during the summer.

Ten years later her introduction to vegetables began with a spirited defence of plainly boiled vegetables with roast meat. 'Foreigners all profess to dislike our vegetables boiled plainly in water, and say very unpleasant things about English cooks in consequence. But, laugh as they may, plainly boiled vegetables are by far the best, if they are served *with* the roast beef of old England. Dressed vegetables are very nice as a separate course'. She echoed Muskett's criticism that Australian housekeepers were far too limited in their choice of them and introduced several 'new' vegetables. Among them were choko (described as having a smooth yellow skin, perhaps a relative of the more familiar green thing); Lima, Tonga and butter beans; okra; and eggplant. Choko was to be boiled and served with white or melted butter sauce. Eggplant could be cooked in the same way; crumbed and fried in fat (noting, however, that the common method 'fried and reeking with fat' had failed to 'captivate the palate of those more hygienically disposed') or, for a more elaborate dish, stuffed and baked. Curly parsley was preferred as 'a much prettier garnish than the ordinary straight leaf'; nowadays the preference is often reversed on the basis of flavour.

She gave only a few hints on kitchen cleanliness (saucepans to be washed in soap and water then scrubbed inside with sand; a wooden spoon used for curry not to be used for other purposes; and instructions for cleaning gas stoves).

Like many other writers of the time, she taught that domestic economy did not mean parsimony. Money could be saved by planning meals wisely, ordering quality ingredients and avoiding waste. She advised readers to use meat trimmings or the bones and trimmings of joints, poultry or rabbits in the stock pot; to trim excess fat from the meat and render it for use in frying or as a substitute for butter; to use cold meat or fish remains for salads or made-dishes; to use bread scraps in puddings; and so on.

> A good deal of judgement is required, in ordering a dinner, to give variety, and to see that the remains of one day's dinner are turned to good account in a savoury made-dish for the next... There are so many possibilities that cooking becomes a delightful surprise instead of the drudgery it is often considered.

The bulk of the 1898 book was divided into 12 recipe sections: soups and purées (51); fish and savouries (72); meat and poultry (164); pastry and sweets (227); bread and cakes, icing &c (90); vegetables (54); omelettes, salads, and savouries (56); sauces (38); eggs (25); jams (24); beverages (14); sundries (18).

Why omelettes, salads, and savouries were grouped together in one chapter (which also included a few soufflés), while other egg dishes were kept separate in another is no clearer than why boiled eggplant was given under vegetables but fried and stuffed eggplant was dealt with under eggs. As she said, 'The possibilities of eggplant are little understood'.

She had nearly all sections of cookery well covered, except for pickles and chutneys (represented only by a sweet pickle of mushrooms, shallots, capsicum and tomatoes called *Sydney relish*) and confectionery (a single toffee *cream candy*).

Mrs Wicken's chapter on fish and seafood savouries was extensive and showed a genuine attempt to come to terms with Australian seafood. As in most books of the time, oysters were the most frequently mentioned seafood item. Lobster (which was more plentiful then than now) was given nine recipes. The most common fish mentioned were bream and whiting; and recipes were given for schnapper, cod, flounder, tailor, blackfish, barracouta and something called Murray plaice. Feeding British nostalgia, she gave a handful of recipes for salmon dishes, of which all but one used the tinned product.

Kitchen Utensils.

There was reasonable variety in the treatment of fish, including deep-fried crumbed bream; a steamed pudding of minced boiled fish, bread crumbs, eggs and cream, served with béchamel sauce; baked rolled fillets of bream in a spicy red sauce (*Fish à la Saumarez*); deep fried codfish balls with melted butter sauce; curried tailor; and tinned salmon in aspic. Most would now be thought over-processed and over-cooked, with eggs and white sauce or its variants appearing too often, but it was a style of cooking seafood that survived in some parts of Australia well into the 1970s. Boiling, baking and deep frying were the favoured cooking methods; grilling was mentioned, but seems to have been confused with baking. The barracouta was 'broiled' on a hot gridiron, a process equivalent to modern dry-frying.

A glance through the chapter of meat recipes confirms that Harriet Wicken expected the meat diet of her readers to be overwhelmingly of beef and mutton, with fowl or veal for an occasional change. There was no shortage of ideas on what to do with the remains of the roast. Rabbit, hare, pigeon, turkey or domestic or wild duck were there for a change. And if the cook had to deal with a calf's head, a sheep's head or a pig's head or even the pig's trotters or the ox's foot, Mrs Wicken had them covered.

The combination of meat and seafood was more popular at the time of Federation than it is now, a product of the abundance of oysters in Victorian London. To plunge one's fork into a savoury boiled pudding of beef steak and oysters encased in suet pastry is one of the great experiences of traditional English dining. The *carpet bag* of beef steak stuffed with oysters lasted in Australia into the 1970s and beyond, but was on an altogether different plane. A recipe for it could be found in the *Goulburn Cookery Book* and in the *Schauer Cookery Book* (as *steak and oyster filling*). In others the *carpet bag* was a piece of steak spread with oysters, rolled up, and roasted.[10] At first glance it seems an odd combination, unlikely to improve either fine, fat oysters or a prime beefsteak without the long, slow cooking that blends the flavours together into something almost ethereal, that is neither beef nor oyster. Perhaps a cook faced with an embarrassment of oysters might be glad of it. The dish has been claimed for Australia, but seems more likely to be North American.[11] Mrs Wicken gave a few meat-and-seafood combinations: *pigeons and prawns, Irish stew and oysters* and *turkey and oysters*. She also put oysters in several meat pies, in the sauce for *stewed breast of veal* and in a *friture de veau* (sautéed veal strips and oysters). The Schauer book added *burnam of fowl*, a dish of chicken and oysters in anchovy-flavoured white sauce.

Among the vegetable dishes were artichokes (presumably the tuberous variety, since they were served fried, *au gratin* or puréed and steamed in a mould), boiled and stewed cucumbers and 21 recipes for potatoes. Turnip tops boiled were 'exceedingly good with roast mutton' and lettuces were 'very good boiled in the same way as cabbages'. Neither recommendation was taken seriously, though the idea of lettuce stewed in a well flavoured gravy had been around for some time (and can still be found in French cookery books). Readers were spared Mrs Beeton's advice that lettuce should be blanched even for summer salads. Beetroot was an accepted vegetable in Federation cooking. It appeared in three main forms: boiled and vinegared (usually cold), boiled with sauce (hot), and as a garnish for salads and savouries.

Her recipes were mostly practical and down-to-earth, emphasising economy as she had defined it (with the startling exception of *lobsters with truffles*), nutrition and presentation. She tried to steer away from the worst features of British cooking towards something that was vaguely, but not obviously, French: good food, handled simply and economically, nicely presented.

Let us sample a 'Kingswood meal'. It is a family dinner, not over-elaborate. We begin with a thick tomato soup, well flavoured with onions, carrots, celery, bay leaf, peppercorns, cloves and a pinch of curry powder. It is puréed and finished with some crushed tapioca that now just glistens through the soup. Served from a tureen, very hot and not at all greasy, it makes an appetising start. It is *Kingswood soup*.

We move straight on to the main course: a substantial and very interesting pie, pushing up a golden crust of puff pastry, made crisp and light with lard. The knife reveals rolls of beef stuffed with chopped kidney and pickled walnuts, gently stewed in rich stock. Hard boiled eggs are there and, scattered throughout – blessed cook! – some oysters. With *Kingswood pie* there is no need for fancy side dishes; let us have potatoes steamed and mashed with milk and butter, fine young carrots partly boiled then stewed in butter, and perhaps some young peas boiled.

Now the pud: a rich and steaming wonder; studded with fruit, standing proud upon the dish in the borrowed splendour of its mould, anointed with its custard sauce. Strictly, it should not follow pie, but we had a fancy for it, and this *Kingswood pudding* is no stodge, lightened with bread crumbs and minced apples. For those more timid there is lighter fare: a fancy dish of sponge cakes filled with jam, modestly cloaked in custard, sparkling with red glacé cherries: *Kingswood cakes*.

We are content; little is wanted for a savoury. A few devilled almonds will suffice, some fingers of anchovy toast. Life can be good in the Colonies.

Victoria

It seems that Victoria was slower than New South Wales to get systematic cookery teaching under way, but not much. It is known that cookery classes were given by a Monsieur Soyer at the Melbourne Servants' Home from 1875 at a cost of a guinea each.[12] In the late 1880s Margaret Pearson, another product of the National Training School for Cookery, London, was giving lectures and public cookery demonstrations in Melbourne. By 1891 her classes at the Working Men's College were attracting more than 100 girls.[13] In 1888 she had published a small book *Cookery Recipes for the People* for the Centennial Exhibition in Melbourne, later editions of which seem to have served as handbooks for her students.[14] Most of the recipes were based on her teaching notes, though she admitted that others were untested. Some of them came from commercial sources and were given complete with the manufacturers' blurb:

> Pure condiments are indispensable. M'Kenzie's White Singapore Pepper is quite reliable, excellent in quality, and the purity is guaranteed.

To modern readers Margaret Pearson's is one of the most satisfying sources of Federation cookery. There was no ostentation or pretence at French cookery; not a mention of truffles. There were not even the ritual offerings of high class English cookery – jugged hare, roast pheasant and such like. She managed to present the common body of ordinary household cookery without the common obsession with economy and plainness, making full use of herbs and spices, calling for cream where it was needed, and showing no fear of peppercorns.

She paid close attention to the basics and gave, for example, one of the best accounts of the *melted butter* so debased by other Federation cooks (and, of course, by those back home, provoking Voltaire's famous jibe that the English had 40 religions, but only one sauce). She pointed out that, as its name suggests, it should be a dressing of melted butter with just a thickening of flour and water to give it substance rather than a water-and-flour sauce with a little butter added.

Her account of the popular bread pudding conceded nothing to those cooks on the lookout for the easy way, but showed just how good the traditional cookery of Federation could be.

By the early 1890s cookery classes were being given for the older girls in a number of metropolitan state schools. The expanding state system later came under Annie Fawcett Story's control. A College of Domestic Economy was founded in Melbourne in 1906 with Mabel Sandes, then aged 24 and a recent graduate of Sydney Technical College, as its founding principal.

Margaret Pearson's recipes

MELTED BUTTER

Dust a little flour over 4 ozs. of butter; put into saucepan with about 1 gill of water; stir it one way constantly with wooden spoon and let it just boil; if the butter is to be melted with cream, use the same proportion of butter, but no flour; stir constantly and heat well, but do not let boil.

BREAD AND BUTTER PUDDING

4 slices of bread cut very thin, 3 ozs. of sultana raisins, 1 doz. Valentia raisins or dried cherries, 3 eggs, Little lemon juice, Little grated nutmeg, 1 gill of brandy, ½ a pint of milk or cream, 2 ozs. of sugar, 4 ozs. currants.

Cut thin slices of bread and butter well, taking off the crusts; butter a melon mould and grease it; garnish the bottom with the large Valentia raisins or with the cherries, putting them in rows; then put in a slice of bread, the buttered side next the shape; then a few sultana raisins and currants; do this alternately until mould is three-parts full; put eggs in basin and beat with sugar; add little grated nutmeg, and lemon juice, milk and brandy; mix well together; pour into shape; put on cover, or tie buttered kitchen paper over top; steam for two hours.

Serve with German or custard sauce.

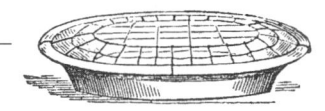

Queensland

Another graduate became a household name in Queensland.

Amy Schauer was born in Sydney in 1871 of German parents. Her father was a cooper. She gained her Domestic Science Certificate from Sydney Technical College, possibly as a student of Harriet Wicken. She began teaching 'cookery and allied subjects' at the Central Technical College, Brisbane in February 1895 and gave classes in invalid cookery at the Mater Hospital. She seems to have become a permanent staff member at the college, as a teacher of cookery, in 1897. Mrs Wicken herself visited Brisbane for a month in July, 1896 to give cookery and domestic science lessons, a visit endorsed by the her employer as 'a friendly and desirable act' to the education authorities of the other colonies.[15]

The *Schauer Cookery Book*, published in 1909, was a somewhat clumsy production.[16] The index was divided into alphabetical sections, but within each section the recipes were listed in order of page number – easy for the compiler, but of little help to users. There was at least one repeated recipe, a few others were plainly out of place, incomplete or jumbled, and the outside cover made the exaggerated claim that the book contained 'over 1600 recipes' – the truth was closer to 1440, still making it the largest of the early Australian collections. It sold out within about six months and was replaced in 1910 with a second edition which corrected many of the errors.

The book lasted in print for many years. Its seventh edition (1931) carried the title *Schauer Improved Cookery Book: Australian and Seventh Edition*. By then it was greatly revised and expanded, had a proper index, and was destined for sale 'in all parts of the Commonwealth,' whereas previous editions had been 'intended principally for users in Queensland'. Interestingly, there was by now no acknowledgment of the book's authorship apart from its title and the claim that it had been received with such universal satisfaction that the author (single) and publishers had been encouraged to issue a new edition.

By 1946 the book was into its ninth edition and had changed its name again, this time to *The Schauer Australian Cookery Book*. It was billed as a book of reference for students taking university public examinations in practical home science (cookery) and for teachers in technical colleges. The introductory section had been expanded further, with greater emphasis on food values and nutrition. Many of the original recipes had been replaced. It carried an apology for being a wartime edition: 'Existing conditions brought about by the war do not allow us to produce this edition in the manner we would desire. For the larger publications... the use of paper of more than one class or weight is unavoidable.' My copy was printed on two distinctly different grades of paper.

A publisher's note to the '12th impression' of 1962, which returned to the original title, eulogised Amy Schauer as 'one of Australia's finest women' and 'a most capable person to compile a Cookery Book for the housewives of Australia', but gave little information about her other than that she taught at the Central Technical College, Brisbane, for over 40 years, was examiner in cookery for the Queensland Department of Education and was commissioned to establish cookery sections in technical colleges 'throughout the country' (presumably rural Queensland). It claimed that after the last of many revisions of the book Miss Schauer had declared herself satisfied with it. This note must have been carried over from an earlier edition, for Amy Schauer died in 1956 at the age of 85. There was no mention of the other original author, Miss M. Schauer (who was, in fact, her sister Minnie, and had accompanied her to Brisbane).

The Schauer style

Hers was the most educational of the Federation books, with some 19 pages of general advice and information and more scattered throughout, though it stopped short of systematic instruction in the basic techniques of cookery. Amy Schauer's approach was that of a teacher rather than of a reformer. Her introduction was a homily on the need for study and practice, beginning with the simple before progressing to the more complex. 'Practice makes perfect in cookery, as in all other concerns in life. Let study and practical work go hand in hand. Strive always to grasp the real essence of the particular recipe and the principle involved in preparing it.' And so on. It ended with the 'five reasons for cooking': to render mastication easy, to render food pleasant to taste, to aid digestion, to combine foods and to economise them by eating them warm. These reasons came without acknowledgment from the 1892 book bearing Mrs Beeton's name.

The chapter on housekeeping began with a lesson on economy and the avoidance of waste: 'It is necessary for the housekeeper to inspect her storeroom and pantry each morning, so that nothing be left that would become stale and unfit for food. After preparing a plain dinner, in which, say, cutlets have entered, see that the trimmings be made into a nice little Irish stew; the crusts from the bread crumbs used in cooking may be baked and ground down, and used as garnishes over fish pies, which may be made from the remains of cold fish and macaroni cheese, etc.' Cold vegetables were not to be wasted: possibilities for recycling them included potato croquettes and salads, mashed potatoes and cauliflower fritters. Left-over peas and beans could be re-heated and served again. Crusts of cheese could be grated for use in savouries. 'If carefulness is practiced, no extravagance need exist, for every scrap may be turned into use, and nothing thrown away.' Even pieces of string should be saved.

Her advice on the storeroom included keeping tea in a lead-lined chest, a practice that would now be considered a serious health hazard. Scullery work amounted to keeping the kitchen and all its equipment scrupulously clean, dry and in good order. The omelette pans and gridiron were not to be washed but there were instructions for cleaning pudding moulds.

There was a general survey of different types of food and their uses ('the ox is divided for cooking as follows ...'). The marketing section included dire warnings on pork which, 'more than any meat, must be chosen with greatest care' and also required more care in its cooking than any other meat, since 'the least portion underdone is more than unwholesome.' She warned that 'it should be withheld from people with weak digestion, as well as invalids generally.' There was advice on choosing pigeons, hares, rabbits, wild ducks and guinea-fowl.

Savouries

Schauer was the only organised book not to begin its recipe collection with soups. Here savouries came first because it was accepted that they had a place before dinner as well as after it. Before-dinner savouries included small dishes of oysters, sardines, caviar, anchovies, plain or stuffed olives. After dinner the savouries were often cheese-based.

> Over elaboration must be guarded against in these small relishes, while, at the same time, careless service must not exist. Therefore serve daintily, and with light and suitable garnish, in tiny dishes of glass or white china, holding just enough for one person; or these are suitable and effective for dotting about the table in larger dishes, say two or three each containing a distinct variety.

A typical oyster savoury was a fried round of bread spread with a paste of cooked chicken, oysters and boiled egg yolk on which was placed a very thin slice of lemon and an oyster, sprinkled with pepper and chopped parsley. Sardine tartlets were made of puff pastry and filled with a mixture of tinned sardines, hard boiled egg yolk, butter and capers. Amy Schauer showed a particular fondness for caviar and anchovies. Caviar was spread hot or cold on rounds of fried bread and garnished in various ways. One of the more elaborate anchovy savouries had a base of toast spread with a savoury egg mixture on which was piled pink-coloured anchovy cream shaped into a cone and decorated with strips of anchovy meeting at the top. Cheese savouries included cheese eclairs, fried balls of grated cheese and whipped egg white, tartlets, biscuits and the popular *straws* of cheese pastry served in little bundles, each held together by a pastry ring.

Soups

Soups were approached methodically and were generally taken more seriously than one might have expected in Queensland. Eight stocks were given: first stock of beef shin and veal knuckle for clear soups; second stock of bones and lesser meat for thick soups; plain stock from bones 'for everyday soups and gravies'; fish stock; vegetable stock and game stock made from trimmings. She also gave an economical stock made from pot boilings. Most of the soups were fairly standard for the time. Among the more interesting were *baked soup*: a 'very substantial winter soup' of stock, beef, rice and various vegetables placed in a sealed jar and baked in a water bath in the oven; *velvet soup* made with sheep's head and served with forcemeat balls of the tongue and brains; and *giblet soup*, made from certain parts recovered from poultry (usually heart, liver, neck and gizzard).

Fish

'Fish intended for cookery purposes must be fresh. On this point there cannot be two opinions.' With this promising start and a few pages of general instructions she gave a selection of basic recipes for fish boiled, baked, fried, soused, steamed, stewed or recycled. These were served with standard white, tomato or curry sauces. There were recipes for fish roes, crabs, prawns, oysters and a couple for lobsters. The prawn recipes give a fair idea of the treatment she gave to seafood: seasoned and rolled in bread; curried with onion and apple; devilled with bottled tomato sauce, anchovy essence, Worcestershire sauce and cayenne; in white sauce; scalloped; or seasoned and served on toast with white sauce.

Roasted or baked?

Amy Schauer gave nearly 20 pages to general information and instructions on meat and poultry: baking, boiling, broiling or grilling, steaming, stewing, braising, wet frying, dry frying, sautering (sic). She was quite particular about the difference between roasting and baking. 'Roasting is cooking before an open fire, and is dying out on account of the construction of the stoves.' Meat cooked in an oven is therefore not 'roast'.

This is too simple. Although roasting was originally by open fire, the essential difference between roasting and baking is that the former cooks mainly by radiant heat, the latter mainly by hot air (unless the oven is very small and tightly closed, when steaming takes over). Herman Senn, one-time chef of the Reform Club in London, admitted three methods of roasting: before the fire, a method confined mostly to England and America; in the oven of 'ordinary coal stoves or ranges'; and in a gas stove.[17] The second method he considered inferior, though it resulted in less weight loss than the first. However, roasting in a gas oven was popular and 'very satisfactory'; the meat was placed under a sheet of flame and the oven space was well ventilated. The cooking medium was therefore very much like an open fire. This advantage was lost from later gas oven designs which were more closed and hid the gas flame.

The popularity of roasting may partly explain the occasional references in Federation cookery books to a tin (Dutch) oven. This was a device for trapping the heat of an open fire. It was a sort of tin box with a polished interior to reflect the heat. One side of the box was open, and faced the fire. The oven was usually fitted with a spit and handle for turning poultry, game birds or small joints. There may also have been hooks on which food could be hung for toasting. In the side away from the fire was a flap that could be opened for viewing the meat or basting it.[18] It was quite different from the large cast-iron pot now known as a Dutch oven. One of the virtues of the tin oven was that

Preserving Pan.

Jelly Bag.

Vegetable Knife.

Stew-pan.

Toaster.

Dutch Oven

Gravy Strainer.

it provided a measure of convenience in open-fire cooking without sacrificing any of the character of roasted meat. Its use seemed to continue for some time after cooking ranges became common in Australian households, suggesting that not everyone welcomed the quite different character of meat baked in a closed oven. Zara Aronson, the most fashion-conscious of cookery writers, recommended the Dutch oven for dishes such as broiled rabbit.

Another explanation for recipes mentioning a tin oven could be that they had simply been copied from old sources, now lost, without adaptation to the new cooking methods.

Amy Schauer explained braising as a 'form of steaming, by which the meat, etc. is subjected to two fires'. This was supposed to be achieved by placing it in a closed braising pan on a gentle heat. The lid of the pan had an indentation to hold live coals, providing the second source of heat. However, she said that braising-pans were 'seldom met with in Australia' and a small boiler, with its lid inverted, was just as good. Senn described the method, noting that it was said to reduce greatly the losses of evaporation and to 'bring out an unusually fine flavour and aroma', but otherwise paid little attention to it. It was a difficult method to use properly without a real fire to provide a supply of hot coals or ashes. Gas stove manufacturers offered a 'braising burner', a sort of inverted gas grill fitted with a handle and fed by a flexible gas pipe.[19] This could be placed on top of the braising pan to provide the top-down heat while the bottom-up heat came from a gas ring or stove-top. The idea did not really catch on, and braising fell victim to convenience.

The method was often imitated by browning the meat and stewing it in a tightly closed pan or by stewing or baking it in a closed pan and then browning it in a sharp oven. The meat was sometimes brushed with a little glaze before being served.

The beef recipes which followed included a pot roast and various dishes of ox tail, brains, heart, cheek, heel, palates and tripe. Mutton, lamb and veal all received detailed treatment, with little left to be wasted. Fresh pork was given less attention, but here also she gave recipes for using up the less seemly bits such as cheek, feet, ears, heart, kidneys and liver – despite concerns about the wholesomeness of pork.

Game

Beyond wonga pigeon and wild duck there was no attempt to deal with Australian game. The Schauer collection was dominated by pigeon, rabbit and hare. It is interesting that both rabbit and hare were occasionally served with the head attached, a practice that many might now consider to be in poor taste. Except for some fish and crustaceans, most creatures are now expected to appear at the table quite headless. Hers was the only book to mention guinea fowl. Pheasant, teal, woodcock and snipe were also mentioned.

Amy Schauer was the pigeon specialist, offering more than a dozen recipes for it. Pigeon pie was a popular dish at the time and appeared in most books. However, the pigeons were often little more than guests in the pie, crowded with rump steak, boiled eggs, usually bacon, and even mince, all sheltering under a generous layer of puff pastry. One can't escape the conclusion that pigeon pie was first and foremost a way of making a couple of little birds 'do' at a large table. The Schauer dish had all these things except the mince. As if to prove the presence of pigeon, a finishing touch was a pair of pigeon legs sticking up out of the hole in the centre. Unhappy pigeon. With a finer sense of aesthetics, but total disregard for anatomy, Zara Aronson suggested three feet. Jean Rutledge outlegged them both by suggesting four or five.

Roast pigeons were served on pieces of toast spread with a mixture of pigeon liver and pâté de foie gras. Pigeons could be 'baked' on a bed of bacon, without added liquid, in a tightly closed saucepan. They could be stewed and served with peas, like a duck, or with other garnishes. For *pigeons a la mazarin* they were partly boned, braised, stuffed with sausage meat, crumbed, fried and handsomely dished. *Pigeons and tomato* had the birds halved, browned and stewed with tomatoes and chillies. However, *pigeons and tomatoes* was a dish on an altogether different plane: for this they were boned; stuffed with forcemeat, mushrooms, pistachio nuts and truffles; rolled and cooked in stock.

They were then sliced, covered with tomato aspic, decorated with pistachio nuts, dished 'on a rice block', surrounded with sliced tomato salad, and garnished with aspic jelly. There was a *salmi* of stewed pigeons garnished with Spanish olives stuffed with pigeon liver; this recipe ended with the interesting annotation: 'Original. Tried.' The pigeon curry included the ubiquitous apple and a cup of thick cream was said to be 'considered by many a great improvement'.

The *Schauer Cookery Book* is difficult to summarise neatly. It was the most comprehensive Australian text book and, except for pickles, chutneys, jams and confectionery, on which it was silent, generally offered plenty of variety. In proportion to its size it gave more attention to savouries and main dishes than the others did. There were plenty of good meals to be cooked from it, but one would have to work hard to make a festive meal. Amy Schauer was not much interested in the *art* of cookery or with novelty; her recipes were plain and her interpretations of foreign dishes generally unconvincing. For more than 40 years she taught her students and the many others who bought her book or attended her demonstrations of competent, conservative, economical cookery. Perhaps no more was wanted of her.

Aunt Eva's book

The pleasure of an old book is doubled when one knows the history of it. My battered copy of the *Schauer Cookery Book* came from my wife's family. It was first owned by great-aunt Eva. Family lore has it that her father was in charge of the glove department of Anthony Hordern's store in Sydney and had been one of the original staff recruited from England. In July, 1901 he was ill in bed when Eva rushed in with news of the 'huge conflagration' that burnt the store down. The news was too much for her father who collapsed and died, leaving Eva, then a young woman in her teens, and her two younger sisters to the care of an aunt in Ashfield. Eva had trouble settling down after this – she was described as a 'wanderer' – and left Sydney. Among other places she lived for a time in Brisbane, where she acquired the cookery book in 1909.[20] She married rather later than was fashionable. Her sister Gladys married a steam train driver, moved to Katoomba and bought the *Goulburn Cookery Book* (1918 edition). She also produced many children, one of whom was Olive, who in turn produced Lynette whom I married, thereby acquiring both books.

And for those who like such things, the circle can be completed. When great-aunt Eva died her copy of the cookery book went to her sister Gladys, who then lived back in Ashfield. Its author was already there. Amy Schauer had spent her last days in Sydney and was buried in the grave of her parents at St John's, Ashfield.

CHAPTER 4

THE CONTRIBUTORS

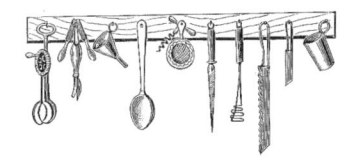

In 1891 a Mrs Longhurst visited Australia to stir up support for the missionary work in Madras being sponsored by the Presbyterian Church of Scotland.[1] Mrs Longhurst, a Scot, had been working with outcast women and children in Palipet and Sholinghur. The mission urgently needed both funds and workers. Her efforts in Australia were rewarded, with several thousands of pounds being raised to assist in the erection of a school and other buildings at the mission. Even more exciting for the New South Wales Presbyterians was the decision of one of their own young women, Mary McLean, a school teacher from Berry, to accept the challenge of going to work at the mission. She wasted no time, and sailed from Australia in December 1891.

Raising the cost of her initial outfit, passage to India and first year's salary (in all, about £150) was one thing; providing for her continuing salary of £120 would be quite another and would take organisation and continued dedication. To provide for this, Mrs Longhurst and several local church leaders agreed that a Women's Missionary Association (WMA) was needed and this was duly launched at a public meeting at St Stephen's Church.

India was not the only field of missionary activity needing support. Missionary outreach was a concern of the church from its early days. The New South Wales Presbyterian Assembly had been active as early as 1864 in mission work in the New Hebrides, where the forced recruitment of Kanakas to work in sugar and cotton plantations in Queensland and northern New South Wales was a serious embarrassment. By the time of the formation of the WMA, missionary work in the New Hebrides was well established, though progress was measured in small steps and there were many difficulties and setbacks to command concern and support from the women at home.

And there was much to be done in Australia. In North Queensland, there was already concern about the plight of some Aboriginal communities and their exploitation by pearl fishers. A mission station had been established there. In Sydney the Presbyterians saw a need for a mission to the Chinese population.

John Chinaman

In the late nineteenth century fear and hatred of the Chinese in Australia ran deep. As the era of convict transportation came to an end in the mid nineteenth century and the supply of convict labour began to dry up, landowners wanting cheap labour turned to importing large numbers of Chinese coolies, mainly Cantonese. They often came on contract, without wives and families and with no intention of staying here after completing their indentures. When the gold rushes started in the 1850s, the Chinese were as anxious as the rest to make their fortunes on the goldfields. Many of those already in Australia, like white Australians, simply left their jobs and joined the rushes. Many more were brought out specifically to provide cheap labour at the fields. For most, the journey out was a nightmare of overcrowding, filthy conditions, scanty rations of poor quality, and generally inhumane treatment at the hand of shipowners. Those who survived the voyage were for evermore wary of white ways.

On the goldfields their strange religious customs, their joss houses, preference for opium rather than alcohol and their physical separation from the white community all made them targets for white suspicion, distrust, hatred and even persecution.[2] The Australian dislike of Chinese immigrants at times flared into violence on the goldfields or in the towns and fuelled a century of discrimination which achieved official status as the White Australia Policy.

After a series of violent incidents, the Chinese drifted away from the goldfields and began to establish themselves in other occupations such as market gardening, commerce and manufacturing. In Sydney Chinese manufactured furniture near Circular Quay, worked market gardens at Botany and brought their produce into the Haymarket, near which they soon established restaurants. They remained rather separate from the European population, to the apparent satisfaction of both sides, leaving no permanent mark on Australian cookery. There were no recipes of Chinese origin in the popular cookery books of the time and very few references to Chinese ways with British dishes.

The New South Wales Presbyterian Assembly, concerned with the conditions under which many Chinese immigrants were living and also for their spiritual needs, opened a church in Foster Street, Surrey Hills about 1893. The WMA undertook to supply the church with an American organ and to pay off the building debt.

With these commitments, fund-raising became an absorbing occupation for the Presbyterian women.

Quong Tart

More than 250 were present when the Association held its first social evening 'in Mr Quong Tart's rooms'.[3] Mei Quong Tart was a particularly colourful character in Sydney community life at that time. Born in the Canton province of China in 1850, he came to Australia as a young boy and was unofficially adopted by a family of wealthy gold miners, the Simpsons, at Braidwood. He was converted to Christianity, naturalised, and joined the Manchester Unity Lodge and the Freemasons. Quong Tart's close association with a number of Scottish families in the district gave him a lasting fondness for all things Caledonian; he delighted in wearing the kilt and in being referred to as 'Mac Tart'. Under the patronage of the Simpsons at Braidwood, he became a successful gold mine operator, but left in 1874 to establish himself as an importer of tea and silk in Sydney.

In the early 1880s Quong Tart began selling quality teas in the Sydney Arcade, handing out samples in attractive Chinese cups and saucers as inducement to his customers. The gimmick was successful and he was soon charging for the tea and serving scones with it. His business flourished and by 1885 he had a chain of six tea houses. His crowning glory was the Elite Dining Hall and Tea Rooms which occupied two floors of the newly completed Queen Victoria Building, then housing the city market. It was a magnificently appointed establishment with trickling ferneries in rock, marble fish ponds of golden carp, hand-painted mirrors, massive Chinese wood-carvings in green and gold and hundreds of fans – all designed to create a 'celestial' atmosphere.[4] All comforts were provided: well appointed lavatories with hot and cold water, writing rooms, smoking rooms and separate rooms for ladies. As in all his establishments, the emphasis was on excellent service.

Despite the 'celestial' atmosphere and names such as 'Han Pan' and 'Loong Shan Tea House', Quong Tart made no attempt to sell Chinese food to Sydney. One went to his rooms to dine on elegant European-style food or to take tea with a variety of sandwiches, cakes, buns or his special scones. Quong Tart's famous scones were not the traditional plain ones. They included sugar and egg, and came out as a cross between the plain sort and the now largely forgotten gem scones. A recipe for them has survived in the *Goulburn Cookery Book*.

"QUONG TART" SCONES

One pound of flour, 2 oz. of butter, 2 dessertspoons of sugar, 1 egg, ¾ cup of milk, 4 teaspoons of baking powder, 1 teaspoon of salt.

Mix flour, baking powder, salt, and butter together. Beat the egg, add milk and sugar, and stir till the latter is dissolved; mix with flour, roll, cut with sugar on the board, and bake in a quick oven.

Missionary enterprise

Eighteen ninety-five was a big year for fund raising. Brimming with enthusiasm for its new cause, the Association held a large 'Exhibition and Sale of Work' in the old Exhibition Building at Prince Alfred Park. (A 'new' exhibition building, the vast 'Garden Palace' in the Botanic Gardens, had been erected for the great Sydney International Exhibition of 1879, but was destroyed by fire in 1882.)

The sale and exhibition were very successful and raised over £1000 – a very large sum, considering that Australia was then in depression. The stall or bazaar and concert had already become hallmarks of all kinds of fund-raising auxiliaries, and the Presbyterians were to return to this good and tried source many times in aid of their missionary ventures.

The Presbyterian Cookery Book

One of the fund-raising ideas came from the Treasurer, Mrs Dawson. She suggested that the women pool the best of their recipes for a cookery book to be offered at the exhibition. The idea was readily accepted. The PWMA Fourth Annual Report (1895) stated that 'a committee was appointed, with Mrs MacInnes as editor, to receive recipes from any ladies who should be willing to send them, and after making a selection to have them published. Messrs. S. T. Leigh & Co. very kindly undertook to print 2000 copies free of charge, provided they had the right to include advertisements, which was granted, and their offer gratefully accepted'.

Mrs. MacInnes was the wife of the Rev George MacInnes, M.A., D.D., a prominent clergyman in the Presbyterian movement in New South Wales. Perhaps it was not merely coincidental that in 1895, the year of the first edition of the *Presbyterian Cookery Book*, he held its highest office, that of Moderator.

The 2000 copies of the cookery book were sold and quickly followed by a second run of 1000 copies – which to the Association was clear 'proof of the excellence of the recipes and the careful

FOR A PERFECT SCONE
A "*Sine qua non*" is the
"ANCHOR" BRAND
SELF-RAISING
FLOUR.

PREFACE.

THIS collection of Receipts for good, Plain Cookery has been compiled for the Women's Missionary Association of the Presbyterian Church of New South Wales, in connection with a grand Sale of Work and Missionary Exhibition, in the Old Exhibition Building, Prince Alfred Park, Sydney. The object of this effort is to pay the debt on the Chinese Presbyterian Church, Foster Street, Sydney, and to clear off the liabilities of the General Assembly's Foreign Mission Committee. The Receipts have been collected from members of the Church, and are all guaranteed by the senders.

M. MACINNES,
EDITOR.

September, 1895.

"Throw physic to the dogs," said Macbeth,
And give me
GILLESPIE'S ROLLED OATS
For Breakfast.

selection made.'⁵ After that, the free run with Messrs Leigh & Co. seems to have run out. The book passed to Messrs Angus and Robertson for more regular distribution, though the third edition was still printed by Leigh.

By 1902 there had been seven editions amounting 45 000 copies and the revenue was contributing to new causes, 'ameliorating the conditions of some of our missionaries, assisting in the purchase of the J. G. Ward mission steamer for the Mapon and Embly River Stations in North Queensland, and in many ways assisting in the more efficient carrying on of our missionary enterprises in India, the New Hebrides, and other parts of the world.'⁶

Recipes from home

One might expect at least the first edition of a cookery book by Presbyterians to be biased towards traditional Scots dishes, but it was not so in this case. The *haggis* was there, as it should be, together with a few others that obviously were either brought from the old country or inspired by it: *Scots broth, Scots woodcock, Scots eggs, Kirkcudbright pudding, Balmoral pudding, Caledonian cream, Scots cake, Thurso cakes, Scots bun, free kirk pudding* and *Rothsay pudding*. *Red herrings, minced collops, hot pot, oat cake, oatmeal biscuits, Urney pudding* and *marmalade* are Scottish. *Cock-a-leekie* (also *cockie-leekie*) was popular enough around the time of Federation and was included in other books, but did not appear in the Presbyterian book for 50 years or so. *Aberdeen sausage* was picked up in the 1902 edition. *Hotch potch*, a marvellous soup of meat and freshly picked young vegetables; *Seakale*, a member of the cabbage family which grows rather like asparagus, and *sowans*, a kind of creamy porridge with a slightly sour taste, made it into other books, but never the Presbyterian. The Presbyterian women even left behind their *rumbledethumps*, the Scottish fry-up of potatoes and cabbage. From the start, the English *bubble and squeak* was given instead. Both mixtures made quite satisfying squeaks and thumps as they came to terms with the heat of the breakfast frying pan – how else did they get their names? – but the *squeak* was preferred in Australia probably because in those days it always had plenty of meat in it.

KIRKCUDBRIGHT PUDDING
(Mysterious pudding)

Take 2 eggs, the same weight of sugar, butter, and flour, a tablespoon of the juice of marmalade. Cream the butter, add the sugar, then the flour, beat the eggs a little and put them in last. Steam in a tin for two hours. Golden syrup may be substituted for marmalade, and a teaspoonful of baking powder may be added.

Why the *Kirkcudbright pudding* was subtitled 'mysterious' must remain its own mystery. It was a plain thing, presumably from the town in south west Scotland, which also gave its name to the famous *Kirkcudbright Grace*, often attributed to the Scots poet, Robert Burns:

> Some have meat and cannot eat,
> Some cannot eat that want it:
> But we have meat and we can eat,
> Sae let the Lord be thankit.

The book was organised into 13 chapters, the largest of which dealt with puddings and pastry. This did not exhaust the subject of sweets, for jellies, creams and fruit dishes were dealt with separately. The second largest chapter gave cake recipes, supplemented by another on biscuits and scones. There were also chapters on confectionery; jams, preserves and (a few) pickles; and summer drinks (you guessed it – all sweet). A further chapter gave two dozen or so sauces, nearly half of which were sweet.

Rather less space was given to soups, entrées, luncheon and other fish and meat dishes.

The omission of a section on savouries from a book on 'good, plain cookery' is not hard to understand; there was probably little call for them in day-to-day family cooking. But the absence of a section on vegetables was most unusual. Notwithstanding Philip Muskett's views, most books tried to put up some show. However, in nearly 600 recipes the Presbyterians were only able to gather one salad and five vegetable made-dishes. Perhaps they thought that plain vegetables required no explanation and that made-dishes of vegetables belonged to a higher class than they had aimed for.

The pudding

The pudding was an essential part of any respectable meal. It was usually hot and often no light matter. The Federation pudding was intended not just to balance the meal with something sweet but to *fill*, and fill it did. Nearly half the sweets in the Presbyterian book are boiled or steamed puddings; and some would challenge the most determined digestion. Some of them were, in effect, steamed suet pastry. The general rule was that 'beef suet makes the richest, and mutton the lightest and most digestible puddings', but these things are relative.[7]

Jam – especially raspberry jam – and marmalade were popular flavourings. The *Hopetoun pudding* was a hefty thing of roughly equal quantities of flour, butter, eggs and raspberry jam, with sugar for good measure. Although lifted with bicarbonate of soda and steamed, it would have been no trifling matter. Others were lighter, but still substantial. The steamed *Balmoral pudding* used a cake-like batter with milk and baking powder and a minimum of fat. It was a plain pudding, flavoured only with a little marmalade or jam, served with jam sauce.

Treacle and golden syrup found their way into a few puddings, ranging from heavyweight suet lumps to steamed 'sponges' lightened with baking powder. Ginger and treacle or syrup have long been a popular combination and it is not surprising that two of the three ginger puddings included treacle (although one of them was marked 'no good' in my 1902 edition). Treacle was sometimes made into a sauce with water, sugar and lemon juice and poured over a plain suet pudding or dumplings ('plain' meaning no sweetening or flavouring of any kind). Jam sauce was used in the same way.

TREACLE PUDDING

Take 1 cup flour, 2 tablespoons sugar, 1 teaspoon salt, 1 teaspoon carbonate soda, 1 large teaspoonful ground ginger, 2 tablespoons butter or beef dripping, 2 tablespoons treacle, 1 cup of milk.

Mix all the dry ingredients; rub in the butter; then add the treacle, and lastly the milk. Steam in a buttered mould 2 hours. To be eaten with custard or sweet sauce. The same receipt is very good made with fruit and a little peel, omitting the treacle and ginger, and adding a little more sugar.

The gradual movement away from boiled suet puddings was quite evident in the range of recipes given in Federation cookery books. Beside – or perhaps above – the flour, suet, dried fruit formulae stood lighter versions of essentially the same puddings: bread crumbs replacing some or all of the flour; less suet; grated apple or carrot or even mashed potato to lighten and moisten the mix. Replacing the suet with butter, including egg and milk, and adding a rising agent such as bicarbonate of soda brought further relief. Boiling the pudding in a cloth was giving way to boiling it in a basin or pudding mould covered with cloth, so allowing the incorporation of more liquid in the mix and reducing the loss of 'flavour and goodness'.[8] For those who could afford gadgets, a 'pudding boiler' was even better. This was a mould with its own lid and was said to be 'cleaner, handier, and more economical to use... and it makes lighter dainties and more digestible puddings'.[9] Later still, the cloth gave way to greaseproof paper and the mould stood in boiling water in a large pot on the stove, with the water coming only part-way up the basin: it was now a steamed pudding. Steaming was more convenient than boiling and cooks who steamed their puddings in heavy closed pots may also have noticed that the slightly higher pressure would raise the cooking temperature and so improve the rising.

> **CABINET PUDDING**
>
> Beat five yolks and one whole egg for a minute or two, add two ounces of sugar. Pour over this three-quarters of a pint of milk brought to boiling point; stir, and strain. Flavour with orange, vanilla, or lemon. Butter a plain pudding mould, and put a buttered paper at the bottom. Decorate with a few crystallised cherries and angelica, washing the fruit in tepid water and sponging it in a cloth. Over this lay a few rounds of Genoise cake or sponge cake soaked in two or three spoonfuls of brandy or liqueur, placing between each layer of cake a sprinkling of fruit (preserved cherries, apricots, and peel cut into small dice; and a few raisins) alternately with six crushed macaroons (three ounces of fruit altogether). When the mould is three parts full, pour the raw custard slowly in, and let the pudding stand for half an hour; then poach very slowly for about one hour and a quarter, or till firm in the centre, covering the pudding with buttered paper. Serve with Sabayon or custard sauce.[10]

The *cabinet pudding* achieved lightness in a different way. At its simplest, it was a rather plain bread and egg custard pudding, with perhaps a few raisins or sultanas, steamed or boiled in a basin. At its best, it was an elegant dessert of sponge cake, macaroon biscuits and sometimes preserved fruit, elaborately decorated with crystallised cherries and angelica, set in rich custard.

Rice and sago were explored in the search for lighter boiled puddings, not always with happy results. The Presbyterian *apple and rice pudding* was a mixture of plain rice and apples boiled in a cloth and served with molasses sauce. The recipe survived into the 1920s, but it could not – or should not – have been popular, and it was later deleted. Cereals were generally more successful in baked puddings. The *George pudding* was a more attractive apple and rice combination: rice boiled in milk, apple purée, egg yolks and whipped egg whites baked in a mould. It was turned out and served with 'a good custard' around it.

The movement away from heavy puddings could be seen in successive editions of the Presbyterian book. It started out with some 66 boiled or steamed puddings (about one in every nine recipes) and few more were added in 1918. The number gradually declined after that and by 1979 it had halved, in what was now a much larger book; of the remainder only a handful were for traditional boiled suet, no doubt left more for the sake of nostalgia than because people were likely to make them.

Baked puddings were increasing in popularity and there was a wide variety of recipes available in the books from which cooks could choose. Recipes were relied upon for puddings and cakes more than for meat and vegetable dishes, since accuracy in quantities, technique and cooking times was often more important. Favourite recipes were marked and used again and again. Nevertheless cooks felt quite free to improvise and adapt. Once they were sufficiently experienced they could take liberties in the realm of baked puddings quite safely, for the main components were simple.

Most were created from four or five basic preparations. Fruit was usually featured in some form: apple was popular, jam was the stand-by. There was often a batter or firm custard mix of milk set with egg, cornflour or both; and nearly always a filler of cereal (rice, tapioca or sago) or of stale bread or sponge cake. Sometimes the filler was on the outside, as pastry. A meringue topping gave a nice finish and an opportunity to use up the egg whites if only the yolks went into the custard. Some puddings called for a sauce to moisten them, to enhance their flavour or simply to make them palatable: a custard thickened with egg yolks or a substitute such as lemon sauce or jam sauce.

Examples from the Presbyterian book are baked *apple and tapioca pudding* served with sugar and cream; *currant batter pudding* with suet, eaten hot with sugar; *cornflour pudding* (thick vanilla custard covered with stewed fruit and topped with meringue) and the famous lemon meringue pie (*lemon tart*).

The age of the jelly was fast approaching, and Federation cooks were preparing for it. Ice was available in cities and towns; gelatine was marketed commercially; jellies were perfect as the alternative sweet for diners who preferred not to attempt the boiled suet pudding. There were crystal-clear fruit jellies, lemon jellies and wine jellies (usually a lemon base with sherry or port). Fine jellies were set in fancy moulds, sometimes with fruit embedded in intricate patterns; fruit purées were set with jelly and moulded; custards were given the same treatment. The results were not yet as gross as they would become a few decades later, but they were practising. *Gâteau of apricots* was a moulded, jellied purée of tinned apricots decorated with whipped cream. *Arrowroot charlotte* was a jellied arrowroot custard set in a mould lined with sponge cake and garnished with jelly or jam.

Lemon sponge was typical of a whole class of jellied puddings that rose to popularity with refrigeration and have now almost disappeared. Essentially it was a lemon jelly into which stiffly whipped egg whites were folded just before it was moulded; the result was a jelly with a spongy texture. A similar thing was done with fruit purée and jellied custard puddings. *Raspberry cream* ought to be made with a purée of fresh raspberries, but usually raspberry jam or jelly was substituted.

THE CONTRIBUTORS 69

Cakes and biscuits

In comparison with other Federation cookery books, the *Presbyterian* had the largest number of cake and biscuit recipes, despite its modest size. It is a good place to look for a general appreciation of the Federation cook's approach to this important kitchen activity.

On the whole, cakes and biscuits were fairly plain. Many were clearly meant for entertaining, but subtleties of texture and flavour, the presence or absence of additions such as almonds or glacé cherries and the proportion of dried fruits were generally what distinguished a cake for occasions from the every-day family items. Federation cookery books show so many subtle variations in mix and method that users – and those they cooked for – really must have appreciated the differences in result. If so, they were connoisseurs of cake to a degree that most people now would not understand.

Lemon essence, currants, candied citrus peel and desiccated coconut were popular additions to biscuits, cookies and patty cakes. Ginger biscuits and oatmeal biscuits were popular. Other recurring flavourings were almonds, caraway seeds and ratafia (almond) essence. Cornflour or rice flour was often added to give a shorter, finer texture. Occasionally carbonate of ammonia was used as a rising agent: the action of heat produced ammonia and carbon dioxide, both gases, with no residue. Hence *ammonia biscuits*.

A few examples from the Presbyterian book will illustrate the range of serious cakes. *Durham cake* was a plain sponge sandwiched with stewed apples. The *cocoanut cake* was unusual, and probably somewhat 'special': three layers of plain cake sandwiched with royal icing and grated fresh coconut. The *Irish cake* was always for special occasions and achieved some status in Presbyterian folk lore because of the number of eggs it required. However, its sub-title pointed more to the Scots' care for expense, and to the overall plainness of their cooking, than to any extravagance in the particular recipe of the Irish. It was a very large cake and not particularly rich eating as pound cakes went, but perhaps one had to be rich to afford the eggs.

IRISH CAKE
(very rich)

Take 2 lbs. flour, 1¼ lbs. butter, 1½ lbs. brown sugar, ¼ lb. citron, 2½ lbs. currants, 18 eggs.

Warm the butter and beat it to a cream, break in the eggs by degrees with the fruit and sugar. Add the flour last. Keep beating the same way and do not take out the hand till thoroughly mixed. Bake about three hours.

There were four versions of *pound cake*, two of them with currants, but none of the recipes was strictly traditional (for that, equal weights of eggs, sugar, fat and flour would be used; if the fat and sugar were creamed properly no rising agent would be required). A fine *exhibition cake* was given, with candied peel and caraway seed, but no indication of which exhibition had smiled on it.

Among the more ordinary cakes were four kinds of *gingerbread*, two very plain cakes named *vanity* (one wonders why) and three versions of *soda cake* (which used bicarbonate of soda as the rising agent, relying on ingredients such as sour milk to activate it). A good sponge cake was greatly appreciated and evidence of a skilful cook. This book gave two versions. In the first, the egg yolks and whites were beaten separately, by hand, for 20 minutes. The second was helped by baking powder, but nevertheless required the cook to beat the eggs and sugar together for half an hour. The *Victoria or jam sandwich* was also there.

Even among basically plain cakes, colour and visual presentation were important. *Day and night cake* had two layers: one dark, the other light. Making a *snow cake* would leave you with eight egg yolks. What to do with them? Make a boiled custard of course – or a *gold cake*. If you made a gold cake first, you might think next, not of snow, but of *silver cake*. The *gold* and *silver* combination was repeated in several other Federation books, and most gave a *snow cake*. For *marble cake* the batter was divided into two portions, one coloured with chocolate and the other left plain; the two were spooned into the tin alternately. *Rainbow cake* had pink, white and chocolate layers. *Nantwich cake* was coloured pink and baked in a tin which had been greased with lard, butter or mutton fat and sprinkled with desiccated coconut to produce a fine coating of fried coconut around the cake. The use of mutton fat is another matter.

From the number of recipes given in most books it seems that small cakes and biscuits were also daily fare. The Presbyterian book gave a number of stand-bys such as *auntie cakes* (lemon patty cakes with cornflour), *cookies* (rather plain biscuits), *lemon biscuits* (flavoured with essence), *light buns* (plain things flavoured with 'almond, desiccated cocoanut, or any other essence to taste'), *luncheon biscuits* (plain), *plain ginger biscuits* and *rock cakes*.

LEMON BISCUITS

Take 1 lb. flour, ½ lb. sugar, ½ lb. butter, 2 eggs, a few drops essence of lemon, 1 teaspoon carbonate soda, 2 teaspoons cream of tartar.

Beat the butter to a cream, add the sugar, drop in the eggs, and beat well. Mix the cream of tartar with the flour, melt the soda in a little water, then mix all together. Roll out, and cut into shapes.

The sweetness index

About 160 of the recipes in the Presbyterian book were for desserts and the same number again were sweet things for tea. Altogether, they made up just over two thirds of the book. In proportion to their size, most Australian cookery books of the time gave only half as much space to sweet dishes; modern health-conscious books may give only a third.

The extraordinary bias towards sweet things in a book that ought to be representative of the popular cookery of the day needs some explanation.

It seems that contributory cookery books generally lie at the high end of the sweetness scale. The *Green and Gold Cookery Book*, compiled in the 1920s to raise funds for Kings College, Adelaide, gave nearly two thirds of its space to sweet dishes of one kind or another. In the late 1930s the *Coronation Cookery Book* by the New South Wales Country Women's Association was healthier, but still well above average, at 47% sweetness. The *New P.W.M.U. Cookery Book* of the Presbyterian women of Victoria was about the same. Cookery books prepared by instructors were more likely to be well balanced, with an emphasis on sustenance and 'healthy' food, than books based on what people actually cooked or perhaps wanted (in the subtly competitive environment of women's auxiliary movements) to be seen to be cooking.

The explanation may lie in the habits of everyday eating. The basic construction of a meal – something to titillate the appetite; something to take the edge off it; the main work of meat and vegetables; and something to celebrate its conclusion – is common enough throughout western cultures. The architectural detail varies according to place, occasion and means, but the idea is the same.[11] Only where scarcity or poverty reduces eating to the bare necessities of subsistence is it altogether put aside.

Modern restaurant dining shows the pattern clearly. At a minimum, the ritual is: a pre-prandial drink; bread to blunt the appetite (quite useful if the kitchen is slow); an entrée if there is time; the main course; and dessert 'to finish' (if the establishment has been canny and not overfed the client). If dessert cannot be sold then coffee and the ubiquitous after-dinner mint will serve to mark the end of the meal. Week-day family meals in busy, modern households may have lost much of their ceremony, but the pattern is still there in a casual, functional form: the after-school snack to take the edge off the appetite; a drink for the adults with something to nibble while dinner is cooking; something sweet to declare the end of the meal or, later, for supper.

No doubt Edward Abbott's 'upper ten thousand'[12] and their successors 40 years later ate very well and suffered no real lack of variety, but in most households the main meal centred on a basic offering of plainly cooked meat and vegetables. The experienced cook hardly needed recipes to boil, roast, grill or stew a piece of meat, to boil vegetables or to make a white or melted butter sauce to pour on them. Only on special occasions would she move outside this accepted formula, and then she might consult a book or wish for a cookery demonstration.

Sweets, cakes, pies and biscuits never became routine in the same way. Ritual offerings such as a plain cake or stewed fruit (*compote* in better circles) with a filler of rice, tapioca or sago existed, but sweet things were *treats*, and variety was important. As cooks quickly learn, cakes and puddings can be unforgiving and need more resort to directions. An onion more or less in the stew will generally not spoil it and the time it takes to cook potatoes cannot be prescribed, only judged. But the amount of gelatine in a jelly pudding can make the difference between rubber and a runny mess; an egg or two more or less in the bread pudding can make the difference between a solid lump and an unusual porridge. Keeping a record of how to make a much-enjoyed sweet concoction was important; it was no accident that scrap-books were high on the sweetness scale.

The competence of a cook was established by her ability to bring out a first class roast with all the customary trimmings, but her reputation would really depend on her cakes, pies and biscuits – the things she would present to callers at afternoon tea or bring to parish suppers, the food of friendship and of celebration. These were the recipes she would trade.

When the call went out for 'good and tried receipts' most people were probably caught up in the novelty of the occasion. It was not so much the idea of Presbyterian women making good whatever shortcomings they saw in the offerings of Mrs Beeton and Mrs Wicken; rather it was a young church launching a missionary venture, needing to raise funds, rallying to the cause, embracing a novel idea. Enthusiasm was in the air and enthusiasm begat celebration. And if the good ladies of the WMA were carried away with the enthusiasm of their project and gave more of celebration than of sustenance in their recipes – more of puddings and cakes than of meat and potatoes – who is to blame them?

Changes

Having completed her task of bringing the little red collection into being, Mrs MacInnes turned to other forms of service and responsibility for the book passed to Clara Kirkland. In the mid-1920s Mrs. Jennings took it over, but seems to have made only minor changes. By 1930 Mrs. Kirkland had it back, this time for a major reorganisation. To the disappointment of the WMA treasurer, the new edition was published 'on less favourable terms', possibly explaining why the book was hardly touched again until Agnes McCallum took it over and produced the great revision of 1950. Mrs McCallum remained in charge until her death in 1983.

Consumer feedback was as important in 1895 as now. It did not take long for the word to filter back to the WMA committee that some people frowned on the amount of space that had been given over to puddings, cakes and other sweet things. In 1902 Mrs Kirkland tried to put the matter right by bringing out a 'Supplement at the close of this volume, consisting of an additional number of recipes, chiefly for meat dishes'.

Only two of the 34 recipes in the supplement were sweet. It took the proportion of sweet dishes from a little more than two thirds of the total to a little less than two thirds – not much of a change, but in the right direction. Each revision brought the sweetness further into line, either by removing recipes that seemed to have served their time or by adding more for soups, entrées or meat dishes. By the time the last cookery convenor rested from her labours, just over half the dishes were sweet – still an unusually high proportion.

There were gradual changes throughout the book. Boiled and steamed puddings gave way to pies, tarts, frozen desserts and novelties for children's parties. Upside-down puddings made an appearance with versions for banana, pineapple and rhubarb. Ammonia and *ratafia biscuits* gave way to the now-famous *Anzac biscuits*. *Angelica cakes*, *auntie cakes* and *tennis cakes* were dropped in favour of *brandy snaps*, *peanut-butter biscuits*, *cornflake biscuits* and even *cornflake macaroons*. *Brandy snaps* should have been included from the beginning; they were popular enough at the turn of the century. With large cakes the story was much the same: *cocoanut cake*, *currant cake* and *railway cake* gave way to *banana cake*, *chocolate marshmallow cake* and new versions of the ever popular sponge. Overall, the number of cakes declined after reaching a peak in 1931. It is perhaps ironic that enthusiasm for making cakes was already waning by the time electric mixing appliances and thermostatic ovens arrived to take the hard work and uncertainty out of the task.

The neglect of vegetables and salads was gradually remedied, though the book never provided much inspiration in these matters. Among the less attractive later offerings was a dish of cooked green beans seasoned, mixed with milk, butter and grated cheese, and baked. Another was *stuffed egg plant with pineapple*: the vegetable was soaked, boiled, hollowed out and baked with a stuffing of its own pulp, bread crumbs, tinned pineapple, butter, egg and milk. Nutmeg, salt and pepper were the seasonings. The changing approach to salads can be seen in the *prune salad* with cream cheese and celery and the moulded jellies of tomato purée. *Chicken Maryland*, veal cutlets stuffed with pineapple and *pork sausages with fried apples* also showed the changing times. The final revision, in 1979, brought back tomato soup, discovered zucchini, pizza, quiche and garlic bread, showed the people what to do with frozen vegetables and introduced the microwave oven.

The book began to take on a broader role than that of a short-term fundraising enterprise. The preface to the fifteenth edition of 1918 shed some light on the reasons:

> The young and inexperienced housekeeper need have no fear of failure, provided she follows carefully the directions given, as the great aim of this book has always been, not only to provide wholesome and economical recipes for capable housewives, but to help those who have not had the benefit of maternal guidance and home training. It is significant that many discerning women have made it a habit to give a copy of the "Presbyterian" Cookery Book to every new bride of their acquaintance.[13]

Of course, this 'great aim' had not been so clear from the very beginning. But the 1895 fund raiser had proven to be enormously popular and, in response to so much favourable public attention, was beginning to expand its horizons and to sort itself out. The sorting-out process brought some useful changes to the way the book was organised, a proper alphabetical index, a section on invalid cookery and others on household remedies, war-time economies and hints. There was a real attempt to provide some general advice on cookery and kitchen management, though by modern standards it might seem wanting.

AUSTRALIAN SALAD

Take 3 large lettuces, 1 bunch radishes, 2 bunches spring onions, 1 cup of finely chopped mustard and cress, 4 tomatoes (skinned), 2 sprigs finely-chopped parsley and lemon-thyme, the chopped whites of 2 hard-boiled eggs.

DRESSING. – The yolks of 2 eggs (having been boiled 15 minutes) beaten with 1 large steamed potato, then add ½ cup of grated cocoanut, 6 sweet almonds (shredded), 1 teaspoonful of mustard, 1 teaspoonful curry powder, ½ teaspoonful pepper, 2 teaspoonfuls salt, 1 cup of cream, and ½ cup of vinegar. The whole to be beaten until quite smooth, then pour on the salad and toss well for 10 minutes with 2 large forks. The dressing must not be added to the salad till just before serving.[13]

Plain though it was, the Presbyterian book has an especially important place in Australia's culinary history. It remained in print for 100 years, for most of this time as a popular source of tested, everyday recipes for many New South Wales cooks. The dust cover blurb of the 1979 edition went so far as to claim that 'throughout the years – from fuel stoves to microwave ovens – it's been kept up to date without losing one ounce of its old-fashioned goodness.' The last printing, a paperback of the 1979 edition, was in 1995.

The value of the Presbyterian book now is as a chronicle of the changing fashions in Australian cookery. It never led the fashions, but was a faithful reporter of them for 85 years. Only in the last 15 years of its century did the ageing WMA allow it to slip gracefully behind the times and feed its readers memories instead.

THE WORKER COOKBOOK

Dame Mary Gilmore (1865-1962) is venerated still by many Australians. Her long and distinguished life as writer, poet and tireless campaigner for a wide range of social and economic reforms has earned her an enduring place in Australian literary and social history. She began her career as a pupil-teacher in the Wagga Wagga district. In the 1890s she joined the New Australia Movement in its attempt to found a utopian colony in Paraguay. In 1908 she asked the editor of the Labor journal, the *Australian Worker*, to include in it a special page for women. He agreed, but asked her to write it herself; she did so, until 1931. Besides many contributions to journals and newspapers she wrote several books of poetry and two of reminiscences, *Old days, old ways* and *More recollections*. Her literary and social achievements were honoured in 1937 with the award of the title, Dame of the British Empire. She died at the ripe old age of 97.[14]

It is impossible in a thumb-nail sketch to do her justice, but our interest here is not with her poems and prose, her patriotism or her campaign for women's voting rights, for the introduction of age and invalid pensions, for child endowment and many other reforms. Our attention focuses on a single small volume which she compiled from recipe contributions to the Women's Page. For here we gain a second glimpse of the people's choice in cookery.

In Mary Gilmore one finds both similarity and contrast with the Presbyterian women full of good works and holy concern for the souls of natives at home and abroad. Both were driven by ideals; both were innovators in their way; both were concerned for the poor and needy; both found in the idea of a contributed cookery book the means of furthering their causes and meeting a practical women's need at the same time. Yet the first book was bred of missionary zeal and Dorcas work, the second of literary leadership and political activism, culminating in her association late in life with the communist newspaper *Tribune*, to which she contributed articles until a few months before her death.

76   A Friend in the Kitchen

The *Worker Cook Book* contained about 800 recipes contributed over several years by women throughout Australia and New Zealand.[15] They were intended to be 'mainly the everyday recipes of Australian housekeepers in working-class homes'.[16] Mary Gilmore claimed that they had been 'collected from books and journals innumerable' and had, in many cases, 'been rectified and improved by the sender to suit the special needs of ordinary Australian cookery'. One need appears to have been answered in the potted meat made for sandwiches: four parts of cooked mutton minced with one of bacon (which 'then tastes like ham'). The frequent use of dripping for cakes and puddings (creamed with lemon or tartaric acid to 'reduce the taste') met an Australian need in much the same way as the use of lard in pastry served the English. There was a whole section on steamed puddings, heralding the end of the pudding cloth age, plenty of recipes for rabbit, and a selection of jams made with the ubiquitous pie melon (including one of melon, carrot and ginger called *household jam*.) The needs of station workers and the shearers whose industrial militancy helped form the Labor movement were well recognised. They also showed the marvellous resourcefulness of the bush cook.

SHED YEAST

I send the following recipe. I have used it for years and never change it:– Boil 4 oz. hops in 2 gals. water till they sink. Wash and cut up 4 lb. good potatoes (with salt, skins and all), boil till they break. Mash them in the liquor. Get a clean kerosene tin and put in ½ lb. flour, and 1 lb. sugar, mix with a little cold water to break the lumps of flour, then strain the potatoes (hot water and all) on to the flour and sugar, and then strain the hops on top of that scalding hot. Stir up. When it has cooled to about 75 degrees in summer and 90 degrees in winter add about ½ pint of old yeast and leave it to work. It will ferment in 4 days, according to the weather. As soon as the head begins to subside put in 2 or 3 handfuls of salt, stir it up and put away in a cool place.[17] It will keep for 6 or 8 weeks in cool weather. Dough up at night, it will be up in 8 hours. One pint of yeast in a gallon water will make 12 ordinary loaves. (Put a handful of sugar in the dough). Mix dough as cool as possible according to temperature (at no time warmer than 90 degrees). I have used this yeast for years, and have never changed it.– "The Jew Boy."

Another special need was for bread. Damper was a necessity in the bush and a last resort at the homestead, but people wanted real bread on the table if they could get it. Without commercial yeast they had to do some interesting things to get it.

Most cookery books gave directions for making bread, often tacked onto the end of recipes for home-made yeast. This was logical, for without first capturing and encouraging some natural yeast the best one could aim for was soda bread. When started, the yeast would be 'grown' in a starch-rich liquid in bottle or tub, according to one's ambitions. A popular mixture for growing the yeast was wild hops, potatoes, flour and sugar. 'Acid' yeasts were made with lemon juice, cream of tartar, tartaric acid, grated apple, or other fruit pulp and juice, together with flour, sugar and warm water. Even banana was used. *Bread lemonade* was an appropriate nickname for a precious, lemony liquid bubbling away in a bottle.[18] When bread was wanted the liquid would be mixed to a batter with flour and left overnight to form a 'sponge'. The next morning the sponge was incorporated into a light dough with more flour and warm water and left to 'prove'. Always a little yeast was kept back as a 'starter' for the next batch. The whole procedure was governed by ritual tested over many years, each cook confident that his or hers, if performed carefully, would never be known to fail. As Mary Gilmore explained it:

> The yeasts given here are those in use by the senders, all of whom are housekeepers making their own bread, or shearers' cooks who also make their own bread. The recipes are given in the senders' own words, and where directions for making bread are added these are put in as well – as the maker of both yeast and bread learns the best methods for either by experience.

Once again the people voted for sweetness; this collection scores about 54%. On the whole, the puddings, cold sweets, cakes and biscuits were not much different from those contributed to the Presbyterian book: plain, everyday affairs with an eye to economy and what might please a family. The *Worker's* readers were not much concerned with preserving dishes in their traditional forms. They only knew two tests: Do we like it? and Can we afford it?

SHEARERS' PUDDING

Put rice or tapioca in a piedish about an inch-and-a-half deep. Fill with milk, and put in the oven after it has cooked for half-an-hour, take the "crust" off the top, sweeten and flavour to taste. Add more milk if necessary, and put back in the oven until thoroughly cooked. The longer it cooks, the richer it seems to get, always providing you don't let the milk dry up. Condensed milk can be used for this. – (R.M., shearer's wife.)[19]

The same tests are clues to understanding also the remainder of the book – the savoury dishes. Mrs Beeton would have called them 'homely' and may not have been much impressed by suggestions like the addition of vegetables to *toad in the hole*. However, the cookery methods were always sound – indeed, no one gave better directions for boiling fish or turkey than did the *Worker*. The food was economical, relying mostly on salt meat and the cheaper cuts of mutton or beef, but economy did not mean having to eat a lot of offal. A festive turkey was allowed; so too was an old fowl. Dumplings were popular as a cheap filler, and when a change was wanted they could be dressed up cheaply by hiding inside each a tomato which was itself stuffed with a boiled egg. *Flappers* were thin squares of dumpling dough dropped in boiling water.[20] There were plenty of pies and meat puddings, and a few oddities such as baked bananas served as an accompaniment to roast beef and *mock marrowbones* (the bones were real; the filling was of minced meat and currants).

What really stood out was the seasoning: the workers were not afraid of pepper or herbs, nor were they concerned about adding a splash of anchovy, tomato or Worcestershire sauce for added flavour. (There were seven recipes for home-made tomato sauce.) They liked their food affordable, filling and tasty.

On the whole, it seems that the workers ate better than the Presbyterians.

CAMP COOKING
Rabbit Stew

To make a stew and have it hot for dinner, though you are away at work (writes a man in a camp), get a 7 lb. treacle tin, then take a rabbit, and, after dressing it, cut it up, and soak it overnight in salt and water to remove the blood. In the morning put it, with a little corned beef, potatoes, onions and seasoning (if you have it), into the treacle tin. Knock a nail hole in the lid (to let out the steam), and put it well down into its place. Put the lot into a kerosene tin, with water nearly up to the top of the treacle tin, and set on the fire to boil while you have your breakfast. Leave your tin and fire after breakfast and go to work. When you come back you will have a hot dinner, all ready cooked. If water is scarce, and you cannot spare enough for the kerosene tin, fill the treacle tin with water, bring it to the boil, and then bed it well in the ashes and leave it. If you suffer from indigestion in the morning, take a seidlitz powder going to bed. You will be alright in the morning, and will remain so till you overwork or overload the stomach again. – Bush Cook.

CHAPTER 5

THE COUNTRY COOKS

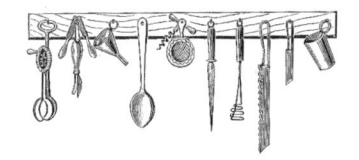

Mina Rawson was one of Australia's earliest writers on cookery and household management. She was born Wilhelmina Frances in 1851, only daughter of a Sydney solicitor, James Cahill and his wife, Elizabeth. Her father died when she was quite young; her mother remarried and moved to a property near Tamworth, New South Wales, where Mina soon learned bushcraft and the independence and initiative that characterised her later life and work.

In 1872 she married Lancelot Rawson and moved to a cattle station west of Mackay, Queensland for five years (long enough to bear three children), then to a sugar plantation at Maryborough (and another child). The sugar plantation soon failed and the Rawsons pioneered a fishing station at Boonooroo near Wide Bay. The work was hard and thankless; Mrs Rawson's own enterprises – poultry, making hammocks and feather pillows, pickling shallots and writing – were, it seems, their only real source of income. They gave up and moved to Rockhampton, where she continued to turn her resourcefulness and practicality into money. After Lance died in 1899 Mina married their former partner in the Wide Bay venture. She died in Sydney in 1933.[1]

Mina Rawson began her publishing career in 1878 with titles such as *The Queensland Cookery Book*, *The Australian Poultry Book* and *The Australian Enquiry Book*.[2] She also wrote short stories, edited the social pages of a Rockhampton newspaper and set down her memoirs. She was one of the most practical of all cookery writers, yet she was clearly no stranger to entertaining and the finer points of table etiquette. The reader could be confident that she had studied her subject well, whatever it was, and had put it into practice, for Mina Rawson saw no reason why a lady should not doctor cattle or take up hammer and nails. She had much to teach, but never lectured; her approach was more like that of a mother passing on the decades of her accumulated knowledge and wisdom to her children.

By the end of the nineteenth century the supply of household help was drying up as girls had abandoned domestic service for the greater freedom of factory work and other forms of employment. Mrs Rawson was well aware of the need for women to manage for themselves. In *The Australian Enquiry Book*, she advised the young housekeeper who had to do all her own housework always to get her puddings and sweet dishes made through the day, that is 'if she indulges in late dinners, as many young wives are obliged to do on account of their husband's business keeping him away all day. If the dinner can be in the middle of the day, so much the better, as tea is an easy meal to prepare, and there need be no greasy plates and dishes to wash afterwards. But in many households the husband takes his luncheon in town and dinner late at home and then, if no servant is kept, everything will depend on the good management of the wife.'[3] The puddings should be left on the sideboard ready to take the place of the previous course; this would avoid the need for the wife to be running from the dining-room to the kitchen during the dinner. Boiled puddings must, of course, be taken up just before serving, but milk puddings were said to be best eaten cold, and were therefore well able to be left standing.

For an insight into Mina Rawson's practical character it is hard to beat her discussion of washing up, which included the following:

> If the man of the house is at all handy at carpentering, the housewife can save herself endless trouble if she will get him to make her a square portable rack for the greasy dinner-plates. I made mine myself, but it was very rough and primitive, and was merely an open sort of box, into which I used to pack the dirty plates and dishes, and standing it in the washing-up tub, pour the hot soapsuds over. I had a strong handle to it, and so could lift it up and down to souse it, and get the plates clean. Then from this I stood it in a large milk-dish, and with a gardener's watering-can rinsed them well with cold water.[4]

The country kitchen

Great changes were evident in the provision of cooking facilities.[5] With few or no kitchen employees, new kitchens were built smaller, with more thought given to reducing the cleaning workload – which nevertheless remained substantial by modern standards. Early kitchens had been kept away from the houses for fear of fire. Now they were more likely to be built into (or onto) their house than to be separate. The modern kitchen very probably had a wood- or coal-burning cooking stove, largely freeing it from soot and smoke and helping to contain the heat of the fire where it was wanted. At the least there was a primitive 'colonial oven' – not much more than a box heated by fire above and below – and at the best a grand cooking range with dampers to regulate the heat flow and a built-in water heater. In the big cities gas cooking was rising in popularity.

Young cooks were warned to know and understand their ovens. Mrs Rawson thought that a stove was easily regulated, but that the colonial ovens, 'so much in vogue all over Australia', were not so simple, and the housekeeper would have to watch everything put into it.[6] Mrs Wicken, on the other hand, thought the modern stove far from simple and urged her students to master it and to make sure they understood its flues and dampers, 'for only in this way will [the housekeeper] be able to successfully cook the dishes she has skilfully prepared'.[7]

In older-style houses, especially in the country, cooking arrangements were generally less convenient. As Mina Rawson put it:

> When I look at the old-fashioned camp-oven and the cross-handled chopper for mincing meat I often think the wives of those times served a martyrdom, and I believe they did just as much, if not more, cooking than we do, with our natty little American or gas stoves and our useful mincing-machines. One great art in cooking, especially in the bush, consists in making the best of poor materials, and in utilizing whatever we find ready to our hands, and in being able to use any oven or fireplace, even an open fire on the ground, with the ashes in which to cook the damper. Nowadays one is seldom called upon to cook by such primitive means, unless when camping out, or newly married, and in a strange land.[8]

Those last words were ominous. As Mrs Rawson was well aware, the romance of courtship in the late nineteenth century generally went hand in hand with preparation for the realities of married life. For most young women there was to be no escaping the practicalities of the kitchen. Man must be cooked for. Preparation for marriage therefore did not always stop at rudimentary instruction in the domestic arts and acquisition of a cookery book and a supply of household linen. She gave some very sound advice to any young lady contemplating married life in the bush:

> Let me suggest to prospective brides that they should stipulate for a stove if marrying a Bushman. A man will promise anything before marriage, very little after. I was wise in my generation, and stipulated for a *stove* and a mangle in preference to a piano, and got all three. In the Bush, where servants come and go like angels' visits, the housewife finds the benefit of the many labour-saving machines now in existence.

Women expecting to set up house in town would also do well to stipulate their kitchen requirements in advance.

We have already had a glimpse of Mrs Wicken's ideal kitchen. Mina Rawson believed that a lady 'no matter how unaccustomed to work, provided she be willing to do it' could do the whole of her housework 'with very little exertion or fatigue' with the aid of a washing-machine, a wringer, a mincing-machine, a knife-cleaning machine, a small kerosene stove, an egg-beater, a scrubbing-brush with long handle, a brass box iron, a mangle, 'a good American stove' and a chain pot-cleaner.

I salute Australia's pioneer women.

The Coolgardie safe, a sort of wooden cage covered in hessian kept damp by strips of fabric conveying moisture from a water container on top, was well established as a cheap and reasonably effective way of keeping perishable food cool (that is, a few degrees below ambient temperature; it very soon 'went off'). Cream separators, butter churns, grinding mills and perhaps cheese presses were important items of equipment in country houses. In the towns refinement took the form of ice boxes to replace the Coolgardie safe, mincing machines, knife sharpeners, a myriad of small gadgets and even, for those who could afford such luxuries, ice cream churns. Among the minor items in a reasonably well equipped kitchen were copper, iron, tinned or enamelled saucepans, omelette pans, gridiron, dish covers, pudding and jelly moulds, pointed strainers, wire sieves, jelly or soup strainer bag, whisks and knives.[9]

The kitchen has always attracted inventors. The colonial kitchen was clearly ripe for reform and then, as now, there was no shortage of enterprising people willing to apply new technology, inventive skills or market cunning to profit from the need for women to come to terms with the reality of doing their own kitchen work. Labour-saving devices found a ready market, so did refinements aimed at improving hygiene. Having to spend more time in their kitchens, women were also attracted to refinements in appearance and amenity; kitchen design began, in a small way, to be more than just a matter of efficiency.

The Kitchen Companion

Mina Rawson's *Antipodean Cookery Book and Kitchen Companion* was published in 1895. It was not as popular as *Schauer*, but saw at least five editions. It was a delightfully down-to-earth little book, written primarily for 'bush' cooks. It gave a good selection of the standard Federation dishes and a fair sprinkling of less common ones. On the whole, writers of early cookery books were not very interested in the finer points of organising collections. Mina Rawson was the least interested of all and made no attempt to organise her recipes and hints. They went in as a jumble, as they occurred to her. Sometimes she lost her way, as when she ended a discussion of salads with the promise 'I will now give detailed directions for a lobster salad' and instead went on to deal with children's meals – the lobster salad appeared nearly forty pages later. The index was no showpiece for the art (listing the lobster salad under 'salad' but not under 'lobster') and only just saved it from being an unusable book.

This lack of organisation was at odds with her practical intentions. She gave plenty of advice on matters such as how to take out 'the yellow stain of perspiration from pillow-cases and gentlemen's underwear' and the use of copper skewers with large iron heads to hasten cooking of a joint. ('The iron head absorbs the heat and conducts it by means of the copper wire into the centre of the meat, and thus enables it to be cooked simultaneously with the outer portions.')

Killing day

Mina Rawson described killing day as 'the most anxious time for a housekeeper on a cattle station'. If killing were done frequently – say, every week – then she had to make sure that all the parts were used in the correct order according to their keeping abilities, so that little was wasted. The killing was usually done in late afternoon. Dinner was fried liver and bacon and, perhaps, sweetbreads. Since very fresh meat is generally tough, the liver had to be sliced and soaked in hot water to soften it. The next morning there were brains for breakfast and a celebratory steak, which would be very tough unless tenderised by some means. In Queensland ripe pawpaw did the job admirably; in other places it would be beaten with a heavy knife.

Large quantities of stock would be made. She recommended the continuous stock pot, kept boiling over a low heat and replenished with water and more meat. When the beef was exhausted, a fowl 'no matter how old' could be added, the trimmings of chickens killed for table, the hindquarters of a wallaby or kangaroo, or small birds. The only rule seemed to be that absolutely no vegetable should be added, or it would cause the stock to ferment. Salt was the only addition, and a desirable one in the absence of refrigeration. Each night enough stock for the following day would be drawn off.

On stations where killing was frequent many 'choice' bits such as the cheek and foot might be wasted simply because they could not be used in time. However, the thrifty housekeeper was expected to pickle everything that could not be used immediately, or to make sausages that could be hung to smoke in the kitchen chimney.

On many stations there was neither the need nor labour for weekly killings; what could not be eaten fresh had to be preserved, and the next killing was not done until all the beef had run out. She observed that 'in old times it was not unusual, on some far out stations, to kill only every three months. Then it was the lady housewife had a chance to show her skill and inventive ingenuity, and, difficult as it often was to provide appetising dishes, I must say there was very great pleasure and some excitement in it.' Beef, pork and even lamb were pickled in brine, hams were cured. Tongues were pickled. Even ox cheek and cow heel were pickled.

The *Schauer Cookery Book* gave a recipe for pickling a large piece of beef with lemon as well as the usual salt, saltpetre and sugar. Once cooked and pressed it was said to keep good for nearly a fortnight – a useful attribute in the country. There was also a *mutton ham* (leg of mutton cured like a ham). Country cooks, it seemed, were interested in almost any method of preserving meat and any recipe for making something edible of the product.

Bush food

Mina Rawson was an advocate of native food, well aware that 'in the far bush the housewife [was] very often at her wits end to know what to do for a change of diet'. She recommended young pigweed as a substitute for lettuce and gave several recipes for pigweed served as a hot vegetable. Young shoots of the 'rough-leaved native fig' could substitute for spinach.

Many white settlers were disgusted at some of the foods they saw Aboriginals eating, but she reminded her readers that 'whatever the blacks eat the whites may safely try.' Witchetty grubs were surely no more disgusting than oysters and, indeed, she thought them delicious, though better 'parched' than raw.[10] There was also 'a large brown grasshopper', which she thought 'very good when parched'. She knew of nothing better than the tail of a young iguana (goanna) 'cooked black's fashion on the ashes'; even large iguanas could be pleasant if taken in the early spring when they would have been feeding on birds' eggs and spring insects. Carpet snakes were very good roasted; unfortunately, there was not much meat on them. And few people in the bush would refuse bandicoot, wallaby or kangaroo.[11] She often salted the last two as a substitute for beef – she thought they were 'almost as good; very much better than what is commonly styled "salt horse" six months old.' From the Aboriginals she was prepared to learn both what was edible and how to prepare it, but native food could also be given the British colonial treatment. Iguana was good cooked, cut up and curried. She thought grubs would be excellent curried, though she hadn't tried them that way.

Mrs Rawson's remarks on preparing game animals were interesting. After giving directions for cleaning them (and 'there is no more distasteful office for a lady to have to do this') she went on:

> All Australian ground game has a strong peculiar flavour, which many people dislike. It can be done away with to a great extent by soaking in vinegar and water, or by burying for several hours.
>
> I have frequently buried wallaby to advantage, as it makes it very tender. Merely wrap it in paper or a cloth, dig a hole three or four feet deep, put it in, and cover over again. Unless left ten or twelve hours it will do no good.

However enthusiastic Mrs Rawson may have been, neither bush cooks nor the Aboriginal people had much influence on the eating habits of the majority of Australians. By 1900 interest in native food had all but died out, except for a few animals and birds regarded as game. While this was a reprieve for the native fauna, the loss to Australia's culture was, it seems, permanent.

THE GOULBURN COOKERY BOOK

'WHILE THERE ARE SUCH GIRLS as this, Australia need never fear. What women they will make!' These comforting words introduced a rather different kind of country cook. They faced the title page of the 1917 edition of the *Goulburn Cookery Book*. Many would look at such an advertisement and smile, for we have turned our backs on so many of the old ways. Yet modern Gwendolines sell equivalent products and little has really changed in the advertising industry. The *Goulburn* is still a good book to cook from – on nostalgia days.

Mrs William Forster (Jean) Rutledge who compiled it, was the daughter of Major Richard Morphy, an Irishman who settled in Australia after serving in India, and of Jane Styles, of Bungonia. The couple lived at Gidleigh, a rural property near Bungendore. Mrs Rutledge died in 1932.[12]

According to Helen Rutledge, Jean's daughter-in-law, the copyright of the book was given to the Church of England, Goulburn Diocese, in 1899. The book was published in almost annual editions – but without revision of the text – for more than 30 years, the price steadily increasing from one shilling to two shillings. By the thirtieth edition 205 000 copies had been sold at a profit to the diocese of more than £6,000, a considerable sum in the early part of the twentieth century.

Helen Rutledge commented that Jean and her husband had a horror of waste of any kind and that late in life she 'became almost fanatical on the subject of over-refined foods'. She wrote a health foods supplement which was added to the 1930 and subsequent editions.

The thirty-sixth edition was something of a curiosity. It was a revision of the original work undertaken by Mrs Walton (Thelma) McCarthy, Domestic Science Diploma, Sydney Technical College, ex-teacher of domestic science in the New South Wales Department of Education, and was published about 1937 under the title *The New Goulburn Cookery Book*.[13] In her preface, Thelma McCarthy said:

> The *Goulburn Cookery Book*, compiled thirty years ago by the late Mrs Forster Rutledge, has achieved popularity, not only in this State, but throughout the whole Commonwealth; it has circulated to the remotest parts.
>
> The sales of this book and the long period of years during which it has been the leading recipe book of the State, are proof of the excellent recipe contents and the efficiency with which the book was compiled.

Thelma McCarthy's revision greatly improved the layout and included oven temperatures. She retained most of the original recipes and added a few new ones, but failed to gain widespread acceptance for it. Helen Rutledge claimed that 'it lacked the distinction of the original'. However, its real fault was that it had kept too much of the original distinction; it was an old-fashioned book launched into a market looking for change. It was dropped from the publishing list after 1945.

The book made a brief re-appearance in 1973 as a commemorative fortieth edition published by the National Trust of Australia. It was a facsimile reconstructed from the second (1905) and fifth (1907) editions, with a short historical introduction. Unfortunately the original advertisements, placed by the merchants and tradespeople of Goulburn, New South Wales, were not reproduced; only brief descriptions of the advertisers were included towards the end of the book.

Jean Rutledge explained the *Goulburn* book thus, in the 1899 preface:

> Although there hardly seems any necessity for another Cookery Book, yet I cannot but think that this collection of recipes will meet a want, especially among the women in the bush, who have often to teach

inexperienced maids, and would be glad of accurate recipes that anyone with fair intelligence could carry out. I have tried to leave nothing to chance, and the vague counsels to "make a nice light crust for a pie," or "a batter as thick as cream," find no place here. However, any dish, to be successful, must be "mixed with brains," and want of care and patience will often spoil the best materials.

These few words and some scattered hints on sauces, puddings, cakes and jams were all that were offered by way of general culinary advice. The book was simply a collection of about 900 recipes and a handful of household hints. The preface acknowledged about 40 sources, including a Miss Futter and the National School of Cookery, London. Probably the book was made up of contributions from friends, recipes gathered or copied from many unnamed sources, and the family scrapbooks.

The layout of the book was typical of the times, with chapters on all the topics one would expect to find in a comprehensive recipe manual and an index in the front which listed the entries strictly in the order in which they occurred. The dishes were generally unexciting, but represented good, practical homestead cookery. As Mrs Rutledge put it, 'many of the dishes are old familiar friends'. She did not take it upon herself to teach or innovate. Her aim of providing a collection of recipes for dishes that country people commonly cooked or wanted makes it a valuable source of information on Federation cooking.

It has been said that her collection was 'suspiciously similar to Eliza Acton's in England more than half a century earlier.'[14] However, comparison of the *Goulburn* with Eliza Acton's final edition (1865) – arguably the one most likely to have been on Jean Rutledge's shelf in 1899, since it remained in print until about 1914 – reveals no more similarity than would be expected between any two comprehensive collections of similar cuisine at about the same point in history. What is more noticeable is the *difference* between the two approaches. Eliza Acton wrote for the well-heeled families of Victorian England; Jean Rutledge addressed herself to an altogether different audience: honest country folk, however prosperous in comparison with their fellows, for whom years in the bush had redefined practicality and economy. They were still essentially *British* and yet seized with the necessity of becoming *Australian*; nevertheless they were beginning to forget – or discard – some of the finer points of table and to adapt their traditional foods ever so slightly to local conditions.

So Jean Rutledge gave her Australians *savouries*, but no *entremets* or *removes*; taught the British of Bungendore how to make do with canned, not fresh, salmon; and presented in a compact little book a large array of traditional dishes that were thought to be suitable for Australian country living.

Mrs Rutledge's chapter on fish neatly demonstrated the problem of living away from the coast or major inland rivers before refrigerated transport. In a determined effort to provide for a fish course when it was wanted, she gave 40 or so recipes, supplemented elsewhere by another half dozen seafood savouries. However, her collection was very different from those offered by the coastal books. Underlying it was the assumption that the country cook could expect little variety: sole, whiting, flathead and mullet were the only raw fish mentioned. She would have to rely heavily on salt, smoked and tinned fish (including tinned oysters and lobster).

On the rare occasions when fresh fish of any quality became available it should be cooked simply – boiled, fried, baked or grilled – because most of the time the emphasis must be on how to make left-over cooked fish, canned fish or possibly indifferent fresh fish interesting, or at least tolerable. There were recipes for tinned salmon in aspic, *salmon balls* of tinned salmon and mashed potatoes, tinned salmon with caper sauce, 'Lord Hopetoun's favourite dish' of tinned salmon gratin spiked with vinegar and cayenne, a steamed pudding of tinned salmon, and stewed tinned salmon. There was also *salmon en papelote* – cold boiled salmon wrapped in buttered paper and reheated – presumably also made with tinned fish.

Jean Rutledge took sauces seriously, giving about three dozen recipes, including almost all the popular ones. Her chapter on sauces began with a sharp lesson on cooking technique. 'Sauces are, as a rule, the stumbling-block of the average cook. Very often the ordinary white sauce is lumpy, pasty, and tasteless, and either too thick or too thin. To make it, do not put a spoonful of flour into a basin, mix with water, and then turn it into boiling milk, adding a lump of butter, and stirring it round two or three times. This is how *not* to make it. The result is a sort of nasty pudding, very uninviting.' The right way, she explained, was to make a roux, add the cold liquid gradually, then stir until the sauce boiled. 'This method takes about a quarter of an hour, and a general servant has not often time for it.' There was a quick alternative, but it would probably have left some raw flour taste.

She gave baking times for beef, veal, mutton, lamb, fresh pork, ham, sucking pig, turkey, fowl, chicken, goose, duck, pigeon, snipe and quail. Her inclusion of the last three must be taken as some evidence that there was a need for them. Beef recipes included favourites such as *beef olives, beefsteak pie, beefsteak and oyster pudding, baked beefsteak and onions, Brazilian stew, Scotch collops, Exeter stew with savoury balls* (dumplings), *sea pie, stewed steak and walnuts,* and *toad in the hole.* Mutton favourites such as *haricot of mutton, hodge-podge, hot pot* and *Irish stew* were there.

HODGE-PODGE

Two and a half pounds of neck of mutton, 2 quarts of cold water, 2 carrots, ½ a turnip, ½ a parsnip, 1 stalk of celery, 1 onion, 1 dessertspoon of salt, ½ a teaspoon of pepper, a pinch of allspice, ½ a teacup of rice, pearl barley or dried peas, parsley.

Have the mutton cut into small neat pieces; remove the fat, and put in a saucepan with the cold water and salt. Boil gently for 2 hours; then skim off the fat carefully; and remove any left on with paper; add the vegetables (cut up into rather small pieces) and the rice. If pearl barley is used, it must be soaked for an hour in cold water, and put on to boil with the meat. Dried peas must be soaked overnight; and if they are used, put a little bacon or ham with the hodge-podge. Boil another hour, and just before taking from the fire put in a teaspoon of finely-chopped parsley. Serve in a hot soup-tureen, and eat with a spoon and fork. Pieces of bread or cold potatoes may be used, with less rice, if liked. This is a capital luncheon dish for cold weather, and is much liked by children. It is a sort of thick soup, or something between soup and stew. If, as often happens in the bush, the men of the house have work that takes them from home all day, this stew, put in a billy-can, is easily warmed for the mid-day meal, and is much appreciated. It can be eaten from a pint-pot with fork and spoon.

She suggested that a leg of mutton could be baked, boiled, stewed, stuffed or cut into steaks (through the bone). One of the curiosities of colonial cooking – and a product of the continuing challenge to relieve the monotony of mutton, beef and mutton – was baked *barrier goose*.

BARRIER GOOSE

One leg or shoulder of mutton, 1 cup of breadcrumbs, ½ teaspoon of salt, ¼ teaspoon of pepper, 1 small onion, 1 dessertspoon of chopped sage, 1 oz. of butter or dripping, 1 egg, or 1 tablespoon of milk.

Bone a well-hung leg or shoulder of mutton; lay it flat on the table, and spread with a stuffing made from the above ingredients. Roll up, and shape as much like a goose as possible. Sew up with strong cotton; put in a baking-dish; sprinkle a little salt and flour over it, and put dripping over it. Bake from 2¼ to 1¼ hours, according to the size of the mutton, basting well at intervals. Serve with a good brown gravy. Veal stuffing may be used instead of sage and onion stuffing.[15]

After chapters on poultry and pork, Mrs Rutledge gave 33 dishes for using up cold meat. They ranged from hashes and curries (both generally better than the Federation average), to croquettes, puddings and pies of cold minced meat. The chapter on breakfast and luncheon dishes included more uses for cold meat, reflecting both the entrenched habit of meat-three-times-a-day and the importance of breakfast to country workers.

One need not look to the *Goulburn* for inspiration on cooking vegetables. Apart from a warning not to over-boil seakale because 'it gets hard and tough' and a recipe for *sauer kraut* that produces merely stewed cabbage – and was quite properly crossed out in my 1917 edition with the annotation 'wrong way' – Mrs Rutledge did not go beyond the basics.

Among the cakes was the house specialty, *Gidleigh cake*, marked as a favourite in my 1917 edition. Recipes for many of the popular cakes of the period were given: caraway, ginger, marble, pound, rainbow, sandwich, sponge and so on, as well as several gingerbreads.

GIDLEIGH CAKE

One pound of flour, 6 oz. of brown sugar, ½ lb. of butter, ¼ cup of treacle, 7 eggs, ¾ lb. of raisins or dates, ¼ lb. of candied peel, ¼ of a nutmeg (grated), 1 teaspoon of baking powder, ½ teaspoon of salt, about 2 oz. of almonds.

Beat butter and sugar to a light cream; add the eggs one at a time, and beat well. Sift flour, baking powder, salt, and nutmeg together, and add to the butter and eggs; then mix in the fruit and candied peel. Put into 2 well-buttered cake tins. Chop the almonds roughly, sprinkle them over the tops of the cakes, and bake in a moderate oven for about 2 hours. This cake bakes very well in a brick oven after the bread comes out.[16]

TO TEST AN OVEN

To test an oven, take a sheet of white paper, and if it only just tinges – that is, becomes a pale straw colour – it is fit for sponge cake, meringues, or anything requiring a slow oven. If it takes the tint of pine wood or deal, the oven is ready for meat or game pies, bread, pound cake, and such things as require a steady soaking heat. When the paper becomes light brown, or the colour of nicely-baked pastry, you may bake fruit pies, Vol-au-vent, &c. When it turns darker brown, about the colour of rather over-cooked pastry, the oven is ready for small pastry. If it blackens, the oven is too hot. This is Gouffé's test.[17]

The importance of preserving fruit when plentiful was underlined by the extensive treatment given to jams, jellies, pickles, sauces and chutneys. Possibilities included *almack*, a purée of plums or other fruit dried to a paste ('very nice for dessert'), barberry jam, guava jelly, shaddock (pomelo) jam and tomato and pineapple jam along with the more common items. There were also plenty of recipes for making one's own confectionery and drinks. The latter included chilli beer, fermented from a syrup of sugar and bird's-eye chillies (which 'may be had from any chemist'), a home-made coffee essence and the usual ginger beer and lemon syrup.

Many cookery books gave recipes for jams, confectionery and drinks, but in the *Goulburn* they were part of a consistent theme of self sufficiency on the farm. In her introduction to the fortieth edition Helen Rutledge noted that country women were taught to be self-reliant. Meat was killed and dressed on the property and what could not be used fresh had to be pickled; milk had to be processed for butter, cream and cottage cheese; pigs, fed on the skim milk, became home-cured bacon and ham ('it was very good eating and quite different from that which is now sold in shops'); mutton fat was clarified and made into soap; eggs, fruit and vegetables were preserved; jam was made and so on.

And if a century of progress has relieved even country people of most of these chores it has imposed upon them instead the necessity of eating the ham and bacon 'now sold in shops'.

A Birthday Dinner

The 1918 edition of the *Goulburn Cookery Book* was the main kitchen reference of my wife's grandmother and was probably the source of many of the dishes that she is remembered serving to her husband during his long terminal illness. The book is well worn, but unmarked apart from her name, a pencilled recipe for coconut ice and the note 'same mixture for date creams without cocoanut'. Unused for many years, it might have been thrown out when Grandma died, but someone thought Colin might like it, he's interested in cooking. True, even in those days before the *gentle passion* took hold, I was glad enough to get my hands on an old cookery book.

When my wife's mother (whose name is Olive) turned 70 in 1989 we celebrated the event with a family dinner at which all the dishes were made from recipes the *Goulburn Cookery Book*. The menu was:

Little pigs in blankets	Beef olives
Olive custard	Pilaff
Oxtail soup	Queen of puddings
Fish pie No 1	Paradise pudding, almond sauce

A Birthday Dinner from the *Goulburn Cookery Book*

LITTLE PIGS IN BLANKETS

Take some large oysters, and season with pepper and salt. Have ready some slices of bacon, cut very thin; put 1 or 2 oysters on each slice of bacon, and roll it up; fasten with tiny wooden skewers, and fry for about 2 or 3 minutes in a hot pan. Do not put butter or any fat in the pan, but see that it is quite hot before the "pigs" are put in. The bacon should be just crisp. Serve on fingers of hot toast.

* * *

OLIVE CUSTARD

One ounce of grated Parmesan cheese, 1 egg, 1 tablespoon of cream.

Mix over the fire till it thickens. Fry some small rounds of bread in butter, spread thinly with anchovy paste, and put a small quantity of the custard on each. An olive farcie to be placed on top of each. Serve *very hot*.

* * *

OX-TAIL SOUP

One ox-tail, 1½ quarts of water (or second stock), 1 stalk of celery, 1 carrot, a bunch of herbs, 10 peppercorns, 1 onion, 3 cloves, salt, 1 dessertspoon of flour, a little dripping, ketchup.

Cut the ox-tail into joints, and divide the large joints at the root of the tail into four. Fry till brown in some good dripping. Add the water, and simmer gently for 4 hours, or till the tail is quite tender. Strain off the stock into a basin; dip the pieces of tail quickly into hot water to remove the fat, and set them aside. When the stock is cold, remove the fat, and put the stock in a saucepan with the vegetables and seasoning. Cook till done. Strain, thicken with the flour, let it boil, add some of the pieces of ox-tail and a teaspoon of ketchup. Serve in a hot tureen. The rest of the tail may be re-heated in a good brown gravy, seasoned with a very little walnut vinegar, and 1 pickled walnut cut into quarters as a garnish.

* * *

FISH PIE (NO 1)

Cold boiled fish, ½ pint of milk, 1 tablespoon of cornflour or flour, 1 dessertspoon of butter, 1 tablespoon of anchovy sauce, salt, pepper, and a little cayenne (if liked), and oysters.

Boil the milk, mix the cornflour with a little cold milk, stir it into the milk, and let it cook for a few minutes; add sauce and seasoning. Remove the skin and bones from some cold boiled fish; mix the sauce with it; spread oysters or prawns over the top, cover with puff paste, bake for about ½ an hour, and serve very hot.

* * *

BEEF OLIVES

One pound of good steak, 1 oz. of suet, 2 oz. of breadcrumbs, ½ teaspoon of salt, ¼ teaspoon of pepper, 1 egg, 1 teaspoon of chopped parsley, a very little grated lemon peel, a grate of nutmeg, stock or gravy.

Cut the steak thin and divide into six pieces; dip a rolling-pin into cold water, and beat each piece out flat; then trim nicely. Cut trimmings up very finely, and add to the breadcrumbs and other ingredients, and make into a forcemeat with the egg. Divide into six portions, place each portion on a piece of steak, and form into a neat roll; tie up each end with cotton. Put a little dripping into a pan, and when very hot fry the olives quickly till slightly brown. Put them into a stewpan, pour on the stock or gravy (enough to barely cover them), and simmer gently for about 1¼ hours. If the steak is tough, they may be simmered a little longer. A few minced olives or a very little bit of pickled walnut is an improvement to the forcemeat. The steak may be divided into twelve portions instead of six, and treated in the same way. Many will prefer the smaller, daintier olive.

* * *

PILAFF

One cup of rice, 2 cups of stock, 1 small onion, 2 tablespoons of grated cheese, 1 oz. of butter, pepper and salt, a very little pounded saffron, if liked.

Chop the onion finely, and fry a pale brown in a little butter; add the rice and stock, cover the saucepan, and let it all simmer gently till the rice is cooked (about ¾ of an hour); put in pepper, salt, and saffron; add the cheese and 1 oz. of butter; stir lightly till the butter is melted. Serve on a hot dish. A very little nutmeg may be grated over it.

QUEEN OF PUDDINGS

Two cups of breadcrumbs, 1 pint of milk, 3 eggs, 1 dessertspoon of sugar, ½ oz. of butter, 2 bananas, or 2 tablespoons of jam.

Boil the milk and pour over the breadcrumbs; beat in the sugar, butter, and yolks of eggs. Bake for about 25 to 30 minutes; then spread the bananas, mashed smoothly with a fork, over the top, or jam may be used instead. Beat the whites to a stiff froth, add 3 tablespoons of sugar, pile rockily over the mashed bananas, and bake till a pale brown. A teaspoon of lemon juice is a great improvement to the meringue.[18]

* * *

PARADISE PUDDING

Quarter pound of apples, ¼ lb. of breadcrumbs, 3 oz. of sugar, 3 oz. of currants, 3 eggs; the grated rind of ½ a lemon, salt, and nutmeg.

Peel the apples and mince them; mix all the ingredients together; add well-beaten eggs. Put the pudding into a buttered basin, tie down with a cloth, and boil for 1½ hours. Serve with sauce.

* * *

ALMOND SAUCE

One and a half ounces of sweet almonds, 2 bitter almonds, 1½ tablespoons of sugar, the yolks of 2 eggs, ½ pint of sweet cream or milk.

Blanch the almonds, and pound them in a mortar till smooth; add the sugar. Put the cream on to boil with the almonds and sugar, and when at nearly boiling point, stir in the yolks of the eggs, but be very careful it does not quite boil, or it will curdle and be spoilt. Stir till as thick as custard. Milk, with the addition of a tablespoon of cream, may be used instead of cream alone. This is an excellent sauce for any light boiled pudding. The almonds may be boiled in the milk till the flavour is extracted, and then strained off before adding the eggs; this makes a more delicate and smoother sauce.

CHAPTER 6

THE SMART COOK

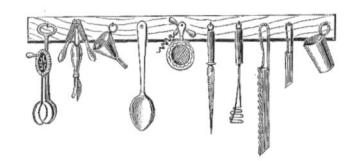

Some collective madness seems to have driven the British in India to adopt a caricature of English society. They dressed for dinner in clothes that were plainly unsuitable for the climate; took their places at table with exaggerated displays of precedence and formality; and gorged themselves on food prepared by Indian cooks in French style for British tastes. This same madness found its way to Australia.

The brutality of the convict era, the naked greed of the gold rushes and the rigours and disappointments of life in the bush did not free white settlers of the need to create a polite 'society'. Many of the traditional values and distinctions that had marked the British social structure before the industrial revolution also formed the basis for Australian society, but here birth, family and education were rather less important. The economic and social turmoil of the nineteenth century had seen many reversals of fortune and social position. Here the unthinkable was possible, indeed almost probable: a person who, a few years previously, had arrived in the country ill-bred and penniless may now have achieved such wealth and influence as to command the deepest social respect. In the bush, land ownership was the primary requirement of social position; in the cities, success in business or the professions or politics were the paths to advancement. Richard Twopenny thought that wealth was the predominating factor and that position was of small account ('though the line is always drawn at shopkeepers'). Newcomers who met the criteria and adopted the manners of gentlefolk were soon accepted into a circle, though Twopenny warned that it was always wise 'to avoid asking questions about or making reference to the earlier days' of people one met. In its way Australian 'society' was as ridiculous in its assumption of the trappings and affectations of the old-world aristocracy as was the raj in India, yet Twopenny defended it. 'The outward and visible sign may be absurd, but the inward and spiritual grace is nonetheless concealed within it.'

Polite society was quick to publish its rules. Few people were born and bred to it and there was a need for generally greater acceptance of social climbing than in Britain. There was thus a greater need for handbooks that would 'enable any one, in whatever circumstances of life to acquire the manners of a gentleman, or the gentle and graceful bearing of a well-bred lady, whose presence will be sought for, and who, by their acuirements [sic], will learn the art of being at home in any good society.'[1] *Australian Etiquette*, first published in 1885, captured exactly the snobbishness which the British class structure had nurtured:

> Society is divided in to sets, according to their breeding. One set may be said to have no breeding at all, another to have a little, another some, and another enough; and between the first and last of these there are more shades than in the rainbow.

It was a comprehensive volume covering manners, morals, dress and personal grooming, all kinds of social intercourse, home culture, letter writing ('an indication of good breeding'), rules for special social occasions and the etiquette of sport.

On home life it was said that 'Home is the woman's kingdom, and there she reigns supreme. To embellish that home, to make happy the lives of her husband and the dear ones committed to her trust, is the honoured task which it is the wife's province to perform.' The rules of correct dress were necessarily general, given the importance of fashion and the rate at which it changed. Advice was given on the practical aspects of personal grooming, including such embarrassments as tartar on the teeth, foul breath, freckles, eyebrows meeting, baldness in men (wear well ventilated hats), blisters on the feet and pimples on the face.

Muttonwool

Although housing never determined social rank it was accepted that the situation, quality and furnishing of one's house would fairly reflect one's standing and means to the extent that practicalities would allow. In the bush practicality dominated; in the cities there was more scope for choice. Twopenny described housing in the late nineteenth century:

> ...the favourite type of Australian house is laid out in an oblong block bisected by a three to eight foot passage. The first door on one side as you go in is the drawing-room, on the other the dining-room. Then follow the bedrooms, etc., with the kitchen and scullery at the end of the passage, or sometimes in a lean-to at right angles to the hinder part of the house proper. This kind of cottage is almost universal in Adelaide amongst the middle and upper middle classes, and invariable in the working-class throughout Australia. In the other colonies the

upper middle classes often live in two-storied houses; *i.e.,* ground-floor and one floor above. Their construction is almost as simple as the cottage, the only difference being that the bedrooms are on the upper storey, and that a pair of narrow stairs face the front-door and take up half the passage-way directly you get past the drawing and dining-room doors. The cottage is not high enough to strike the eye, but the squareness, or more properly the cubeness, of these two-storied houses is appalling. They look for all the world like houses built of cards, except that the cards are uncommonly solid... The strong light of the sun has the effect of a window-tax in limiting the size and number of the windows... Shutters are not much used. Venetian blinds are more common. On a hot summer day it is absolutely necessary to shut all windows and draw down the blinds if you wish to keep at all cool... Nearly every house that can afford the space has a verandah, which sometimes stretches the whole way round. The rooms are usually lofty for their size, in winter horribly cold and draughty, in summer unbearably stuffy in small houses, the science of ventilation being of recent introduction... As a rule, the kitchens are terribly small, and in summer filled with flies... In a few larger houses the fashion has been adopted of making the kitchen a mere cooking galley, the cook preparing the dishes and doing all that does not require the presence of fire in a large back-kitchen. Happily every house has a bath-room, though it is often only a mere shed of wood or galvanized iron put up in the back-yard. In many of the poorer households this shed does double duty as bath-house and wash-house, or the wash-house consists of a couple of boards, with a post to keep them up, and a piece of netting overhead to keep the sun off.

As already noted, Twopenny's generalisations may be treated with some caution. He wrote at length on the contents of Australian houses, but his description was in satirical vein. It was aimed mainly at men who could afford ostentatious houses but had not the taste to furnish them decently, and whose concern was more with display of costly articles, especially in the public rooms, than with comfort or decorative art. So Muttonwool's carpet was gaudy and stiffly patterned, his mantelpiece of 'regulation white marble'. The chair backs had been 'carved out into various contortions of a horse-shoe, with a bar across the middle which just catches you in the small of the back, and is a continual reproach if you venture to lean upon it' and the fabric is 'specially manufactured for the colonial market'. There was a collection of useless (but expensive) tables, a Louis XVI clock, a pair of ornaments to match, and so on.

At the other end of the social scale he claimed that a working-man could furnish a four-roomed cottage for 27 pounds and gave a price list to prove it, though he overlooked many details essential to household comfort such as bed linen and kitchen equipment. He began with the wrong assumption; the interior of the home was the woman's kingdom, as Mrs Aronson well knew.

The journalist

Zara Aronson (née Baar) was born in Sydney of Jewish parents and educated in England, Germany and Sydney. She married Frederick Aronson in 1864 and became active in various charities, including the Red Cross. An original member of the Women's Literary Society and National Women's Council, and Foundation secretary to the Society of Women Writers of New South Wales, she edited the women's pages of *The Sydney Mail* from 1897 to 1901. Among others, she edited the fashion pages in *Town and Country Journal* and *The Sunday Times* (Sydney). After World War I she established the Mary Elizabeth Tea Rooms in King Street, which she ran until the 1930s, and published the *Mary Elizabeth Cook Book*. She was awarded the O.B.E. in 1936 and died in 1944.[2]

When 'Thalia', as she was known to her many newspaper readers, published *XXth Century Cookery and Home Decoration* in 1900 she offered her book 'humbly to the Australian public in the belief that a scheme of Housekeeping and House-decoration peculiarly adapted to these Colonies has not yet been attempted, and is widely needed'. Her claim must have rested on the few home decoration pages at the back of her book, for at least two colonial household management manuals had been in print for some years and she certainly did not write the first cookery book.[3] And this really was a cookery book: of 300 pages of text, all but 35 were cookery and several of the remainder covered household hints of the kind routinely included in such books.

From the first page she projected quite a different personality from those of the strident, censorious Philip Muskett, the more restrained, schoolish Harriet Wicken and the practical, self-sufficient Jean Rutledge. Thalia's orientation was public relations – what do my readers want to know? what will they find interesting? – rather than laying down the law to them or carping on the errors of their ways. The result was a book which was less representative of popular Federation cookery than most others, but more modern – altogether a charming collection.

The preface was addressed 'To my readers' and continued in that vein. 'With a view to assisting my numerous Australian friends – both in the cities and in the country – I have collected the recipes and compiled this work, hoping that, by its introduction, the agreeable and acceptable art of Cooking may be brought within the means and into the homes of many hitherto without some of its benefits.' What a difference from Dr Muskett! Here cookery was not dominated by concerns of economy – though the recipes were by no means extravagant. It was not overly concerned with a healthy diet (the book was above average on both the *sweetness* and *vegetable* scales) or of method, though her explanations were as full and detailed as any. Here the main theme was that cooking could also be an art. Thalia brought art to Federation cookery.

The art of cookery

The art of cooking is pleasant to both the practitioner and the diner. To the former, gathering interesting and novel dishes from many sources, including 'reliable epicures', and presenting them with an eye to fashion and beauty is a satisfying occupation. The latter, freed from the dullness of average Australian cookery, is delighted by the variety it affords. Mrs Aronson described these dishes as 'dainties', anticipating the fashion of daintiness that swept through British and Australian cookery two or three decades later.

> 'You will find [the recipes], I venture to say, a delicious collection, which, if followed with care, will prove a happy addition to the average housewife's culinary library. Amongst them appear many dainties, accompanied by garnishes that have hitherto only been known to English and Continental households, but which with a little study will soon become acceptable dishes of our colonial homes.'

Her ancestry and European education are evident in the more than usual sprinkling of Jewish and German dishes.

The charm of this book comes not only from its chatty tone and the culinary curiosities it presents but from the way it blends the fashion and practicality of cookery. Thalia brought fashion to cookery. She taught her readers how to give a 'smart' luncheon and an elegant dinner. But she did not omit 'the general simple cookery dishes – those that come into the ordinary home life.'

She began with a page or two on housekeeping for middle class households. The keys to success seemed to be consistency and routine in ordering the daily cleaning tasks and service of meals, kindness to servants (while making sure they always understood who was mistress) and careful attention to household accounts.

In case the relevance of housekeeping to federation and its idealist sentiments had escaped her readers, Thalia concluded: 'We can also admit that when people grow refined, first in their food fancies and their homes, the other characteristics of culture follow in due time. To ensure this we must cultivate the home and its management, and regard housekeeping as a desirable addition to our daily lives, and an interest that will assist in the success of a growing federated continent.'

Mrs Aronson's recipes covered the full range of household cookery, with scattered notes on general method. It was one of the most varied collections, offering plenty of interest and novelty, many of the popular Federation dishes and a few unaccountably dull ones. Her soups included kangaroo tail, three of cucumber, walnut (which she said was German) and several of mock turtle. With seafood her emphasis was on applying known treatments to local fish. For example, she told readers that in the colonies, whiting, schnapper or sole were best for fried fish. Her recipe for fried fish was the 'Jewish method, in oil'. Her *bouillabaisse* was made with bream, lobster and whiting. Other varieties mentioned were mullet, perch and eels. There was little resort to tinned or preserved fish, except for fried whitebait, or to satisfy British cravings for fried sardines and broiled herrings for breakfast.

She encouraged Australian cooks to give more attention to entrées:

> To many cooks the mere mention of the word entrée produces an effect that borders on scaredom. Indeed, the ordinary plain cook at once thinks that a very superior class of high-class cooking is demanded – a class that appears quite beyond *their* culinary education. Now, it is not one whit more difficult to prepare a dainty entrée – or, for the matter of that, a series of entrées – than it is to, say, roast a joint properly...'Now, therefore, let me give you a few entrées that are not in every cookery book, and yet, in my opinion, quite within the power of the average intelligent cook.

The promised recipes included *an entrée of veal or chicken and mushrooms; sheep's tongues and spinach; kidneys à la reine; sauté kidneys; kidneys and mushrooms; cutlets in aspic* and *white fricassée of lamb*. She suggested that a few other cutlet and veal dishes could also be used as entrées.

Meat and vegetables

Mrs Aronson gave the most detailed advice on the art of carving:

> Firstly, regarding the position of the carver. Standing is quite unnecessary, provided the chair is high enough so that the work can be done comfortably seated. The dish, which must be large enough to hold the entire joint when carved, should be placed near enough to the carver to prevent a moving of the dish or an awkwardness in the movements. And of all things it should be arranged that no string or

skewer is left in the meat when it is brought to the table. Neglect of this particular may cause no end of annoyance.

Take first the position of the meat. Large birds, such as geese and turkeys, should have their heads set always to the left; smaller birds, like partridges and grouse...

...should have their heads set always to the right? No, they simply went to the back of the dish. Daintiness had not reached new heights; this was about convenience. She assumed that all carvers were right-handed: the meatier part of the bird or joint should therefore be on the right, the fiddly parts would be dealt with in the kitchen, to be returned in made-dishes at a later meal. So a roast pig was placed with its head to the left and a calf's head was placed with its face to the right. Her care was both for nicety – that the bird or joint be carved neatly, evenly and without fuss or contortion on the part of the carver – and for efficiency – that the remains be returned to the kitchen in such a state that the cook might be able to make good use of them.

Mrs Aronson completes our picture of the lengths to which Federation Australians went to satisfy their enormous appetites for meat. It is pretty

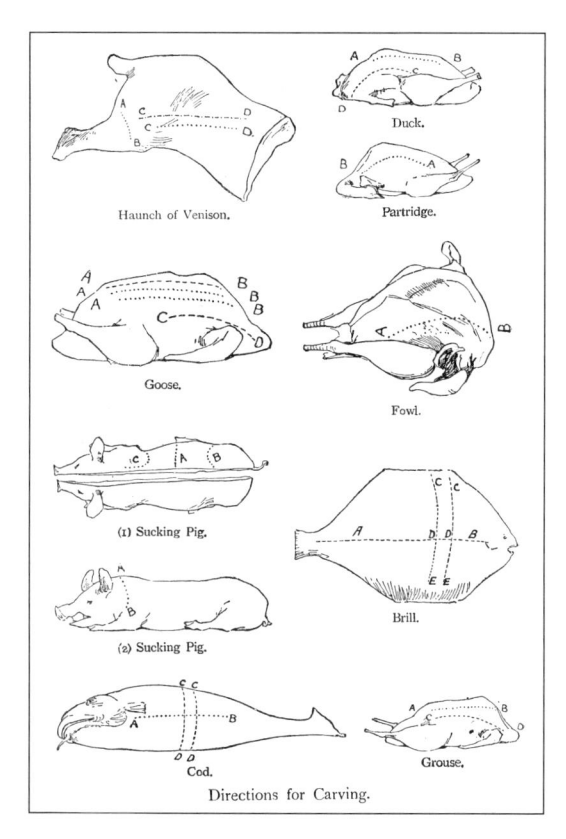

Haunch of Venison.

Duck.

Partridge.

Goose.

Fowl.

(1) Sucking Pig.

Brill.

(2) Sucking Pig.

Cod.

Grouse.

Directions for Carving.

clear that the main work in a formal meal was very often a roast joint or roast poultry, and sometimes both, and that the creative use of left-overs was an important culinary skill. We know that keeping meat in fresh or tolerable condition before the widespread availability of refrigeration was a real problem to which the ice chest was but an imperfect solution. In the country there was little choice but to kill and pickle or to buy meat in large quantities – again, mostly pickled.

Despite the monotony of pickled beef, pork or mutton day after day, many people acquired a kind of liking for it and continued to ask for it from their local butcher for decades after any need for chemical preservation had disappeared (the same can be said, of course, of dried and smoked fish in Europe). Some of the made-dishes ceased to be mere conveniences of economy and became popular in their own right. The meat loaf, for example, once a means of using up cooked meat remains, was adapted to fresh meat and lived on.

Although by the 1920s joints were still commonly and routinely sold – for the tradition was well entrenched – there was general availability of fillets, steaks, chops and other small cuts, and the local manufacture of a range of processed meat such as mince, fresh and smoked sausages, pickled and cured meats, and brawn was widespread. The *Australasian Butchers' Manual* commented that 'the legislation of to-day, dealing as it does with labour, wages, etc, compels the master butcher to look to the profits obtainable from by-products of the trade', and it even included recipes for *Melton Mowbray pies* and sausage rolls.[4] The advent of domestic refrigeration was beginning to make the purchase of several days' needs of small cuts practical.

To a Federation cook the joint offered both economy (as distinct from cheapness; for that a bullock's heart could be bought) and challenge. 'With a little trouble, one can easily avoid the monotony of a cold joint served up for several successive meals.' Mrs Aronson's suggestions included taking a slice off the thick end of a leg of mutton, dividing it into cutlets and serving them crumbed and fried with tomato sauce, a thick onion sauce, a purée of peas or haricot beans, or a good plain gravy. The knuckle end could be stewed with onions and celery (and rice 'if the liquor is liked thick'). 'The undercut of a sirloin will make a nice dish of fillets; the rest can be roasted.' The fillet could be stuffed with bacon, onion and herbs, browned in butter with minced bacon, onion, garlic, carrot and herbs, then left to simmer in tomato purée and beef gravy. It was served on a platter with its sauce and boiled macaroni or tiny new potatoes (baked) and 'little groups' of carrots, peas and white beans. The fillet could also be treated in the 'Swedish mode': marinated in olive oil, onions, parsley, bay leaves, salt and pepper, then roasted. It is interesting that the gravy collected from roasting was served *under* the fillet – a modern fad for serving food 'on a sauce of...' is at least 100 years old.

Among the other meat dishes were *Moscow cutlets (a smart luncheon dish)* of neck of mutton braised, glazed with aspic and presented elaborately on a mould of aspic and a *macedoine* of vegetables in mayonnaise. *Lamb à la Neully* (sic), described as 'a dainty dish', was breast of lamb boiled, boned, stuffed with oysters, rolled, braised and dished on a bed of spinach with its sauce. Hare featured in three recipes: roasted, roasted by the German method (marinated with 'white cooking wine, or, if wanted for a smart dinner, with Moselle') and jugged (in this case with stout, port and red currant jelly). A whole chapter was given over to veal, with dishes ranging from pressed veal in aspic and a galantine through various treatments of cutlets to dainties such as *wiener schnitzel, veal olives* and *vol-au-vent* of veal. However, her taste for daintiness did not exclude calf's head, feet, tongue and brains.

Miss Cook's steamed mutton and rice was a good example of a style of cooking that has all but disappeared in Australia. With a couple of minor improvements, it would make a simple and satisfying winter meal for modern families. The water is quite unnecessary; it only dilutes the gravy, which was apparently not served up with the meat. If lamb is used instead of mutton, the gravy will not be too rich and can certainly be served with the meat. And a sprinkling of provençale herbs would do no harm at all. It is a dish that makes one wonder how Australians, in learning so much about cooking during the past hundred years, have forgotten so much.

STEAMED MUTTON AND RICE (Miss Cook's)

Put into a stewing jar three pounds of neck of mutton, two carrots, a small onion and turnip cut into dice, two teaspoonfuls of salt, a saltspoonful of pepper, a tomato, some peas, and half a pint of water. Cover the jar and stand it in a saucepan of hot water, and keep boiling for three hours. Put a border of boiled rice round a dish, place the mutton in it, the chopped vegetables in a heap in the centre of it, and sprinkle over some finely chopped capers or parsley.

'Steaming' was not really featured in any of the Federation books, except for the elegant jugged hare and rabbit which were cooked in a similar way. It was the town equivalent of *The Worker's* 'camp cooking' in a treacle tin. Amy Schauer gave the general method and a couple of recipes and Jean Rutledge gave a kangaroo or wallaby version.

Although it was then going out of fashion, the *kangaroo steamer* had been one of the great successes of colonial cookery. Abbott gave three quite different recipes for it, all of which required the meat and flavouring ingredients to be simmered with little or no liquid very slowly in a tightly closed container.[5] The first came from an unnamed lady who combined 'in her own person the desideratum of literary ability with becoming attention to household affairs'. The second was labelled as a 'prize recipe' and attributed to Mrs Sarah Crouch, wife of the respected Under-Sheriff of Tasmania. A useful feature of Mrs Crouch's recipe was that the finished *steamer* could be packed into preserving jars and sealed; in this way it would keep good for 12 months or more. She won a prize medal for it at 'the Exhibition of 1862' in London. In the same year the dish was presented to a dinner of the Acclimatisation Society in London and was pronounced excellent. There was talk of its introduction to the Navy and of the acclimatisation of the kangaroo to France to enhance the cookery of that country. The third recipe for *steamer* was Abbott's own. Later in the book he gave a recipe for *kangaroo ham*, also by Mrs Crouch, which won a prize medal at the same exhibition and was able to 'keep good for years'.[6]

> **STEAMED KANGAROO OR WALLABY**
> **(From the *Goulburn Cookery Book*, 1899)**
>
> Kangaroo or wallaby, salt pork or bacon, 2 or 3 onions, ½ wineglass of ketchup, 1 claret glass of port wine, pepper, salt.
>
> Cut the kangaroo into pieces about the size of a small veal cutlet, and slice the pork or bacon. Put a layer of pork at the bottom of a gourmet boiler or earthenware jar, then a layer of kangaroo, then onions. Season with salt and plenty of pepper. Continue these layers till all is used. Cover with a cloth, and then put on the lid; see that it fits well, so that no steam escapes. Put the pot in a saucepan half full of boiling water, and cook for 4 hours. Half an hour before serving, add the ketchup, and 20 minutes afterwards a claret glass of port. Serve with a dish of hot boiled rice.

In the following recipe Zara Aronson, explaining in one sentence 'the correct French mode of cooking a chicken' might have generated some controversy among French readers. It is hard to believe that she ever tested it.

The Civil Service Company's Stores in Pitt Street, Sydney did not take up advertising space in the book, but Mrs Aronson gave them a good plug anyway, with later footnotes explaining that forcing bags for decorating dishes, also truffles, chillies, gherkins, angelica and pistachio nuts – all recommended as garnishes for various dainties – could likewise be purchased there.[7]

> ### CASEROLE OF CHICKEN
>
> Slightly fry some meat, add stock, wine, and seasoning and let it gently stew till done; cut up a fowl and two or three slices of ham into dice, toss these over the fire till a nice brown, put into the casserole about one quart of chicken stock, three eschalots, bay leaf, thyme, parsley, green onion, lemon peel, peppercorns, half a dozen mushrooms, two or three tomatoes, cut and seeded; boil all for twenty minutes, then place the fowl in the casserole, and wash out the pan in which the fowl was fried with a gill of port or claret; pour this into the casserole, cover the pan down closely, and cook in the oven in a pan of boiling water for thirty to forty minutes, according to the size and age of the bird; when cooked, thicken with roux, dish with fried croutes and slices of lemon; serve on a dish or the casserole jar.
>
> Casseroles are earthenware jars, used frequently in France and Spain for cooking purposes. They replace our stewpan, as they can be sent direct to table, requiring no re-dishing. They can be purchased at the Civil Service Company's Stores.

Like many other Federation writers Mrs Aronson was severe in her criticism of the neglect of vegetables, but her concern was less with their dietary value than with their presentation:

> Housekeepers always more or less welcome vegetables as a pleasing addition to their *menù*. Yet there are few who understand the actual simple art of cooking and dishing them correctly. Indeed, as they are sent to table in the general household and the ordinary hotel they are often neither a "thing of beauty" nor an item of taste – simply and solely a mass of greens with a dash of salt and such a superfluous supply of water that frequently a somewhat hungry person leaves the vegetable on his plate and eats his dinner without it.[8]

Notice the implication that 'his dinner' is the meat; the vegetable is an adjunct.

> With this picture before me, can you wonder that the verdict has gone forth that vegetables to be really tasteful must be cooked with as much care and consideration as even a pudding or a cream? You must in reality regard your vegetable as an "entrée," which, if you might wish, you could even serve as such. That is, as a separate course, either before or after the meat. In fact, on the Continent, and often now even in smart English households, the method of serving vegetables

with meats is quite a thing of the past, and classed in the same category as other ancient customs. This preface will, therefore, make you understand that instead of a vegetable being only a minor addition to a dinner or luncheon it becomes a "thing apart," and consequently a delicious adjunct.

She concluded that 'the additional cooking is, after all, but very little trouble – only a somewhat superior method, which turns the ordinary insipid vegetable into a dish of extreme delicacy'. She failed to move popular opinion. The idea of serving vegetables as a separate course never caught on except for formal, multi-course meals. Nor did the more elaborate treatments ever replace simple cooked vegetables; such dishes remained in the province of special occasion menus.

Nevertheless, her many suggestions for dressed-up vegetable and potato dishes were interesting. They included carrots in aspic 'for cold meat or game', spinach with buttered eggs and tomatoes (presumably a luncheon dish), *queen of turnips* (ball-shaped turnips boiled, served on creamed rice with cream sauce and a pretty garnish), a 'dainty dish' of creamed cabbage and a second dish with a dainty name (*chou à la crème*), beetroot with cream sauce, Jerusalem artichokes cooked in the French mode (parboiled, stewed in butter, wine and sugar; claimed to be delicious), mushroom fritters and patties, stewed cucumbers in a sauce of eggs and cream, and tomatoes stuffed with prawns. Salads included one of boiled eggs, lettuce or watercress and nasturtium blossoms and one of watermelon with 'plain salad dressing'.

Puddings à la mode

Zara Aronson divided sweets into 'puddings and pastry' and 'simple puddings'. The first included many of the British favourites, one or two standard French, American and German imports and a few patriotic offerings with Australian names. One might have expected the vanguard of daintiness to decry boiled suet puddings, but it was not so. The simple puddings included some as economical as boiled macaroni and custard and *rice milk*. She described the latter as 'simply rice boiled in milk till quite done [then] piled up in a rough-looking mass on a dish' and served with cinnamon and sugar. Others seemed to be no simpler than similar dishes given in her previous chapter. There were also batter puddings, half a dozen meringue desserts, junkets, and three fruit mincemeats, one of which included real roast beef. Christmas pudding was included with the 'simple' puddings.

In a separate short chapter she gave a few 'pretty sweets made with oranges', perhaps reproduced from a feature article she wrote for a newspaper. Any of them would have sat nicely on an elegant table, but none was unusual for the time. There was an *orange sponge* of jelly whipped with a whisk until frothy and set in a mould. The whipping had to be 'constant', and took about half an hour. Another was a moulded pudding of orange jelly embedded with orange segments and pistachios filled with layers of whipped cream alternating with the jelly. A pudding of oranges in custard, topped with meringue was very much like the *bridal pudding* then in circulation.

A chapter of 'superior sweets' included *eclairs, maids of honour, gâteau Saint Honoré, baba au rhum* and half a dozen fancy dishes dressed like little baskets. All of them called for considerable time and trouble in the kitchen, particularly the baskets, which were exercises more in decorative art than in cooking and would have made stunning displays at table.

MAIDS OF HONOUR

Mix with a quart of fresh milk two well-beaten eggs. Put these into a saucepan with a quart of boiling water, pour in some lemon juice, and as the curd rises, take it off and place it on a sieve to drain, mix the curd with the yolks of four eggs which have been well beaten, a large cupful of clotted cream, the peel of a lemon rubbed into some sugar, a little pounded cinnamon, quarter of a nutmeg grated, six ounces of currants, well washed and dried, and a glass of brandy. Mix well, and bake in patty-pans, buttered and lined with a light French puff paste. They will take about twenty minutes to bake, and will make twenty-four delicious cheese cakes.

Jellies and creams were especially attractive to students of daintiness and Mrs Aronson gave them a whole chapter. At the end of the twentieth century, with the advantages of processed gelatine, food processors and refrigeration, and jelly crystals for those who cared more about their time than their product, it is not so obvious why jellies and creams were considered to be something of a challenge to the cook. Although gelatine was widely used in the Federation period, the old way of making jelly was still valued. Zara Aronson gave both methods.

To make a decent classical jelly the cook would start with a calf's foot or two. This was simmered and skimmed for six hours or so, then strained and set aside overnight. Next morning every particle of fat had to be removed, then the stock was boiled up with wine, lemons and sugar. Fruit could also be included. Egg whites and crushed egg shells were then whisked in and the mixture boiled again; the suspended particles that would otherwise cloud the jelly were trapped by the egg white as it coagulated. This produced an unsightly mess of scummy egg white and shell grit in a crystal clear liquid. A yard of muslin was tied to the legs of an up-ended kitchen stool and the mixture gently poured in and left to drip through into a basin – on no account could it be hurried or helped. The mixture was not then simply left in its basin to set: it was more likely to be set in a fancy shaped mould of glazed earthenware together with stewed fruit of some kind, elaborately arranged.

TO SET A MOULD WITH FRUIT, Etc.

Take a pint mould, melt a pint of jelly for it in a *clean* pan. Get ready the grapes, cherries, pistachio nuts, strawberries, or whatever it is that is to be set in the jelly. Wash out your mould with hot, then cold, water. Put the mould on broken ice; put in a flat basin. If you cannot have ice, allow a longer time for each portion to set. Pour into the top of the mould with a spoon enough jelly to cover it thinly. When this has set, lay it on its side, pour in jelly to cover that, and let it set also. Do this till the mould is coated thinly all over with the jelly. Then stand the mould upright again. Place some fruit in any sort of pretty design in the top of the mould; pour in more jelly to just cover the fruit. Let this set. Put in more fruit, taking care to arrange and contrast the colours, etc., and cover with jelly and let it set. Keep on repeating this until the mould is full, level with the top.[9]

A chocolate cream, made from a base of egg yolk custard, melted chocolate and commercial gelatine, would also be set in a fancy mould, turned out and decorated with whipped cream, glacé cherries, chopped wine jelly or whatever. Fruit creams were either made simply of a purée of fresh or stewed fruit (rubbed through a fine hair sieve), whipped cream and gelatine, or on an egg yolk custard base, to which cream might be added. However, making a cream by the simple method did not mean taking short-cuts with its presentation.

Mrs Aronson gave more attention to dessert fritters than most, offering the smart cook some bold possibilities for astonishing her guests. Among them were some unlikely fruit subjects, *custard fritters* – squares of well-set steamed egg custard dipped in batter and fried – and *lemon fritters* of bread soaked in lemon-flavoured egg mixture and fried.

> **LEMON FRITTERS**
>
> Beat three eggs without frothing them, sweeten and flavour them with lemon rind, and add a tablespoonful of rum. Cut from a loaf of bread, without the crust, slices one-third of an inch thick. Stamp them into small fancy shapes with a cutter, dip into the mixture, and then soak until they have absorbed as much of the egg as possible. Lift the fritters out carefully with the slice, and fry in the same way as pancakes. Put them on a hot dish, and sprinkle thickly with powdered white sugar. Serve very hot. These fritters take about five minutes to dry, and, if preferred, they can be flavoured with orange-water instead of lemon-rind.

She gave a good selection of cakes, including a group of special 'confectioner's cakes' such as *potato cakes* (given as 'the Sydney A.B.C. recipe'). These were made of sponge biscuits hollowed and filled with custard, sandwiched in pairs, coated with almond icing and rolled in powdered chocolate to look like potatoes. The likeness was completed by poking little 'eyes' in their skins with a skewer.

Her book led the field in the variety of recipes incorporating fresh fruits. More than 30 were mentioned, including black, red and white currants, citrons, cumquats, gooseberries, mulberries, quinces, shaddocks, rose hips and water melons. Among the curiosities were gramma and lemon jam, carrot jam, rose hip jam and walnut jam: she could afford to include such things, as her section on jams and preserves, with more than 80 offerings, was more extensive than others. The nearest rival was the *Goulburn*, at 43 recipes, which concentrated less on the *art* of preserving than on the practicalities of making the most of what grew on the property.

Mrs Aronson's after-dinner savouries included the usual fancy concoctions of anchovy and cheese and a few novelties.

The dainty domicile

The few pages on home decoration seem almost to have been aimed at correcting the vulgarities of Muttonwool. They certainly illustrate nicely the late colonial mood of breaking away from the heavy formality of the Victorian age. 'Old fashioned, heavy ideas on decoration are fast being superseded by simple modes, carried out with brightness and colour and delicacy of tints, that appeal to the eye directly one enters a home.' Beginning with the hall, she commented:

> ...I do not mean "a gloomy, marble-tinted wall, an ugly, multi-coloured oilcloth, a hallstand and two chairs, and nothing more!" No. This style is happily becoming as extinct as "marble mantelpieces and green Venetian blinds," which, to me, are absolute horrors of ordinary houses.

So she went through the home, room by room, offering her suggestions for art, fashion and good taste. Her theme was that dainty decoration, making the home a pleasing space to live in, did not require great expense or ostentation. Indeed, home decoration and art amounted to much the same thing. Zara Aronson brought art not only to the dining room, but into the living-room.

Her ideal drawing-room was small, 'very daintily furnished, accompanied by an air of comfort and homeliness. It has yellow walls, bordered by a frieze to correspond... A quaint side-window is of cathedral glass, and when properly carried out is charming, and a rest to the eye from the usual glare proceeding from an ordinary window. The cosy corners, now so much in vogue, should be upholstered in a brocade (which should harmonise with your wall paper) or velveteen of a golden brown. The same for hangings and chair-coverings. Also add a shelf over the fireplace for all your bits of favourite china, and have it painted ivory white to match the other woodwork in the room.'

What a contrast to Muttonwool!

It was almost customary to launch a new cookery book with a slight apology. Mrs Aronson's was the prettiest, if inconsistent with her opening claim. 'Yet a few of you may say that of the making of Cookery Books and Household Guides there is no end. Probably there never will be...'[10] As if to prove this, she later produced two more, *Mary Elizabeth*, which I have not seen, and *The Excell Cook Book*, a small budget-style book first published in Western Australia.

The *Excell* was nicely attuned to the needs of its likely readership. In her introduction, which she addressed again 'To my readers', Mrs Aronson summed it up as one which would commend itself to households 'where it is desired to have originality, excellence (without extravagance), and economy, allied to tasty and easy cooking.'

Surely that also sums up the smart cook.

CHAPTER 7

The Hotel Keeper

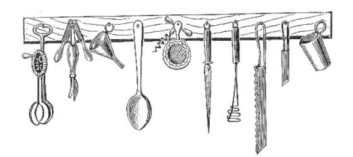

The accommodation on Church Hill

Almost as soon as they arrived at Sydney Cove the British settlers began to lay out plans for a substantial town.[1] The site first selected for the Governor's residence was the crest of a hill south of the Rocks. The main street of Sydney was to sweep past it in a south-westerly direction. A little down the hill, just to the north-east, was marked on the first town plan as 'Ground intended for the Church'. Although work on a church started officially in 1793, progress was slow and the rather plain, barn-like structure that was finally dedicated as St Philip's in 1810 hardly justified the wait. In 1848 work commenced on a new St Philip's, the handsome stone building which stands on what is now the west side of York Street. It was to crown a hill of churches. The first Scots' Kirk had been built a little to the south-east, in 1826. St Patrick's Roman Catholic Church, completed in 1844, stands to the north-east.

However, the vision of Church Hill was never fully realised. The main street took a different course and Government House was built elsewhere; the prime site originally selected for it became first, the manse for the Scots' Church, just across the road in York Street, then in 1836, Petty's Hotel, one of Sydney's most respectable establishments and a favourite meeting place until it closed its doors in 1950. And much of the 'Ground intended for the Church' never saw ecclesiastical use. A long strip of it lying along the east of the Church Hill road, now Lang Street, became caught up in the larger power struggle between Captain Macarthur and Governor Bligh, for Macarthur had managed to obtain a lease of it and Bligh was determined to return it to the Crown. The matter was not resolved until Bligh was deposed and his replacement, Governor Macquarie, proclaimed the land to be reserved for 'a handsome square' to honour Queen Charlotte. Macarthur gave up his claim in the face of this noble purpose, but the 'handsome square' simply became Charlotte Place and eventually gave way to the present Grosvenor Street.

In the early 1820s the government erected three two-storey stone buildings roughly in the middle of the once-disputed land; their intended purpose is unknown. Joseph Underwood bought them at public auction in 1826 and turned them into fine mansions. When he died, the middle house served for several years as the first Presbyterian College in Sydney and was then occupied in 1842 by the Royal Bank of Australia, an enterprise of the colourful Ben Boyd, who also launched a whaling venture at Twofold Bay and established Boyd Town. His bank crashed in the late 1840s and the site became the Government Treasury for several years, long enough to receive the first gold escorts from Bathurst in 1851.

The southernmost building first housed the *Australian* newspaper, founded in 1824 by William Charles Wentworth and Dr Wardell. From the 1850s it served as a boarding house until, in 1882, it became an 18-room licensed premises known as the Wentworth House Family Hotel. Destroyed by fire in 1888, it was rebuilt with 32 bedrooms and opened as the Wentworth Hotel in 1890.

In 1901 it changed hands again when Hannah and Donald Maclurcan took over the lease and licence of the Wentworth and set about making it one of Sydney's leading hotels.

Born in the Hill End district of New South Wales in 1861, Hannah Maclurcan had come from a family of hotel keepers. At 17 she was said to have been managing the Club Hotel in Toowoomba for her father. From 1894 she and her husband, a retired Master Mariner, ran the Criterion Hotel in Townsville before moving in 1896 to the Queen's Hotel, which they built up to a very respectable establishment.[2]

Donald Maclurcan died in 1903, but Hannah continued the business and gradually expanded the hotel. By 1912 she had increased the number of rooms to 83, formed the business into a company and bought out the freehold. By 1923 she had added 'a palatial ballroom' capable of accommodating at least one thousand guests and had taken over the former Treasury building. The

Wentworth prospered and so did its proprietress – a grand house and a matching lifestyle marked her out as a woman of considerable substance and style. When economic depression and construction of the harbour bridge approach severely affected profits in 1930-31, she responded in style by reducing tariffs and installing an indoor golf course in the hotel's palm court to entice back guests. She retired as Managing Director in 1932 and died in 1936. She was followed by her son, Charles, who later became Managing Director of the hotel.

The history of the Wentworth after Hannah Maclurcan is like that of many great city institutions. The family interest was sold in 1950 to Qantas, which kept it going as a luxury hotel but also made it the airline's city passenger terminal. In 1966 the site succumbed to redevelopment and the Wentworth moved to its present location in Chifley Square, where it has survived further changes of ownership.

Mrs Maclurcan's Cookery Book

Here we may see Federation cookery through the eyes of a hotel keeper.

If there are any objections to using a hotel keeper's recipe collection as a source of information about the common threads of Federation cookery – for it is certain that the Wentworth was not the common eating house of average Australians – then the popularity of the book overcomes them. *Mrs Maclurcan's Cookery Book* first appeared about 1897 in Townsville, with a second edition soon following.[3] The third was published in 1899 in Brisbane, Sydney, Melbourne and Adelaide, though its northern origins were still very evident in the number of advertisements from Townsville and other Queensland suppliers.

Her recipes became very popular and continued in print for many years, though later editions which I have seen, such as the twentieth (1930), were simply rehashes of the early collection in more economical bindings.

The sixth edition of 1905, used as the main reference here, followed the same structure as the third, but was much enlarged. In all, some 217 recipes had been added, including three dozen seafood dishes. For editorial – but not reader – convenience most of the additions were made in little blocks here and there, generally in the appropriate chapters but with no particular concern for order. At the very end of the book – with even less concern for reader convenience – 84 additional recipes now appeared in a supplementary section with chapter headings such as 'fish', 'curries, 'salads', 'puddings and creams' and 'cakes'. In the third edition recipes and hints had been numbered, pages had not; the sixth was paginated, though the index continued to reference entries by number rather than by page. And the contents table was dropped to avoid drawing attention to how messy the book had become. Among the new recipes was one which clearly owed its existence to her Sydney days, *pudding à la Wentworth*, a plain milk and egg jelly topped with a thick syrup of orange and lemon juice.

The sixth edition contained a glowing testimonial from the Earl of Kilmorey:

> Mrs Hannah Maclurcan is personally well known to me. In a place like Queensland, where one hardly expects the perfection of cooking and hotel management, it was my good fortune to come across the Queen's Hotel, at Townsville, when my experience of Mrs Maclurcan, the then Proprietress, satisfied me that she could not only superintend cooking, but could talk about it and write about it to perfection.

Although it was the least representative of the Federation cookery books, it was by no means eccentric and contained a large body of dishes that were straightforward to make and quite typical of the period. And that seems to be the secret of its success. The core of the book was, of course, traditional British – despite the claim of the *Towers Evening Standard* that it 'treats only how to cook Australian products, so that there is no waste space given to the unattainable'.[4] To this Hannah Maclurcan added her ideas on seafood, tropical fruits – both, presumably, developed during her time in Townsville – and game, and a few recipes developed for the hotel dining room. These extras, which were her distinctive contribution to the body of Federation cooking, apparently meant little to the public, for many of them were later excluded from the 'popular' editions. Even so, she deserves credit as one of the pioneers of Australia's adaptation of British and European cooking traditions. She was not a teacher, and gave no general instructions on methods of cookery, just a few scattered comments, a table of cooking times and a selection of household hints. However, she offered her readers an extensive selection of menus derived from her experience as a hotel keeper.

Seafood

Perhaps the most striking feature of *Mrs Maclurcan's Cookery Book* was its variety.

In proportion to its size it gave more attention to seafood than any other Federation book except the *Art of Living*, but led the field in the variety of seafood mentioned. It did not tell what to do with blackfish or barracouta – Harriet Wicken did that – or with garfish, gurnet, mackerel, smelt, sturgeon or trout – Isabel Ross obliged there (though why she thought sturgeon was useful in an Australian book is a mystery).[5] And, curiously, neither told how best to deal with bream. However, a cook in happy possession of barramundi, *bêche de mer*, eel, perch, plaice, schnapper, turbot, or whitebait could turn to Mrs Maclurcan for help. Recipes for oysters, lobsters, crabs and prawns outnumbered those in other books. There were also more for salmon, of which some were plainly intended for the fresh article and others to be made with cooked or tinned fish.

MRS. MACLURCAN'S
COOKERY BOOK

A Collection of Practical Recipes specially suitable for Australia

BY

H. MACLURCAN

SIXTH EDITION
REVISED AND ENLARGED

GEORGE ROBERTSON & COMPANY,
PROPRIETARY, LIMITED,
MELBOURNE, SYDNEY, ADELAIDE, & BRISBANE.
1905

SPRATS (A nice way of cooking)

1 tin sprats; toast; 1 wineglassful of good whisky.

Mode. – Place three or four sprats on a plate about an inch apart; then place another layer the opposite way, and so on till you have four layers; pour the whisky over the sprats and light it; allow it to burn out; carefully place the sprats on hot toast and serve.

Like Jean Rutledge, she solved the problem of the shortage of fresh fish 'on stations and inland towns' by providing plenty of recipes for tinned fish – in this case, a whole chapter, including three for tinned lobster. The *grilled salmon* made from a tin demonstrates how acutely the scarcity of fresh fish, and particularly the familiar British varieties, must have been felt: what a poor substitute it must have been for the glory of grilled fresh salmon!

BROWN STEWED FISH (Jewish)

½ lb. dark treacle; ¾ pint porter; 3 lemons (juice); 4 lbs. fish; 1 dessertspoon vinegar; 2 onions; 1 teaspoon ground ginger; 1 bunch sweet herbs; nutmeg; allspice; cloves; pepper and salt.

Mode.– Choose four pounds of nice fish, wash and dry thoroughly. Stew a crust of bread and the onions in porter with the herbs.

When tender take out the crust and put in the fish with the spice, and add the treacle and vinegar slowly until the fish is nicely cooked; serve cold with slices of lemon.

The voice of the turtle

Turtle soup deserves mention. One of the exotica of elegant Victorian tables, it lingered in up-market Australian cookery and was served to the Duke of Edinburgh in Sydney as late as 1965. Something going by the same name was being marketed in tins and was considered a delicacy, though its consumption was more often an exercise in gastronomic pretension than in gastronomic fulfilment.

The original *Mrs Beeton* gave a recipe that went on for three pages; the list of ingredients began 'A turtle'. By 1861 it must have already become a hopelessly costly dish, for the same book also gave two recipes for *mock turtle soup*. The better of these was made with calf's head, vegetables, lemon, sherry or madeira and forcemeat balls. A cheap alternative used veal knuckle and cow heel. The two recipes given by Zara Aronson owed much to Mrs Beeton. Amy Schauer gave a calf's head version. Harriet Wicken suggested a compromise: half a calf's head *and* the veal knuckle.

Despite the ready availability of turtles in northern Australian waters, only Hannah Maclurcan recognised fresh turtle as a possibility in the colonies. She gave a recipe for soup using 'stock made from the turtle' and green turtle fat; no methods were given for preparing the meat or for serving it separately. Apart from that, the nearest she came to a turtle was her suggestion of Skinner's tinned turtle fins on toast. Amy Schauer offered a soup made of tinned turtle soup (Skinner's preferred) stretched with brown stock and finished with lemon juice and best sherry.

Game

The chapter on game showed Hannah Maclurcan at her most distinctive. She gave four dozen or so recipes – about the same as Amy Schauer, but in a smaller book – and provided easily the greatest variety. Rabbit, pigeon, hare, pheasant, duck and quail were common in recipe books. Whether they were so common on tables is another matter. Kangaroo appeared as kangaroo tail soup and wallaby was roasted or jugged. There were recipes for broiled or roasted partridge and for roasted teal and wonga pigeon. But only she gave recipes for black-cock (roasted), lark (roasted or in a lark and oyster pie), 'pigmy goose' (roasted, with oyster stuffing), ptarmigan or white grouse (roasted), scrub turkey (roast), wild goose (larded and roast; the remains in *salme* simmered with onion, chopped ham, lemon, cloves and claret) and wild turkey (roast with liver stuffing or the remains in *ragoût* – much the same, in this case, as the *salme*). Given the determination of the more respectable British settlers to continue to enjoy in Australia the game they were used to in the old country, and therefore to import many varieties perhaps better left at home, Hannah Maclurcan's selection provided a reasonable balance between Australian and British game.

Vegetables and fruit

Hannah Maclurcan gave a respectable amount of space to vegetables, and one of the widest selections, but was by no means a campaigner for them. There were a few curiosities worth mentioning. Green bananas were boiled in milk and served with white sauce and toast as a vegetable, or curried. Bananas were more esteemed as vegetables than they are now; several books mentioned them. There was a recipe for celery fritters for which the vegetable was first boiled, then battered and fried in dripping. Chokos were boiled, sliced, crumbed and fried. Three recipes were given for eggplant, then called *bringhall* or *egg fruit*: grilled in slices, baked 'exactly the same as you do a potato' or stuffed with minced cooked meat and baked. Mrs Maclurcan suggested that pawpaw could be used as a vegetable as well as a fruit. When green it was plainly boiled and served with butter; when just turning ripe it was baked. Pumpkin tops (young shoots) were boiled and served like spinach with poached eggs. Sea kale was also boiled. Finally, there was a nicely garnished dish of radishes with white sauce.

The selection of fruit recipes included *mulberry cream tart* and *mulberry snow cream*; *rosella pie* and *rosella cream* (a jellied milk pudding); *banana cream* (bananas in custard) and *banana trifle*. Four fruits not found in the other books were granadilla (pie, cream, jelly and ice); mango (jam); pawpaw (pie); and prickly pear (jelly). And a final curiosity: cherry tomatoes stewed with lemon and sugar, served with boiled rice, custard or blancmange. But she was not the first to suggest tomato as a sweet. Harriet Wicken thought tomatoes made a delicious sweet simply sliced, sprinkled with sugar and served with cream and Margaret Pearson had suggested a tomato jelly.

A touch of ginger

Hannah Maclurcan's time in Queensland showed through clearly in her use of ginger in savoury dishes; there seem to be few which she didn't think could be improved by the addition of a little of it. For example, it appeared in soups such as barley, mutton, chicken and kangaroo tail, in fish dishes such as *savoury stewed fish, soused fish* or the rather interesting *brown stewed fish (Jewish)*, given in two versions. It was added to stews such as *haricot ox tail, stewed calf's feet (with lemon sauce and forcemeat balls), stewed beef and mushrooms* and *stewed giblets and lemon sauce*. It was included to good effect in several dishes of remains, such as *hashed goose, stewed chicken and rice* and *ragout of wild duck*; and in pickles and chutneys.

At the sweet end ginger was less obvious, but appeared in the near-mandatory suet treacle pudding (here called, amazingly, *French sponge pudding*), ginger cake and gingerbread; and in jams such as vegetable marrow jam and pie melon jam. And, of course, there were three recipes for ginger beer and one for ginger wine.

Justice von Liebig

A dozen or so of Mrs Maclurcan's recipes called for *Liebig's meat extract*, one of the forerunners of the modern stock cube. She introduced it thus:

NORTH QUEENSLAND MEAT EXPORT COMPANY'S LIEBIG'S EXTRACT OF BEEF

In private houses where there are not many servants kept, Liebig's Extract of Meat is most useful for cooking purposes in every way; it gives very little trouble for soup-making, entrées, gravies, sandwiches and many other things. It saves time, money, and in many cases temper. It promotes the appetite and assists digestion. No house should be without it. It is especially attractive to the capricious appetite of an invalid. It is already recognised by the cooks of the leading hotels, as well as housekeepers in private life, especially in summer, when we have such hot weather, as being always ready and good.

> **IMPROVED AND ECONOMICAL COOKERY.**
>
> **USE**
> # Liebig Company's Extract of Meat
>
> For BEEF TEA and for strengthening and improving the flavour of SOUPS, SAUCES, GRAVIES, and MADE DISHES.
>
> Every Jar should bear the above signature in blue across the label.
>
> Forty pounds of prime lean Beef are used in South America to make one pound of Extract; the value of which in England would be about thirty shillings.
>
> PERFECT PURITY ABSOLUTELY GUARANTEED.
>
> *COOKERY BOOKS sent free on application to*
> **Liebig Extract of Meat Company, Limited,**
> 9, FENCHURCH AVENUE, LONDON, E.C.

Mrs Maclurcan used this versatile paste in two recipes aimed at the 'capricious appetite' of invalids: boiled sago flavoured with meat extract, and a savoury custard of milk, egg and extract.

Justice von Liebig was a German chemist whose main contributions to science were in the application of organic chemistry to agriculture and research on animal nutrition, in the 1840s. His theories had considerable influence on culinary thinking in Victorian England. In particular, his work on protein led to his name being given to a commercial beef extract made to his specifications, which later became *Oxo*.[6] Eliza Acton's 1865 edition gave Baron Liebig's method of extracting beef juice under the heading *Extract of beef; or, very strong plain beef gravy soup* and the comment: 'this admirable preparation is not only most valuable as a restorative of the best kind for invalids who require light but highly nutritious diet, it is also of the utmost utility for the general purposes of the kitchen, and will enable a cook who can take skilful advantage of it, to convert the *cold meat* which often abounds so inconveniently in an English larder, from our habit of having joints of large size so much served, into good nourishing dishes, which the hashes and minces of our common cookery *are not*, though they may answer well enough as mere varieties of meat.'[7]

It was during the period from the 1840s to about the turn of the century that questions about the effect of temperature on cooking meat (whether immersed in liquid or dry) were settled for most cooks. Liebig was influential in this debate. In the 1865 edition of her book, Elizabeth Acton, stated that 'Baron Liebig and other scientific writers explain clearly the principles on which the nutriment contained in fish or flesh is best retained by bringing the surface of either when it is cooked, into immediate contact with *boiling* water, and then (after a few minutes of ebullition) lowering the temperature by the addition of cold water, and keeping it somewhat below the boiling point for the remainder of the process.' Miss Acton also acknowledged his influence on methods of roasting: 'Baron Liebig ... says that roasting should be conducted on the same principle as boiling; and that sufficient heat should be applied to the surface of the meat at once, to contract the pores and prevent the escape of its juices; and that the remainder of the process should be *slow*.'

Some time later Marie Sugg, in a book on cooking by gas, observed simply that 'the main point to be considered is whether it is desired to keep in the nourishment and flavour, as in boiling beef, ham, fish, etc. for the table, or to extract that nourishment and flavour, as in soup, broth and stock making. In the former case, the water must be boiling before the cooking is begun; in the latter, it should be cold'.[8] Her book carried a full page advertisement for *Liebig Company's Extract of Meat*, advising readers that 'forty pounds of prime lean beef are used in South America to make one pound of Extract ...'

It is hard to forget that Hannah Maclurcan was a hotel keeper; dishes such as *bêche-de-mer soup*, *grilled turbot a la Vatel* (mussel sauce and crayfish garnish), *turtle fins on toast*, *lark and oyster pie* and *punch a la Mascotte* (a frozen purée of peaches and cream laced with liqueurs) serve as frequent reminders. She offered grand dining to those who could afford it. However, Mrs Maclurcan earned her place in Federation cookery not because of the high class recipes she offered, but because she also understood the needs of everyday family living. She knew well that after roast lamb on Sunday, Monday would bring:

Cold Roast Lamb and Salad
If any Vegetables left, fry them, if not, Mashed Potatoes
Stewed Fruit and Rice

CHAPTER 8

THE GAS COOKER

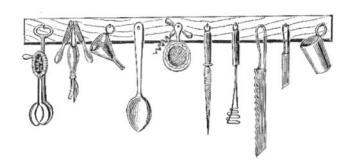

Reticulated gas was first used for lighting streets, shops and houses. The first gas company, Australian Gas Light Company, founded in Sydney in 1837 by Ralph Mansfield, a former Methodist missionary, began to supply gas from Darling Harbour on Queen Victoria's birthday on 24 May 1841.[1] The Melbourne Gas Company was formed in 1850. Most other capital cities followed quickly: Hobart in 1857, the South Australian Gas Co. Ltd in 1861 and the Brisbane Gas Company in 1865. Perth got its first gas in 1884.

The use of gas for cooking seems to have begun, in a tentative way, as early as 1842 in Sydney. However it was several decades before the method was marketed seriously. The gas cooker seems to have been introduced to Melbourne in 1873 by a Mr R. A. Walker and to Sydney by the Australian Gas-Light Company about the same time.[2] At the Intercolonial Exhibition in Melbourne in 1875 gas cookers from five Australian manufacturers were shown, and by this time Walker had sold more than a thousand units.

Some appreciation of the impact of gas cooking on Australian households can be gleaned from a slim volume written in 1875 by Alfred Wilkinson, Chef de Cuisine of the Athenæum Club in Melbourne, and published the following year. It is widely regarded as Australia's second cookery book and may fairly claim to have been the first available in Australia on cooking with gas.[3] It was presented by the author 'with the firm conviction that there exists a real want of such a book written especially for this part of the world, not that there is an insufficiency of Cookery books in circulation, but as, in the majority of cases they have been written specially for Europe, they only partially meet the requirements and resources of the Australian colonies.' He acknowledged the determination of the colonists to perpetuate in Australia the cookery of the old country – a determination encouraged and sustained by the skill of adaptation which became a hallmark of the country cook.

The Athenæum Club was one of the first to install a gas cooker and Wilkinson had already come to the conclusion, after two and a half years' experience, that 'no hotel should be without one'. However, their real future lay in private houses: 'the day has now come when the cumbersome machinery of wood, coals, ashes, poker and shovel, are to be done away with; when the fuel conveys itself into our houses, requiring nothing but the spark of ignition to instantaneously supply us with the exact amount of heat we require for any given purpose of cookery.' The case for switching to gas rested undeniably on its cleanliness, economy and suitability for Australia's climate, which for at least half the year required artificial heat only for cooking and laundry purposes.

He dismissed the three popular objections to gas cookers. The first, that they were expensive, could only arise from carelessness and mismanagement. His own experience had shown that they were economical of fuel, caused less loss of weight of meat in the process of cooking, and saved labour. The second, that they created a bad smell in the house, was a problem of installation, overcome by placing the cooker in a fireplace or under a tin canopy vented into the fireplace. The third, that they would not bake pastry well stemmed 'entirely from want of knowledge in their management'; strict attention to the printed instructions issued with the stoves and a little experience could not fail to overcome this difficulty. And there he pointed to a problem that has attended the marketing of kitchen appliances ever since.

The new gas cookers quickly gained popularity. In 1880 the Metropolitan Gas Company in Melbourne offered three Walker models for hire. Within ten years there were 12 000 out on hire, though many of them had to be returned a few years later when the full effects of the depression were felt.

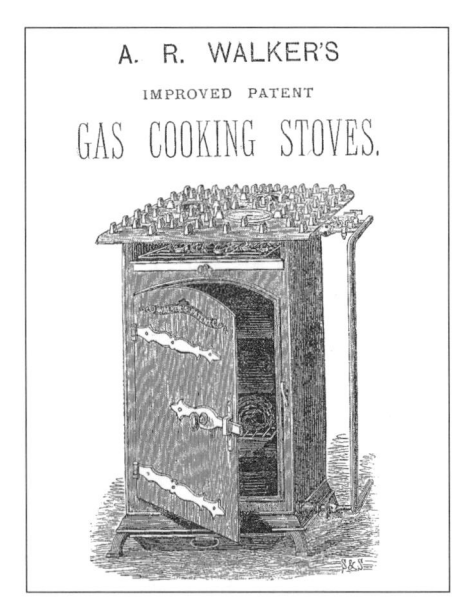

To popularise gas cooking, the supply companies sponsored public demonstrations aimed at showing women both the advantages of this clean and convenient cooking medium and how existing recipes could be adapted to it. In 1885 the Australian Gas Light Co. assisted Miss Whiteside to give two lectures at the gas exhibition in the Town Hall, Parramatta.[4] Mrs Wicken hired the Temperance Hall in Sydney for the same purpose.[5] Isabel Ross is recorded as having given demonstrations for the gas company in Melbourne in 1891 and in the same year a Miss E. M. Cook was lecturing in cookery at the Australian Gas Light Company's rooms in Parramatta.[6]

COOKERY CLASS RECIPES

Mrs Ross returns us to the domain of teachers, but with a difference. Her teaching activities were more commercial: in addition to public cookery demonstrations for gas companies she gave private classes in schools, convents, hospitals and any other organisations which wished to have them. She was employed by the Metropolitan Gas Company, Melbourne, one of whose advertisements ran along the following lines:

THE ADVANTAGES
of Using a Gas Cooking Stove

YOU CAN SAVE TIME
Prompt meals at all times; no waiting whilst the fire burns.

SAVE LABOUR
No raking out of the grates. No carrying of coal and wood. No ashes. No constant running to the kitchen to see if the fire is burning.

SAVE DISCOMFORT
By using gas for cooking the kitchen can be kept cool in summer.

SAVE MONEY
Cooking by gas is economical, because fuel is only used when necessary, and in strict proportion to the work, whereas coal ranges use fuel all day long, and as much coal is used to cook a chop as to roast a sirloin of beef.

Meat cooked in a Gas Stove loses much less weight than if baked in a coal range.

Isabel Ross was yet another cookery writer who gained her credentials from the London School. She boasted 'two gold medal diplomas and one silver medal diploma – all first prizes' – from the Cookery and Food Association, London, together with 'first class testimonials from well-known French chefs in the West End of London' (without, unfortunately, explaining what she did to earn them) and from various organisations. Beyond these brief details little seems to be recorded about her.

Cookery Class Recipes was first published about 1900. My copy is of the second edition (1907), a soft cover version printed for her cookery classes in hospitals. The cover was subtitled *Cookery Handbook for Nurses* and carried the assurance that it was approved by the Royal Victorian Trained Nurses Association, though this cheerful information did not appear on the title page. Lessons in invalid and convalescent cookery had become an accepted part of the training for this profession.[7] The chapter on sick room cookery, with the further approval of that body, followed an advertisement for a substance called *Falières' Phosphatine*, the chief uses of which related to natural or artificial nursing, weaning of infants, nourishment of mothers and nurses, food for growing children, infantile diseases, and cases of debility and convalescence; it was also recommended for the aged. The last page of recipes offered a *blanc mange*, a custard and a pudding made with it; this page was obviously a late addition.

The sick room chapter also included recipes using peptonised milk, but these do not seem to have been add-ons for the hospital edition only. (Peptonising, as explained in one of Philip Muskett's medical works of the time, was a process for predigesting cows' milk to make it more closely resemble breast milk in composition. Peptonised milk was considered to be 'exceedingly valuable in the treatment of many infantile digestive disorders'.)[8]

In all other respects the cheap nurses' edition seems to have been the same as that offered to the general public, down to the uneven type-setting, the charming art nouveau whole-page chapter headings and six or seven little picture engravings that had nothing to do with food or sick rooms but simply popped out as pleasant surprises. There was the usual scatter of advertisements, among which gas appliances were well represented.

One might describe this book more in terms of its scatter than its organisation. The recipes were grouped into sensible chapters, but in the alphabetical index many recipes were out of order, making them difficult to find. The problem was compounded in the second edition where there was some reordering of existing recipes plus additional recipes, miscellaneous afterthoughts and a few pages of phosphantine recipes for use in the sick room, without corresponding changes to the index. Inclusion of a list of *index errata* added to the confusion without filling the gaps.

It made 'no pretensions to being a Cookery Book in the strict sense of the term', but a representative collection of recipes from her classes that would also be useful, she hoped, to ordinary Australian households. She need not have been so modest. Apart from a larger-than-usual selection of invalid and convalescent recipes and a very few references to gas, it was quite typical of Federation cookery books. It gave one of the most comprehensive collections of popular dishes, though it concentrated on the formal meals. Scant attention was given to cakes and biscuits, pickles and chutneys, jams and jellies, and none to confectionery, despite the vigorous demand she must have faced in her cookery classes and demonstrations for such things.

As we shall see, some of its recipes were rather too pretentious for everyday dining, but it was not alone on that score. Her cookery was the most 'French' of the eight books, both in the number of dishes that pretended to French titles and in the understanding she displayed of genuinely French dishes.

Cookery Class Recipes was a respectably healthy collection. It scores a low 27% on the sweetness index. The proportion of its recipes given over to vegetables and salads was second only to the *Art of Living*; in variety of vegetables introduced it matched Mrs Maclurcan.

There was plenty of interest and variety. It gave the only cheese soup (with Parmesan, not Stilton or Cheddar). *Potage à la Bagration*[9] (after the Russian general who fought Napoleon) was a pleasant soup of flounder and shrimp tails in a curried stock enriched with cream and egg yolk. There was a slightly sweet almond and rice soup – an interesting contrast with the only other Federation almond soup, Mrs Rutledge's, which was flavoured with onion and celery.[10]

Isabel Ross gave more savoury sauces than anyone else, ranging from the ubiquitous *melted butter* to *périgueux* and *financière* sauces, both *sans accents*, complete with truffles and madeira. The last two were grand sauces for Australian tables, and she did not hesitate to cut them down to size. In the first, she suggested that Sauternes could be substituted for the essential Madeira; in the second she was content with 'Madeira, Champagne or equivalent of good colonial wine'.

Her approach to fish was generally to cook it simply, and not too long. She dealt with a wide range of seafood, including five varieties not mentioned in other books. From a writer called Ross it is no surprise to find four recipes for fresh herrings, including one with oatmeal. 'Herrings are fried in this way in the West Highlands of Scotland, where they are to be had in perfection.' Boiled salmon ('as fresh as possible') was also offered in the Highland fashion. She well understood how to grill salmon and would surely not have tolerated

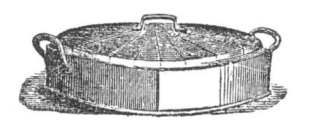

Lord Hopetoun's favourite dish. The most unusual fish dish was perhaps *Fish pudding (B)*, of which the *Art of Living* gave a poorer version.

> ## FISH PUDDING (B)
>
> Line a basin with good suet crust, and fill it up with alternate layers of scollops of cold cooked fish, slices of hard-boiled eggs, and good, white sauce, seasoning each layer with pepper, salt, chopped parsley, and grated shallot, and a little nutmeg, and a few chopped capers. Two or three pounds of fish will make a large pudding, and the sauce must be rather thick, and spread very thinly over each layer of fish and eggs. Cover with paste, tie a cloth over, wetted and floured, and boil or steam steadily for three hours. Serve with good melted butter sauce.

Sweetbreads were much more popular at Federation than they are now. Isabel Ross almost made a specialty of them, giving 13 recipes, including braised, broiled, crumbed, truffled and set in aspic. The esteem in which she held them is best illustrated by *Ris de Veau à la Périgueux*. The happy sweetbreads were first soaked, blanched, washed, dried, pressed and studded with truffle slivers of equal size and shape. They were then laid on a bed of bacon, vegetables, herbs and peppercorns with some good veal stock, topped with bacon and baked slowly with frequent basting. After being brushed with half glaze they were browned in the oven (or so it appears; the recipe is unclear on this point), then arranged nicely in an entrée dish with a little périgueux sauce and some small poached quenelles. The sick had to be content with their sweetbreads simply soaked, blanched and roasted or braised.

Among the dainties were patties or 'bouchées' of oysters, crayfish, lobster, bone marrow, truffled chicken breast, game, sweetbreads or brains. There were also various timbales (which, according to Mina Rawson, were often 'thimbles' to the cooks)[11] of forcemeat or some other mixture steamed in little dariole moulds: *petits pains au chasseur*, for example, were made of a forcemeat of hare with a little madeira sauce. *Huîtres farcies* were not, fortunately, stuffed oysters, but oyster shells stuffed with fish forcemeat, in the middle of which were whole oysters, one per shell. Cold entrées were mostly things decorated in aspic, mayonnaise or chaudfroid sauce.

On the whole, her entrées were more interesting than typical. The same was true of game dishes, of which there were plenty, including grouse, plover or widgeon (a freshwater duck).

Made-dishes included the common (*Irish stew, beef olives* and *haricot mutton*), the refined (galantine of chicken and rabbit pie) and the daring (curried calf's head and roasted or baked bullock's heart). All these were lumped in with luncheon and breakfast dishes. Turkish *dolmas*, among Australia's culinary discoveries of the 1970s, were also there; and the recipe would turn out a passable product, providing one ignored the suggestion that lettuce might be substituted for vine leaves 'if more convenient'.

Mrs Ross treated vegetables with respect and care, but made no great fuss about them. Apart from traditional items such as cauliflower gratin, braised cabbage and stewed mushrooms, she dealt with an interesting collection of less common vegetables. These included boiled green corn (which could be done in milk 'if liked'), four ways of cooking Jerusalem artichokes, and instructions for cooking brussels sprouts and salsify, a white root vegetable somewhat like parsnip. Neither brussels sprouts nor salsify were mentioned in other books. For the Scots she gave a version of *kalcannon*, a mixture of potato and cabbage steamed in a mould. And for the lazy or desperate, directions for reheating tinned peas.

There was nothing very remarkable about her desserts – a collection of hot puddings and pastry, moulded jellies and creams, a couple of ice creams and some fruit compotes – except that they demand an explanation of rissoles.

The rissole

Few Australians have not met the rissole: that fried ball or patty of seasoned ground beef, usually flavoured with minced onion, often crumbed, sometimes stretched with soggy bread. There is no need to make them; most butchers offer ready-to-cook versions. Perhaps you remember that they used to be made with cooked meat or with tinned fish. Recipes are hardly needed, but are not hard to find. The *Presbyterian* gave five, ranging from the simple crumbed patties of minced cooked meat and mashed potatoes, through a salmon and bread crumb version to elaborate and unlikely constructions of cooked kidney slices sandwiched with slices of boiled egg yolk and ham, bound together with melted butter sauce, crumbed and fried. Hannah Maclurcan gave one of tinned salmon, one of cooked veal and one of spinach. Amy Schauer gave six, including one of fish roe, baked. *The Art of Living* had one of meat and one of fish.

Two books took a different approach. Zara Aronson's rissoles were a mixture of oysters and white sauce baked in puff pastry. Isabel Ross gave four versions, all of them enclosed in puff pastry, all of them fried: chicken, marrow, oysters and – jam!

> **JAM RISSOLES**
>
> Roll out any trimmings of puff pastry very thin. From this stamp out with a paste cutter as many rounds as are required. On each of these place a little apricot or any other stiff jam; damp the edges, fold over the paste, and press it down with the fingers that it may be well closed; cut it again with the same cutter, egg, crumb, and fry in moderately hot fat. Cook gently till a good colour, drain, roll in sugar, and serve. If many rissoles are required, roll the paste out thin, cut it square, and place at equal distances apart small portions of jam. Fold the paste over the jam. Press it round each rissole, first damping the paste, stamp out, and fry.

Did these two totally misunderstand the humble rissole (like a later recipe for *Italian rissoles* that actually made a fairly standard *risotto*)?[12] No, they understood exactly what a rissole is – or was. According to *Larousse Gastronomique*, the rissole is made of 'pastry (of different kinds, but mostly puff pastry) with filling of different sorts of forcemeat, often made in the shape of a turnover and generally fried in deep fat'. It may also be baked. They used to be called *roinsolles* and were known as early as the thirteenth century, when they were a kind of pancake fried in butter or dripping. The filling of chopped meat came later. Isabel Ross was entitled to include a jam version; *Larousse* lists one filled with a 'marmalade' of apples.

The others, who got it wrong, may have taken their lead from Mrs Beeton. Her recipe for beef rissoles was for the cold meat version: finely minced remains of roast beef, bread crumbs, herbs and lemon peel; bound with egg; 'divided into balls or cones' and fried. Eliza Acton's book shows evolution at work: she gave two recipes – or, rather, general methods – introducing the first with the explanation that *rissoles* is 'the French name for small fried pastry of various forms, filled with meat or fish previously cooked'. The first of her rissoles was of exactly that sort. The second was for *very savoury English rissoles*. These were made by encasing a little pounded chicken meat in a general forcemeat such as we might now stuff in a chicken (bread crumbs, herbs, lemon rind, butter, egg) and frying the result in butter. She commented that 'these *rissoles* may be egged and crumbed before they are fried'. In time, the meat in the middle was to become more important than the forcemeat casing.

In the 1820s the accomplished, but entirely fictional, Mistress Dods gave only the fried puff pastry version – showing that the Scots generally preferred the French to the English.[13]

Going further back, to 1730, Charles Carter, 'lately Cook to His Grace the Duke of Argyll, the Earl of Pontefract, the Lord Cornwallis, &c' gave several recipes 'to make resoles, sweet or savoury, of fish, flesh, or fowl'.[14] He began thus:

> You must make Resoles in a Mould, and of several Fashions, as Fish in an Escollop, or Dolphin sweet in Hearts, and savoury in any of the Moulds: First, for Savoury; you must make hot Butter-paste, not rich, and sheet your Moulds, and fill them, not too full, with any of the before-mention'd savoury Forc'd-meats; close them, and cut them round with your Jag or Chissel; and these you may either fry or bake...

The 'before-mention'd' included a paste of veal, suet or marrow, fat bacon, onion and bread crumbs bound with eggs and seasoned with salt, pepper, nutmeg, thyme and parsley; a similar paste of capon, turkey, pheasant or partridge; and one of sweetbreads, oysters, marrow and bacon with bread crumbs, egg yolks, cream and herbs. He also gave fillings in similar style based on boiled eggs, oysters, lobsters, and artichokes.

Isabel Ross knew what rissoles were about.

RISSOLES OF CHICKEN

Roll out some trimmings of puff paste very thinly. Then with a paste cutter cut as many rounds of paste as are required, leaving them large enough to form a nice sized rissole when folded over. On each of those rounds place a small portion of chicken croquette mixture. Brush round with beaten egg, fold the round of paste so that it forms a half-moon shape. Press the edges neatly together, and cut them again with a fluted cutter; spread the rissoles on a lightly floured cloth. Plunge into moderately hot fat, and fry. If the fat is too hot, the paste will not be properly cooked. The rissoles may be egged and crumbed before being fried.

For the chicken mixture: Six ounces of cold fowl, two ounces of ham, yolk of one egg, one ounce of butter, one ounce of flour, one gill of stock, a small teaspoonful of chopped parsley, small piece of shallot (grated) if liked, a pinch of salt, pepper, cayenne, or grated nutmeg.

Put the butter into a small saucepan, add the flour, off the fire, mix smoothly, pour in the stock, and cook well over the fire till the sauce leaves the sides of the pan, stirring constantly. To this sauce add the fowl and ham finely minced, the parsley washed, dried and finely chopped, the seasoning and the yolk. If the preparation is too stiff, add another yolk[1], stir over the fire for a minute, merely to set the egg. Mix thoroughly... and leave till quite cold.[15]

CHAPTER 9

THE ADVERTISERS

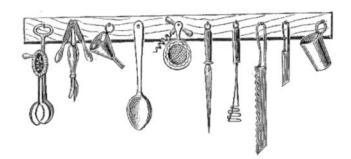

Among the first things one notices on opening almost any old cookery book are the advertisements. The practice of selling advertising space in books generally suited publishers by helping to keep retail prices down and thereby to increase sales. It suited marketers, since the readership could be predicted very accurately. Food brands, food sellers, kitchen equipment, household equipment, health care products, toiletries and beauty products, furniture and home decoration, household and life insurance, even private schools could be marketed effectively through cookery books, since these were all matters in the province of the housewife. The books' purchasers did not seem to mind being targeted in this way; no doubt they found some the information useful.

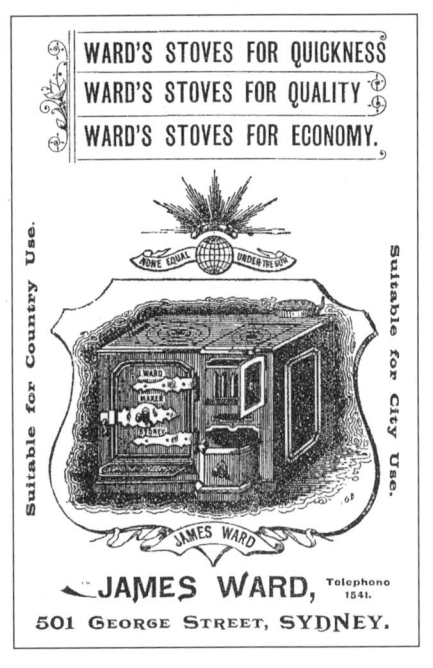

Conscious that most cookery books would remain in use for many years, the marketers usually designed their advertisements with the aim of establishing long-term loyalty to products, brands or suppliers. However, this did not rule out the mention of specific appliance models or even prices. The market changed quite slowly, and no doubt it was assumed that even an old advertisement could influence a potential buyer to inquire about the latest models and prices.[1]

The old advertisements offer useful insights into the kinds of equipment and commercial preparations that were available to Federation cooks and the things that were important in the management of households. Some of them make interesting reading – more so, at times, than the recipes themselves.

Advertisements often emphasised purity and quality, and not without good reason. Widespread adulteration of food was a rising concern in the second half of the nineteenth century. Tea was one of its targets, with claims that spent tea leaves were exported to China for reconstitution with Prussian blue and turmeric. The addition of chemical preservatives was a growing cause for alarm. A test of yellow- and orange-coloured sweets in Melbourne found that most contained lead chromate, a poisonous yellow pigment. Adulteration of milk by removing cream or adding water was common. As well as being a form of adulteration, the practice enabled manufacturers and dairy producers to get away with unsanitary conditions and many of the additives were actually harmful. Attempts to legislate for food purity began in Victoria in the 1860s, but the first effective regulation, the *Pure Food Act*, did not come until 1905.[2]

> **To Detect the Adulteration of Milk.–** Take a long slender bottle thoroughly cleaned and dry. Fill with suspected milk, and stand in a cool (not cold) place for forty-eight hours, when all foreign fluid will be precipitated. The sour milk will fill the middle of the bottle, and the fatty substance will float on the top. Sometimes there will be a layer of cream, then a layer of albumen, an artificial device to make the milk look rich; then will come the soured milk, and the bottom will be the foreign water.[3]

The battle between margarine and butter became a public issue in the 1880s. James Barry of Fitzroy was convicted of selling oleomargarine (also known as *butterine*) as pure butter from 'The M Butter Shop'. The incident provoked considerable public debate in which the nature and quality of the product, the conditions under which it was manufactured, its fitness as a substitute for butter and its commercial description all featured. If any understanding emerged from the controversy it seems to have been that butterine was not actually harmful, but should not be sold as butter. It did not take long for the dairy industry to enter the debate, demanding that the product be banned.

SINGER SEWING MACHINE.

The Latest Model sold on Instalment.

No Cover, as the head disappears and the stand forms a neat table.

Sold only by SINGER AGENTS.

THE SINGER MANUFACTURING COMPANY.

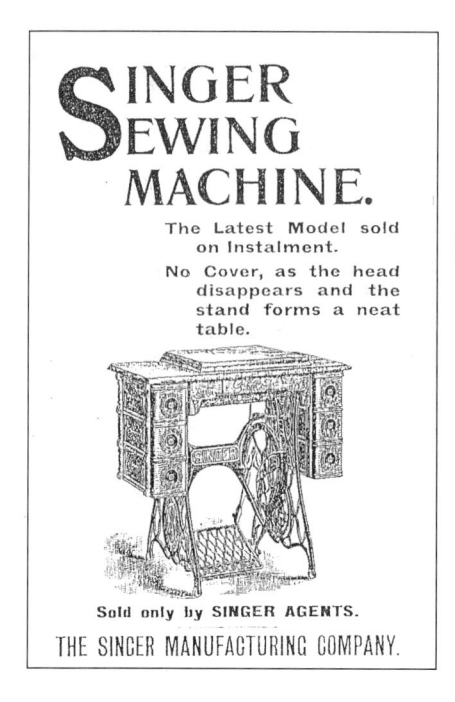

ARNOTT'S MILK ARROWROOTS Light, Nourishing, and Easily Digested. "The Children's Biscuits." Specially manufactured for the delicate digestive organs of Infants and Invalids.

For Young and Old.

ALBERT HAYDON, Champion Juvenile Cyclist of Australia. Aged 7 years, Son of Mrs. Haydon, 98 Henderson-road, Alexandria, near Sydney, N.S.W. Fed from birth on Arnott's Milk Arrowroot Biscuits.

As we now know, the matter was never quite settled, but the *Margarine Act* of 1893 was the first attempt. It required that all such products be labelled 'Margarine' and that shops selling them display a notice to that effect. The colouring of margarine was forbidden and quantities of less than 2 lb were to be cube-shaped for easier recognition.[4]

Selling the goods

Looking through the old cookery books turns up many advertisements for products still known, and for many that have long been forgotten.

The Art of Living had a few advertisements, among which the only culinary products likely to be remembered were Fry's malted cocoa and Harper's oatmeal, rolled oats and – just possibly – *Farine*.

Harriet Wicken's 1891 edition included an advertisement for Rose's lime juice cordial and, in a forerunner to Gertrude of Goulburn, there was an engraved likeness of Sydney Shepherd Smith of Pyrmont, NSW, aged six months, weighing in at twenty-seven-and-a-half pounds. 'This fine child,' the advertisement proclaims 'was brought up (as many thousands of others have been) on Arnott's *milk arrowroot biscuits*, the children's health food'.

As a fund-raiser, the Presbyterian book had more reason than most to carry advertisements. The front cover advertised Fry's cocoa and Bonnington's

134   A Friend in the Kitchen

Irish Moss; the preface was surrounded with mini-advertisements for *Anchor* self-raising flour, Gillespie's rolled oats and table jelly tablets, and Khedive coffee. It demonstrates one of the common methods used in cookery books of the time, to establish loyalty to products and brand-names. Throughout the book short slogans were printed in the head and tail margins of every page, for example 'Eat Parsons' Flaked Oatmeal', 'Eat Parsons' Pure Jams'; 'Wade's Cornflour – Purest and Best', 'Wade's Cornflour – Delicious with Stewed Fruit', etc. The frequent repetition must have had some effect and eventually perhaps even the stewed-fruit-and-cornflour took on.

Zara Aronson's book advertised Cadbury's cocoa ('absolutely pure and a perfect food') and *Germea* porridge (backed up by some recipes). The *Bovril* advertisement claimed that this product had been 'the life of many a brave boy' in the Boer war.

Mrs Maclurcan's Cookery Book advertised Schweppes drinks; table plate from Hardy Brothers; Moët & Chandon Champagne, Lindeman's wines, Martell brandy, Wolfe's Schnapps and Gibson's teas. Also represented were Liebig's meat extract; and a product called *Yolkova*. The latter was said to be a substitute for eggs; it was, in fact, a food colouring agent. Arnotts were in it with their famous milk arrowroots again, this time featuring Albert Haydon, Champion Juvenile Cyclist of Australia, aged seven years.

Predictably, Isabel Ross gave most advertising space to gas cooking and heating equipment. Few of the food brands she advertised would now be

"FORCE,"

The Great Warm Weather Food.

Will not overheat the Blood. Develops Brain and Muscle. Soothes the Nerves.

Eat "**Force**" if you suffer from Indigestion or Insomnia.

"**Force**" is recommended by the leading Physicians.

Delicious Dishes made with "**Force**."

"**Force**" may be used as breadcrumbs for fish or cutlets, and saves a great deal of time.

Egg puddings made with "**Force**" are very nutritious and especially good for Children and Invalids.

THE TASTE THAT CAN'T BE COPIED

Concentrated *Sunshine*

Tender Dew-Laden Leaves all plucked in the early morning sunshine of the East for your eventual enjoyment.

KING TEA

GOOD TO THE LAST DROP

COMPARE KING TEA HANDSOME FREE GIFTS.
WONDERFUL VALUE FOR WRAPPERS.

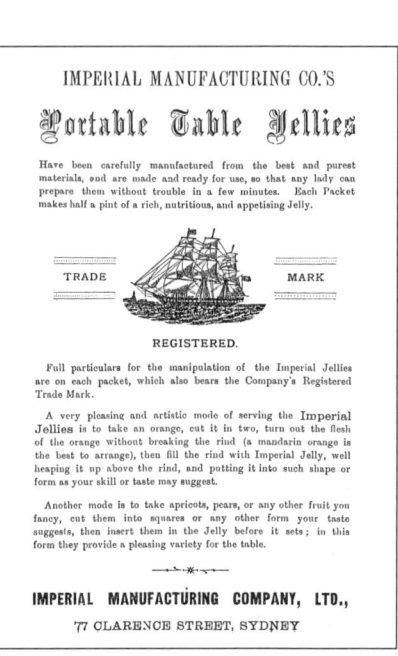

remembered except Hutton's 'celebrated' *Pineapple* brand hams and bacon and Lea & Perrin's sauce. Commercial jelly crystals made an appearance, leading the way to all those awful jelly puddings. And, as the ultimate persuasion to use Brown and Polson's cornflour, readers were assured that 'His Majesty the King uses it.'

The Schauer Cookery Book began with an advertisement for Fry's cocoa ('recommended by the medical profession as a wholesome and refreshing beverage'), followed ominously by one for headstones, monuments and crosses. It ended with 'the Pawpaw treatment', billed as 'the new cure for tumours, cancers and all internal and external inflammations'.

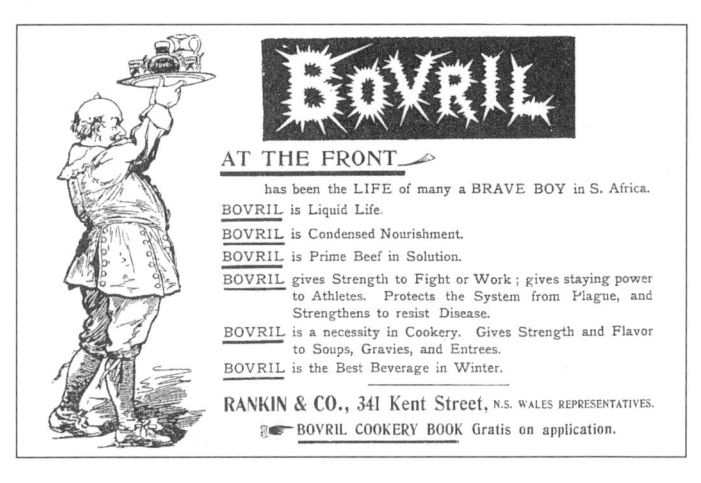

CHAPTER 10

Festivities

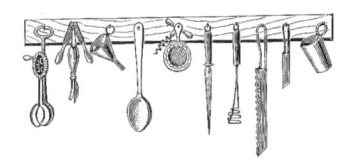

Yin and Yang

Two great principles shine forth from all good cookery: nurture and celebration. Nurture finds its fundamental role in feeding, its higher role in caring. It is expressed as practicality: awareness of the limitations of time, equipment, cost and skill. Nurture food is wholesome, free of affectation, lovingly prepared to satisfy and please. Food that simply fills insults the eater.

Celebration takes its festal role for joyous occasions; its daily role is thankfulness. Celebration food stimulates and delights. It may be uncommon – the celebration of novelty or newness – or commonplace – for old favourites may also be celebrated – but in every meal is some small celebration. Food that titillates but does not satisfy is futile.

Simple quality has often been its own celebration to those who appreciated it. Special occasions have also been celebrated with rare or costly ingredients, little known foreign dishes, the invention of new dishes, feats of technical difficulty, unexpected combinations of food, displays of vast quantity, elaborate decoration and theatrical presentation. Most of these can be found in some degree in the special dishes of Federation cookery. In ordinary households the theme of celebration was most often expressed in fantasy by dressing up the ordinary ingredients of daily fare with fancy names and pretty garnishes

Cooks through the ages have found many ways of expressing the theme of celebration according to the importance of the occasion, their skill and the available resources. But the highest achievements of the kitchen blend art and practicality together and satisfy in both realms at once. This is the goal of the best of cooks: to present the most wholesome, interesting and attractive dish that can be produced with the materials, equipment and time at their disposal.

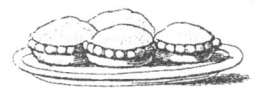

Putting a name to it

One of the delights of old cookery books is the way they named dishes.

An obvious way to name a dish is with a short descriptive title that indicates any ingredients being featured, the cooking process and perhaps the general group or course to which the dish belongs. *Stewed steak with walnuts* or *boiled coconut pudding* are quite satisfactory and there can be no objection to *cabbage and bacon soup* on the grounds of its name alone. But the temptation to improve a dish with a fanciful title was irresistible and the results ranged from romantic through commonsense to ridiculous.

Look and feel

Sometimes appearance suggested the name. *Apple snow* is a reasonable description for a pale mousse of sweetened apple purée and whipped egg white, and gives a better sense of what the dish is like than does, say, *German apples* which is made in much the same way.[1] Sometimes presentation is more important than substance and if one must serve apricot halves in circles of whipped cream on slices of sponge cake then a name such as *eggs on toast* or *apricot eggs* seems as good as any.

Other dishes named, more or less successfully, for their appearance include *anchovy cushions*, *sardine tablets*, *turkey corks*, *apple hedgehog*, *apple transparency* and *rice snowballs*. Perhaps the modern commercially prepared *potato gems* owe their origin to Hannah Maclurcan's recipe of the same name.

POTATO GEMS

4 cold potatoes, 2 oz. Flour, Cayenne, Salt, 1½ oz. Butter, 1 tablespoonful milk, 1 egg, Parsley.

MODE. Rub the potatoes through the sieve; put the butter in a saucepan; when dissolved stir in the flour, cook for a minute without browning; add the milk; stir (off the fire) till it thickens; add seasoning (pepper and salt), and then stir in the potatoes and drop in the egg; blend thoroughly and make very hot. Have ready some boiling fat, drop in rough pieces of the mixture, and when a nice brown take out; drain on paper for minute; pile high on a hot dish, and garnish with parsley.[2]

The 'feel' of food was captured in such names as *Feather cake* or pudding, light and spongy with whipped egg whites. 'Velvet' was sometimes used to describe dishes that aimed for an especially smooth, caressing texture: baked puddings of egg yolk and cornflour custard topped with meringue; cold spongy puddings of lemon and sherry jelly with whipped cream; and cakes. The same logic was probably responsible for the *velvet soup* made from sheep's head.

Origin

The country or region of origin – real or supposed – was often used to distinguish dishes. *Scotch broth*, *Irish stew*, *Cornish pasty*, *Welsh rarebit* and *Russian salad* are well known. Less well known were *Aberdeen sausage*, *Scotch woodcock*, *Yorkshire brawn* (pig's head and feet) and *Irish quail* (baked potatoes filled with prawns and white sauce, which Mrs Maclurcan suggested as 'a nice little dish for supper'). Many puddings came from or were named from the old country: Arundel, Durham, Essex, Glasgow, Jersey, Kirkcudbright, Lindisfarne, Manchester, Nantwich, Olney, Oxfordshire, Southport and so on. *Tomatoes à la Siberia* (skinned tomatoes in mayonnaise) were probably someone's idea of a culinary joke.

The practice of place-naming spread to Australian towns and cities: sometimes it was no more than a convenient way of identifying a recipe, but there also seems to have been some conscious attempt to localise the cookery. Harriet Wicken took it most seriously; her book has at least 17 obviously Australian names – though it is impossible to say in each case whether she intended to honour the place or its namesake.

One could imagine an 'Australian' meal. There would be *Brisbane puffs*, *Sydney soup*, *Fish à la Tasmania*, *Sydney eggs* (boiled eggs layered with bread crumbs and melted butter sauce, baked), *Adelaide sausage* or *Sydney pie* (minced steak layered with vegetables, topped with mashed potato). The meal would undoubtedly finish with a suet pudding and there was plenty of choice: *Melbourne pudding* or *Mittagong dumpling*, a boiled suet and dried fruit dumpling made inside out, with its sauce of lemon and honey in the middle. Others were named after Grafton, Casino, Camden and Bundanoon. For tea there might be *Maitland cakes*, *outback buns*, *Sydney buns*, *Brisbane cake* or *South Coast drop scones*.

More seriously patriotic were the few dishes named 'Australian'. These included a tomato soup which was little different from *Sydney soup*, a mixed salad and a pudding. Hannah Maclurcan's *Australian salad dressing* was a kind of white sauce with eggs, vinegar and mustard; she also gave 'another way' with oil, milk, vinegar, mustard and egg yolks. Both were of the general class sometimes called *boiled salad dressing* which were not supposed to be boiled at all, but stirred in a jug standing in gently simmering water only until thickened by the egg yolks.

Harriet Wicken gave an *Australian trifle*; a *rarebit* with anchovy paste and cayenne pepper (Australia is a hot country); and an *Australian drink* of ginger beer and port.

One might have expected the Federation itself to have named a few celebratory dishes, but if it did, they never achieved fame. Fanny Fawcett Story recorded *Federation pudding* and *Federation scones*; Ina Strickland named her cookery book after the Commonwealth; hardly anyone else bothered.

An Australian Meal from Mrs Wicken

BRISBANE PUFFS

½ lb. flaky pastry; ½ gill gravy; ½ lb. various cold meats; 2 hard-boiled eggs; pepper, salt and parsley.

Take different kinds of meat, such as bacon, tongue, corned and fresh meat, and put through the sausage machine; mix with the gravy and seasoning. The pastry must be very light and flaky and rolled out into very thin squares. Put in each some of the meat and a slice of egg, close over, brush with raw egg and bake in a quick oven, arrange on a dish, garnish with parsley sprigs, and serve hot.

SYDNEY SOUP

½ doz. Tomatoes; 1 Carrot; 2 Small Onions; 12 Peppercorns; 1 fagot (sic) Herbs; ½ teaspoonful Salt; 2 quarts Stock; 1 oz. Butter; 1 oz. Cornflour and ½ oz. Tapioca; 1 cup of Green Peas; Curry Powder; ½ teaspoonful of Sugar.

Put the butter into a saucepan, slice up the onions and carrot and fry them in it with the herbs, peppercorns, and a good pinch of curry powder. Mix the cornflour with a little stock and pour it over. Slice up the tomatoes and add them with the boiling stock; stir until it boils, and then simmer slowly for an hour. Rub through a sieve and return to the saucepan. Add the salt, sugar, and the tapioca; stir until this becomes transparent and thickens the soup. Put in a cupful of cold boiled peas; boil up and serve.[3]

FISH À LA TASMANIA

1 Codfish; 3 ozs. fat Bacon; Shred of Onion; 1 Egg; ½ gill thick Sauce; 1 oz. Bread Crumbs; 1 teaspoonful Anchovy Sauce; Pepper; Hot Fat.

Cook the fish in the oven, and flake it up; mince the bacon and onion, and mix it in with the crumbs and seasoning; mix into a paste with the sauce and egg; roll into balls, cover with egg and bread crumbs, and fry in very hot fat; pile in a dish, and send melted butter sauce and anchovy to table with them.

ADELAIDE SAUSAGE

1 Breast of Mutton; 1 lb. Pork Sausage Meat; ½ pt. Brown Sauce; Egg and Bread Crumbs.

Take all the bones out of a breast of mutton and trim off some of the fat; lay in it a nice sausage meat; roll up and sew into sausage form with string; brush over with egg and bread crumb and bake in a tin for one hour, basting frequently; put on to a hot dish, draw out the string, pour round some sauce or gravy, and serve.

MELBOURNE PUDDING

¼ lb. Suet; 4 tablespoonfuls Raspberry Jam; 1 teaspoonful Baking Powder; ½ lb. Flour; 1 gill Milk; 1 teaspoonful Carbonate of Soda

Chop the suet finely, and mix it with the flour and baking powder; stir in the jam; dissolve the soda in the milk, and mix the pudding up quickly; press it into a well-greased basin, and boil four hours; turn out, and pour round a wine sauce.

AUSTRALIAN TRIFLE

1 doz. Bananas; 1 doz. Oranges; 1 Cocoanut [sic]; Sugar to taste; ½ pt. Boiled Custard; Whites of 4 Eggs; 2 ozs. Citron Peel, or a few Pistachio Kernels.

Peel the bananas and slice them up; lay them in a deep glass dish; take all the peel, pith and pips from the oranges, slice them up and lay them over the bananas, sprinkling in plenty of sugar and grated cocoanut and the juice from the oranges; pour over a cold boiled custard; make a meringue mixture with the whites of the eggs and sugar, spread on the top; blanch and chop the pistachios or citron peel, and sprinkle on the top; if possible, stand on ice for an hour before serving.

Royal food

Zara Aronson offered a steamed *patriotic pudding* of soaked bread, suet, jam and eggs served with 'sherry or whipped sauce' – but the question 'old country or new?' springs to mind. Patriotism was often expressed as veneration of the monarchy, and royalty was therefore a popular theme for naming dishes. Queen Victoria was very well represented by her anchovy canapés, her sausage rolls of cold cooked chicken or tongue, her soup (cream of barley, a recipe for which was found in her own scrap-book), her fish fillets (rolled, baked with bread crumbs and butter) and her pudding. The last was all things to all subjects: a steamed bread and jam pudding; a light batter with raisins, boiled in a mould; a light steamed pudding with almonds and citrus peel; or even a moulded pudding of jellied custard, biscuits and apricot jam, royally decorated. Victoria's consort, Prince Albert was honoured with two puddings: a plain steamed one and a cold one of apples baked in custard, topped with meringue.

VICTORIA PUDDING
(*Schauer Cookery Book*)

Quarter of a pound of butter, quarter of a pound of sugar, 5 ounces of flour, 1 teaspoon baking powder, 2 ozs. of chopped peel, 1 oz. of blanched and chopped almonds, 3 eggs. Put the butter and sugar in a basin, cream well together with a wooden spoon; add the yolks of the eggs one by one; then the flour, peel, almonds; beat the whites of the eggs stiffly, and mix them in lightly; put the mixture in a well buttered mould, cover with buttered paper, and steam for three hours.

Victoria's reign ended with Federation. Edward VII saw out the remainder of the Federation period, but his only mark on Australian cookery was to inspire the rather plain, though popular, *Prince of Wales* patty cakes made with a mixture of wheat flour and cornflour.

Other apparently royal dishes included a thick *Battenberg soup* of beef and vegetables, *Windsor pies* (mutton), *Balmoral pudding* (steamed, with marmalade), *George pudding* (a baked sponge of boiled rice and apple purée, set with eggs), baked *Windsor pudding* of apple and pastry, and a plain *Windsor cake*.

Foreign titles

Foreign language titles were called upon when a touch of ostentation was required to dress up either the occasion or the dish. The language was almost invariably French, with scant regard to grammar and accents. *Croustades de parmesan* were cheese tartlets. *Bouchées à la reine* were chicken patties. *Pailles à la Yarmouth* were cheese pastry straws sandwiched with bloater paste. More often than not, a word or two of French was added as a garnish to an English name. Consider *réchauffé of lamb* for left-over roast lamb reheated in gravy, *rolled fillets of sole au beurre* or *sweetbreads aux champignon*.

Giving foreign titles was a challenge that sometimes led to interesting results. Hannah Maclurcan's *rosetti* was a brave attempt at risotto. Even the less common English dishes sometimes gave trouble, like Zara Aronson's *sauced fish*, a respectable recipe for soused fish.

Travel food

I am not aware of any published modern recipes for *roadside hamburger, railway pie* or *airline club sandwiches*. This is good. But a hundred years ago, when transport was very much slower, some of the foods associated with travel became popular in their own right, and recipes were circulated. The most obvious ones were *railway pudding*, a cake-like pudding sandwiched with jam; *railway cake*; and *sea pie*, a stew of beef and vegetables topped with suet pastry. The pastry was steamed right in the saucepan, on top of the stew. *Sailor's pie* was similar. There was also a very plain steamed *cabin pudding*.

RAILWAY CAKE
(*Goulburn Cookery Book*)

One and three-quarter cups of flour, 1 cup of sugar, 2 eggs, 2 tablespoons of butter, 4 tablespoons of milk, 2 teaspoons of baking powder, ½ teaspoon of salt, essence if liked.

Rub the butter, powder, and salt into the flour; beat eggs and sugar well together; add milk, and mix into the flour. Bake in a flat tin in a quick oven.

Johnny cakes are easily overlooked, perhaps because, according to Henrietta McGowan, their proper name was *journey cake*.[4] There was no general agreement about what they were. Edward Abbot gave the name to a kind of damper made of scalded 'meal' and baked 'before the fire' (to distinguish it from *ash cake*). The *Goulburn* gave them as very plain fried scones. Later books helped to put them in their proper place. *The Worker* gave a Texan recipe of corn meal, flour, milk, sugar, lard or butter, eggs and baking powder. There were no directions for cooking them, though the list of ingredients do not suggest campfire cookery. One may assume that they were cooked on a girdle or in fat.

Fed on Fancy

Some dishes seem to have been named in a flight of fancy or with a touch of whimsy.

Bubble and squeak was a popular breakfast dish. *Pish pash*, a legacy of the Raj, was diced cooked chicken or other meat reheated with boiled rice and a little butter and gravy. Fried or poached eggs covered in a tomato sauce were called *eggs in purgatory*, and may have seemed so to those who believed it a culinary sin to put tomato sauce on or near eggs. To begin one's day in contemplation of a pair of *ox eyes* was fair retribution for a night of hard drinking: they were eggs baked in circles of fried bread.

> ### OX EYES
> (Goulburn Cookery Book)
>
> Slices of bread, eggs, a little cream or rich milk, pepper and salt, butter.
>
> Cut the bread into slices rather more than ½ an inch thick; cut out in rounds with a paste cutter about 3 inches in diameter, taking smaller rounds from the centre with a smaller cutter, about 1½ inches in diameter. Fry these rings lightly in butter; do not let them get hard. Butter a dish well, lay in the fried rings, pour a very little cream on each to moisten them, and put very carefully a raw egg into each ring; season with pepper and salt, and put a little cream on the top of each egg. Bake in a hot oven till the whites are set, but not brown. They may be garnished with crisped parsley.

The purgatorial theme continued with *devils* – the term was applied to almost any dish visited with the fires of hell and of pepper. They were very popular and included almonds, biscuits, chicken livers, chicken legs, crab, oysters, prawns, sardines and whitebait, as well as left-over meat and poultry. A typical *devil mixture* was mustard, Worcestershire sauce, chutney, oil, anchovy and cayenne pepper.[5] A *wet devil* was made by reheating cooked meat in a spicy, peppery gravy; *devilled bones* were the legs of last night's roast poultry coated with a devil mixture and grilled.

Oysters rolled in bacon, skewered and grilled made a delightful appetiser. Sometimes they were called, simply, *oysters and bacon* but more commonly they were *angels on horseback* or *little pigs in blankets*.

Toad in the hole has disappeared from Australian tables except as an occasional conscious act of nostalgia. Edward described it as 'a piece of meat baked in a dish of batter'. The meat could be beef steak, chops, sausages or cooked mutton and was usually cut into pieces. The batter was much the same as Yorkshire pudding, poured into a dish of smoking hot dripping. It was always a humble dish, but if the dripping was good it could be a tasty way of stretching out a small amount of meat. The question remains, why 'toad'? The only (dim) light I can shed on it is to note that Hannah Glasse (1747) gave a recipe for *pigeons in a hole*: pigeons baked in a light batter. She said it was a 'good dish'. To many English *toad in the hole* was soul food.

Tipsy cake was a pudding of sponge cake soaked in sherry and surrounded with custard. Hannah Maclurcan's version was more elaborate than most: it had the cake layered with a mixture of almonds, currants and sultanas, stuck all over with slivered almonds and decorated with whipped egg white. She also gave a *tipsy pudding* of sponge cakes spread with jam, soaked in sherry and baked in egg custard, on top of which a meringue was then cooked.

A few other fanciful names were *poor knights of Windsor* (bread fingers soaked in a milk and egg mixture, fried) and *fat rascals* (a kind of girdle scone with currants). *Puftaloons*, rather like deep-fried scones, were also known as *moon balls* or, showing that the two names mean the same thing, *puff de lunas*.[6]

Romance

Romantic names were popular: *angel's cake* (a feather-light white sponge made either as a whole cake or as patty cakes), *angel's food* (a lemon-flavoured jellied milk pudding) and steamed *paradise pudding* (of apples, bread crumbs, currants and eggs) fed the world above. The fairy realm was taken care of with *fairy cakes*, *fairy baskets* and *fairy delights*. Princesses were romanticised in a light and frothy custard sauce and a fancy soufflé of jellied orange custard and whipped egg whites. The queen had her rich patty cakes (*queen cakes*) and her plain patty cakes (*queen buns*, made with dripping instead of butter in times of drought), her *savarin* (yeast cake soaked in liqueur-flavoured syrup, filled with cream), her sponge (*queen cake*, with lemon peel and almonds); and, standing rightly among the glories of British cookery, her pudding. The *queen of puddings* (also known as *queen pudding*) became one of the popular sweets of early twentieth century Australian cookery and inspired a whole class of similar puddings – some good, but none surpassing it.

The romance of love was present in seductive little biscuits called *cheese darlings*, in *kisses* (cornflour biscuits sandwiched with jam), *kiss pudding* (boiled coconut custard topped with meringue) and *love balls* (cornflour cookies). *Othellos and Desdemonas* were made of patty cakes sandwiched with custard. The Desdemonas were the ones coated with white icing and dotted with chocolate; Othellos were appropriately coated with chocolate icing and dotted with white. It gets worse. There were *puits d'amour* – wells of love – hollowed out patty cakes prettily decorated and filled with good things such as preserves, liqueur and whipped cream.[7]

The *bachelor's buttons* were little round biscuits rolled in sugar; he was also not without his cake and his pudding. The latter was generally of the boiled type with apples and currants and is said to have induced a gentlemen to 'pop the question' to the young lady who made it;[8] perhaps its passing similarity to *paradise pudding* was not merely coincidental.

Other curiosities
Here and there one finds other oddly-named dishes in want of explanation.

Hooghly rice and banana cream stirs the imagination if not the appetite. It was a dish of plain baked bananas, uncreamed in any sense, in a border of pink boiled rice, unsweetened. Perhaps it took its name from the Hooghly river in north-east India. It would be interesting to know what the dish was like before it reached Australia.[9]

Mrs Maclurcan regarded *country captain* – a chicken curry – as 'Indian'. Modern writers are not so sure; suggestions include East India via North America, and Singapore. One may guess at the origin of *parliaments* (crisp biscuits with currant and lemon peel filling); but who was *brown Betty*?

Decorative arts
The artistic presentation of food reflected the formality of the late Victorian era, the rising flamboyance of the Edwardian period and the flowing elegance of *art nouveau*. It was an age where a meal was an occasion – for those who could afford to make it so – and every dish had to be complete, a thing of beauty that could grace the elegantly laid and decorated table. Appreciation of the visual presentation of dishes was an essential part of fine dining, and even household cooks were expected – as far as circumstances would allow – to dish up daily meals attractively arranged and garnished. Beauty was added to the food by way of design – the order, colour and neatness imposed by the artistic cook – more than it was found to emerge from the natural properties of the ingredients.

Height was important in stating the importance of the dish: if the chops could be made to stand upright, so much the better; then they might each wear a little paper crown. Anchovy fillets arranged vertically around the side of a cone of savoury whipped cream demanded more attention than those lying flat on a *croûton*, however tasty. At formal dinners the Victorian custom of laying out the dishes in pattern was still practised. A hundred years later elaborate presentation, now almost exclusively the province of professional cooks, is less formal and relies more on the intrinsic beauty of ingredients.

Zara Aronson advised her readers to 'aim at simplicity, neatness, judicious blending of colour and delicate tints... to improve what might otherwise be very ordinary dishes'. However, what she had in mind went well beyond what now passes for simplicity. For a modest dish of veal cutlets, she suggested that the meat be trimmed into neat shapes, crumbed and fried, placed on grilled slices of tomato and arranged in a circle on an entrée dish around a neat mound of boiled macaroni which had been tossed in butter and parmesan cheese. Any remaining space would be covered with sauce.

Garnishes

Amy Schauer suggested that cold joints could be garnished by surrounding them with alternate slices of beetroot and lemon; on each slice of beetroot could be placed a small Maltese cross of lemon and a tiny sprig of parsley. Tinned or bottled fruits could be decorated with a tiny cherry in the centre of each, surrounded by four small leaves of angelica.

Boiled eggs were popular garnishes and were used whole, halved, quartered or sliced, the yolks chopped or sieved, the whites chopped. Forcemeat balls and dumplings often added interest and substance to soups and stews; quenelles provided a touch of class to a special soup. Shredded lettuce, parsley or cress was almost indispensable as a garnish for savouries, sandwiches or salads. Tomatoes sliced or stuffed were valued for their colour.

Cucumber and lemon slices were popular because they could be worked easily into neat designs or borders and would sometimes complement the flavour of the dish. Other vegetables were used as garnishes whole, shaped, sliced, cut into matchsticks (*julienne*) or little cubes (*macédoine*). Some combinations of food and garnish were dictated by custom; for example, lemon with fish, grated horseradish with roast beef, and sliced oranges or green peas with duck. When ostentation was the dominating consideration one might apply to the Civil Service Stores or to some similar establishment for a small tin of truffles.

Sweet garnishes included meringue, cooked or uncooked; nuts, especially almonds and pistachios; dried fruit, especially raisins, sultanas and currants; crystallised fruits; angelica and citrus peel. Cakes were often decorated with designs piped in coloured icing from a forcing-bag.

> **F. LASSETTER & Co., Ltd.,** THE LEADING *Universal Providers*
> SYDNEY,
>
> STOCK every requisite for High-class Cookery, and have the best assortment of Jelly, Pudding, Aspic, Cake. Ice, and other Moulds; also all the latest improved Machines for Raisin Stoning, Apple and Peel Slicing, Coffee Roasting, Mincing, and Knife Cleaning Machines, etc.

For cold dishes, savoury or sweet, there was the ubiquitous jelly. Crystal clear aspic jelly, sometimes coloured, cut into fancy shapes and displayed around the dish; food coated with aspic to make it sparkle; elaborate moulds of aspic filled with neatly arranged meat, fish, vegetables and boiled eggs in almost any combination. There were the *chaudfroids* – often misunderstood and abused – of white sauce, brown sauce or mayonnaise combined with aspic jelly to make a thick coating sauce that would prevent dainty morsels from drying out, and provide the enterprising cook with endless scope for further decoration. Sweet jelly offered endless possibilities for fancy presentation in its own right, incorporated into trifles and cake fillings or cut into shapes for decorations.

Colour

Attractive presentation went well beyond the physical arrangement of food in eye-catching ways. Colour was important. Gravies had to be a rich brown; if necessary, they were made so with caramel (burnt sugar). White sauces were made red or pink with beetroot or tomato, green with spinach or parsley, yellow with carrot or egg yolk. Colour was so important that it was often considered independent of the flavour of the food. Commercial food colourings – especially carmine, derived from the cochineal insect – were popular and were used extensively to provide a colour wanting from the food ingredients. Consider, for example, Zara Aronson's 'summer luncheon dish' of vegetable marrow. The marrows were split lengthways, hollowed, boiled, chilled and filled, rainbow fashion, with a savoury purée of cooked broad beans which had been artificially coloured pink, green and yellow. *Rainbow cake* was a favourite: a slab cake in three layers of chocolate, pink and white or pale yellow.

The brilliance of beetroot made it an obvious choice for garnishes and decorative dishes, providing its propensity to 'bleed' was dealt with in some way – either by keeping it separate from other components or by adding it at the last possible minute to prevent the unsightly spreading of colour to neighbouring components in a dish. However, neither approach could possibly work for the popular dish of beetroot in white sauce or the salad of beetroot and macaroni given in both *Kingswood* and *The Art of Living*, where the colour must begin to leach through the other ingredients from the very moment the beetroot is added, marring the appearance of the dish. Mrs Wicken revealed the mystery: the object was often not to present a stunning visual contrast of red and white, but a vivid display of red (like *borsch*, in fact). The dish was left to stand until it took on 'a good colour'.[10]

Lobster coral was a proper garnish for fish, and was mentioned by a number of early twentieth century writers.[11] It was made by drying the coral (ovaries) in a slow oven, pounding it, then rubbing it through a fine sieve. It did not keep for long. Lobster spawn was sometimes substituted, but it also had a short shelf life. Zara Aronson suggested that coralline pepper bought ready prepared, achieved much the same result, and could be kept always at hand.[12] Lobster butter was made by mixing butter with powdered coral or spawn – or with powdered lobster shells, as often found in classical French cookery. If none of these were available, Federation cooks were not above using a few drops of carmine.[13]

Novelty was occasionally sought by presenting food 'in surprise': prawns or sardines rolled in buttered bread; sausages encased in mashed potato, crumbed and deep fried; or a pudding with some hidden or unexpected filling. The surprise was never breathtaking. Perhaps the most convincing was Hannah Maclurcan's pudding – providing one could work out how to fit a pint of ice cream inside a pint of cake and to coax a 'blaze' from very cold brandy. It was, at best, a gentle bombe.

SURPRISE PUDDING
(*Mrs Maclurcan*)

1 pt. sponge cake; 1 pt. ice cream; 1 gill best brandy.

MODE:– A stale sponge cake is best for this; scoop out all the centre and fill with ice cream, turn over into an entrée dish, then pour the brandy over it, and just before putting it on the table light the brandy and allow it to blaze.

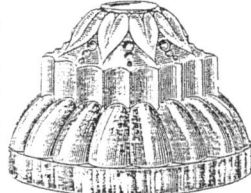

A celebration of nostalgia

In the winter of 1980, at the end of a dinner of French regional dishes at the Canberra Wine and Food Club, we lingered over coffee and an excellent *sauternes*, talking of future dinners. Why not do a traditional Australian dinner? Posing the question in the negative showed fine judgement, for the common response was 'what could one eat at a traditional Australian dinner that wouldn't be boring?' It seemed that everyone had strong opinions on Australian cooking: dishes that had been condemned without trial, favourite dishes from childhood, or hated ones. So, as the wine did its work we confronted the question that would finally lead to this book.

Gordon talked of roly-poly, that glorious English stodge of suet pastry spread with jam, rolled in a cloth like a large sausage, and boiled heartily. We joked a little and I recalled my grandfather's story of a household in which it was *not* boiled in a cloth. As the little boy explained to the parson who had been invited home for Sunday dinner, 'We're getting roly-poly for pudding. Look! Mother's wearing only one stocking!' Stockings were very much thicker then, so the story has some plausibility, but calico was certainly preferred. Jam was not the only filling one might find inside a roly - it could contain anything sweet that pleased the cook and used up what she had to hand.

An Australian dinner was a compelling idea. The next morning I sat in the wintry sun and planned, drawing on the oldest book I had at the time, the *Schauer Cookery Book*. The dinner was presented in the autumn of 1982, when I was Foodmaster. It was made up of mainstream dishes rather than the curiosities or novelties that are the decoration, but not the substance, of tradition. With a single exception they were English. We began with *angels on horseback*, then took *Sydney soup*, followed by *chicken and tongue croquettes*. The main course was of whole fillets of beef braised on beds of vegetables, with their gravy. After that was a salad, with cheese.

And we rejoiced in roly-poly. Gordon made the roly. Feeling his way around the kitchen bench and commanding a dozen pairs of willing eyes, he made it with real suet, rubbed in by hand. And every stocking was accounted for.

Celebration from the Schauer Cookery Book

ANGELS ON HORSEBACK

Sprinkle oysters with lemon juice and cayenne pepper, roll each oyster in a very thin strip of bacon; pass a skewer through a number of rolls, place on a tin plate in a hot oven until nice and crisp. Serve two or three on narrow fingers of hot toast to each person, garnish with a little lemon and parsley.[14]

BRAISED FILLET OF BEEF WITH VEGETABLES

Tie up a fillet of beef neatly with string, and put it in a stew-pan, the bottom of which has been well buttered, and lined with thin slices of fat bacon, and two onions cut in slices. Let the fillet fry for about twenty minutes, then barely cover it with stock; bring to the boil, and add a small onion stuck with cloves, a turnip, a carrot, a bouquet garni, and whole pepper and salt. After this let the meat simmer very gently indeed for one and a half to two hours. For the garnish take equal quantities of peas, French beans, artichoke bottoms, and new carrots and turnips; cut the latter with a vegetable cutter to uniform shapes, and cook them each separately in some consommé. Strain off about three quarters of a pint of the stock from the fillet of beef, and pour it on to a brown roux, made with one ounce of flour and an equal quantity of butter; stir till it boils, add a small piece of glaze, and then let the sauce boil fast over a fierce fire till sufficiently reduced. Add a little colouring, if necessary, and pepper and salt to taste. Dish up the fillet of beef, glaze it with the sauce, and arrange round it the above vegetables in small heaps. Send up the rest of the sauce in a boat.

JAM ROLY POLY

Make ½ lb boiled suet pastry, roll out thin into an oblong piece; spread with jam, leaving a margin of an inch all round, then roll up; put into a scalded and floured cloth, tie at each end, and in the centre; plunge into boiling water, and keep rapidly boiling for 2 hours; serve with jam sauce.

BOILED SUET PASTRY

Sift ½ lb of flour into a bowl with a pinch of salt, and a small teaspoonful of baking powder; rub in well ¼ lb of beef suet cut and chopped very finely; work into a dough with half a cup of water; knead till smooth; then roll out the required size on a floured board. Boiled suet pastry used for beef steak puddings, fruit puddings, roly-polys, apple dumplings, etc., must be kept covered with boiling water while cooking.

The dishes were standard but the meal was celebratory. For many the rediscovery of the past was even better than novelty. A special pleasure was the conversation, rich with recollections of meals gone by and discussion of what dishes might have been included in an old-fashioned menu. Many might have been included, but for practicality or delicacy; at least their omission could be the opportunity for another dinner, and on this we all agreed. I date the gentle passion from that meal.

CHAPTER 11

PRACTICALITIES

We have seen some of the fantasy and art of Federation cookery. Its practicality was even more important.

We see practicality at work in the way cookery writers often gave more than one recipe for a dish: 'beef olives 2' or 'another mode' or 'another way'. Giving multiple recipes was not necessarily the mark of an indecisive writer. Often there were several accepted ways of making a dish, and giving additional versions provided insurance, since it was common to publish untested recipes. Writers rarely admitted to this frankly, but they were not slow to recommend a recipe they knew to be good or one of their own devising, generally by including in the title or sub-title a comment such as 'excellent', 'very good' or 'my own recipe'. Zara Aronson, the journalist, enjoyed browsing recipes. Passing on several interesting ones at once was no more than a service to her readers. Her book was rich with examples.

Popular dishes spawned many variants, both in method and result, as cooks experimented, adapted to what ingredients were to hand, expressed their own preferences, or sought to please their employers or families. Recipes were also changed through carelessness or forgetfulness and were not always passed on accurately. By giving more than one version of such dishes, a writer could meet the needs or tastes of a wider range of user; she therefore gave three versions of *chocolate pudding*, marked '1 – simple', '2 – rich', and '3 – very good'.

Safety in numbers

If a recipe were known, but not well known, there would be uncertainty about how to make it, and therefore interest (and perhaps safety) in having several versions. The savoury cheese pudding *fondue* (sometimes *fondu* in early Australian books) is an example. It was usually something less than a French soufflé and bore no relation to the Swiss fondue popular in Australia in the 1960s. Zara Aronson gave four versions, including a curious recipe which followed generally the accepted method of making a soufflé, with a couple of rather doubtful exceptions: the flour, butter and milk for the white sauce were cooked together without the preliminary step of making a roux, and the egg yolks were thrown in to take their chances from the beginning. Her *cheese fondu 2* was copied without acknowledgment from Abbott's book, complete with his instruction to 'serve hot, for cold fondu is unbearable.'

As recipes were tried and passed on, each cook felt free to adapt them for personal taste or convenience. An ingredient may be omitted or made optional, another may be substituted. At other times the improvement may be to put back a near-vital ingredient, such as an egg, that someone had thought could be done without.

Practicality sometimes meant convenience. *Cup puddings* were baked or steamed in cups as individual serves. However, *cup cake* usually meant that the measurements were in whole-cup amounts, for the convenience of the cook. The idea was taken a step further in the *Goulburn Cookery Book's* offering of *one, two, three, four cake*: one cup of butter, two cups of sugar, three cups of flour and four eggs. Another convenient measuring system recognised that in the natural order of things hens do not lay eggs in standard sizes. Some recipes followed the approach of this *Sunday pudding*: 'Take two eggs, the weight of the eggs in flour, butter and sugar...' Since kitchen scales were usually of the balance-and-weights variety it was a simple matter to put the eggs on one side in place of the standard weights and balance them against each of the ingredients on the other.

This recipe from the *Australian Worker* illustrated another form of convenience:

MEAT PUDDING (BUSH RECIPE)

Mince cold meat with onions, and flavour with pepper and salt. Have a jam or other tin, and cut off both ends, so that you have a pipe. Now take your pudding basin, and put in the greased bottom of it a layer of the following mixture:– Three tablespoons of meal, four of flour, one of suet, pepper and salt to flavour, one egg, an onion cut fine if liked, baking powder and milk to make a nice batter. Set the cut tin over the batter and fill with the meat, surround with batter, and then draw the tin out, leaving the meat in place. Cover with more batter, set the basin in a saucepan of water, and steam three hours. Made with fruit instead of meat, and with sugar and spice instead of pepper and salt in the paste, this makes an equally nice, sweet pudding.[1]

Fast food

The demand for convenience had not yet altogether supplanted the belief that a good dinner was worth the time spent preparing it. However, in practice 'a good dinner', as the Victorians liked to think of it, was already sliding graciously towards the golden age of mythology. It was sustained by the wealthy for as long as they could still afford to maintain large domestic staffs. It was held as an ideal by the middle classes, whose cook or maid – if either could be afforded – never seemed quite up to it. It had always been irrelevant to the poor.

We continue to venerate a good dinner, but more in its absence than as a daily experience. Modern household cooks are encouraged to believe that only on special occasions – Christmas, family celebrations or entertaining friends – need any serious effort be put into meal preparation; and not always then, for the hospitality industry has become a widely accepted alternative for such occasions. Modern cookery books emphasise the quick and easy methods, the hasty combination of a few currently fashionable ingredients and, generally, the substitution of 'flair' or 'imagination' for effort.

Federation cookery writers recognised that help in the kitchen was limited, that taking pains with one dish often required short cuts to be taken with another, that busy cooks appreciated being shown 'an easier way'. And they were not single-minded in their pursuit of quality.

Then, as now, short-cuts were popular. Then, as now, people were prepared to accept some astonishing concoctions in the name of haste or convenience. Scattered throughout the old books were shorter or simpler methods for most dishes and no doubt cooks took liberties with their favourite recipes when the occasion demanded. In meat cookery it would usually be easy to find a dish that could be done in the time available. Harriet Wicken's *hasty mutton*, slices of cold cooked mutton reheated in a quickly made sauce and dished up in a circle of mashed potatoes, is an example. If time was short, vegetable made-dishes were out, boiled vegetables in.

Sometimes a pudding had to be produced in a hurry; it might be the occasion for *quick pudding* or *hasty pudding*. Such sweets were never better than they deserved to be, but they were popular. Plain suet dumplings took only minutes to prepare and could be put on to boil as soon as dinner was served. They would be ready in twenty minutes and were usually served with treacle, golden syrup or butter, lemon juice and sugar. It was important that they be served immediately, steaming hot; they would soon become leaden and unappetising.

The possibility of saving time in the mornings by doing away with a cooked breakfast in favour of a convenience meal of the modern sort was not even acknowledged in Federation books. Nevertheless, breakfast recipes were kept simple and emphasised the use of left-over cold meat, vegetables, gravy and even stale bread (in bread fritters, for example). Many savoury breakfast dishes made heavy use of tomato sauce (which gets its zip from its high acid level) and of sharp sauces and condiments such as mustard, curry powder, Worcestershire sauce and anchovy in various forms. It was accepted that some compromise was necessary in the matter of sauces: while cooks who took liberties with the 'correct' way of making roux-based sauces at other times were roundly denounced, the general use of bottled sauces and condiments at breakfast was acceptable. Quickly prepared sweet breakfast dishes such as fritters and pancakes were also in the convenience class but had to be served immediately or they quickly revealed their shortcomings.

Another time when the cook might be caught short was at afternoon tea. The country housewife who could turn out a batch of perfect scones or tea-cakes without notice and without the slightest fuss became almost legendary in the early part of the twentieth century. The books had recipes for such occasions. Some short-cuts were permissible; after all, if visitors arrived unexpectedly they could not expect the best. Hannah Maclurcan gave a 'quick' version of the popular *sandwich cake*, in which the wet ingredients were beaten in one bowl then poured into the dry ingredients in another. The mixture was baked quickly in two tins in a hot oven, the parts were sandwiched with jam and the cake was eaten while still warm. Harriet Wicken's *surprise cake* contained no surprises – indeed, no filling at all – but was a very plain slab cake that could be made quickly when one was surprised by guests. Mina Rawson's answer to being caught short was *hurry-scurry cake*, a plain thing for which all the ingredients were simply stirred together and baked in a soup plate.

Inventiveness

A resourceful cook is seldom deterred from serving up a desired dish by the lack of some essential ingredient. Australian cooks were adept at finding substitutes or devising imitations, often with an eye to economy. We have seen that mock turtle soup was rather more common than real turtle soup. *Mock bisque* was a thickened purée of tomatoes – 'a very nice soup if carefully prepared' – and contained no trace of the crustacean or shellfish usually thought necessary for a bisque.[2] Nothing was sacred; Zara Aronson gave a method for making *pâté de foie gras* from calf liver (at least the truffles were real, if tinned).

The monotony of mutton and beef was sometimes relieved, ever so slightly, by little games of make-believe.

PRACTICALITIES 155

The leg of mutton which Jean Rutledge called *Barrier goose* was known to others as *colonial goose*. What the meat lacked in goosiness had to be supplied by the imagination and the sage and onion stuffing. Cold mutton recooked slowly in a sauce of port wine, red currant jelly and lemon took on a passing similarity to a hash of venison; so it became *Australian venison*.[3] A beef steak rolled up with sage stuffing and baked under a thick layer of pork fat became *mock duck*.[4] Amy Schauer presented beef shin stewed with vegetables and herbs as *mock hare*; the similarity to hare would have been slight.

For dessert, a light batter pudding could be baked on a saucer with jam and dished up as *imitation omelette*.[5] A thick cornflour custard, lightened with whipped egg whites, could be moulded and served as *mock cream pudding*.[6] Finding a substitute for fresh cream was a continuing challenge. Most modern mock creams are of whipped butter and icing sugar with various additions. Federation mock creams were generally based on a cornflour custard or milk jelly (sometimes both), whipped. They were less rich, but could be fluffier.

What to do with the remains

> The great cold meat question is such an important one to housekeepers that I feel sure a few hints on this head will be acceptable. So many nice tasty dishes may be made from the remains of a cold joint if one knows just the right way to prepare them.[7]

In this way Harriet Wicken introduced the art of 'using up'. It was an important matter for the Federation cook. Roasts were popular and the rules of polite conduct at table generally forbade the service of joints and vegetable dishes that were just big enough. Left-overs were inevitable and had to be used in the interests of economy, since waste was condemned even in wealthy households. Used creatively, they could provide variety in the daily fare.

Amy Schauer gave some basic rules: already overcooked meat should not be stewed; undercooked meat should not be fried; only the best parts should go into a hash; the 'inferior' parts should be minced; and, almost always it seems, flavour enhancement by way of some strong gravy, bottled sauce, curry powder, pepper or vegetables was needed.

Federation cookery books provided plenty of ideas, even whole chapters or sections, on what to do with cold meat; others scattered the recipes through sections of breakfast and luncheon dishes, entrées, savouries and so on. *Kromeskies* were small meat croquettes rolled in bacon, battered and deep fried. Sausage rolls were made of minced cooked meat and would have been rather better eating than what passes for a sausage roll now. Tomatoes and potatoes were often stuffed with a mixture of minced remains. Thick mulligatawny soup was sometimes made with cooked meat. A homely fish pie could be made with the remains of a boiled fish layered with white sauce and potatoes or with tomatoes and bread crumbs. *Shepherd's pie* is still remembered, if not eaten, by many Australians; in Federation times it was made of cooked meat moistened with gravy, covered with mashed potato, baked like a pie.

Apart from *bubble and squeak*, breakfast dishes included meat, chicken or turkey croquettes; an omelette filled with cold meat and gravy; *potato nests* filled with a mixture of meat and gravy; various savoury mince concoctions; *devils*; and *cutlets*. The *cutlets* were of two sorts. Real cutlets were thick slices of cold veal, beef, mutton or even poultry or game seasoned, crumbed and fried. Another sort was made of a mixture of minced cooked meat – or, it seemed, almost anything that took one's fancy – bound with gravy or thick white sauce and cut into shapes, crumbed and fried like a real cutlet. Cutlets were not limited to the breakfast table; the better preparations were quite acceptable as a luncheon dish or an entrée for dinner, providing they were dished and garnished in a style fitting the occasion.

Hash

Unfortunately, the great virtue of hash – its ability to give second life to cold cooked meat of almost any kind – led to much abuse; eventually it acquired a name as bad as 'cold shoulder.'[8] Few now think of it as any culinary masterpiece, but such it was when made properly. The meat, as rare as possible (saving the well done portions for something else) should be *very* gently heated in a well flavoured sauce. The quality of the result depends on the quality of all the ingredients and the care that is taken. The *miroton* – one of the glories of French everyday cookery – was, essentially, a hash. Jean Rutledge misunderstood the dish altogether and gave it as a sort of meat loaf. Isabel Ross got it more or less right. *Miroton* is made by sweating some sliced onions in butter, adding slices of cold cooked beef (boiled beef was traditional) and a little brown sauce and setting the dish, tightly covered, to simmer over a very gentle heat until the meat and onions melted together. *Salmi*, an old French dish, in its pure form was made of game which was first partly roasted then finished (sometimes at the table) in a special wine sauce. As often as not the English made it as a modified hash – game remains recooked in gravy with a few spices added and finished with port and a squeeze of lemon.

Cooked meat could also turn up in pies, as a baked meat loaf or as a macaroni and meat pudding, a once popular dish that has now disappeared from Australian tables. The pudding usually included tomatoes or cheese layered with the boiled macaroni and cooked meat, and could be boiled in a basin, steamed or oven baked. An obvious virtue of the pudding was that it could make a substantial and tasty dish from even a small amount of meat.

Foreign food

Scattered throughout Federation cookery books are some recipes that might easily be passed by as mere curiosities except for the insights they provide into how Federation cooks approached unfamiliar ingredients, dishes and cookery ideas. The British were capable of taking in foreign dishes and embracing novelty with something approaching enthusiasm, though new dishes were invariably adapted to their tastes and, in the process, lost much of their original character. In fact, the results were often awful. Some of these awful dishes became immensely popular and most of them found their way into Australian books.

Whatever the French may say on the matter, their cookery probably suffered least damage in the United Kingdom. The geographic closeness of the two nations ensured that no interpretation of French method remained untested for long.

A single dish illustrates the fortunes of French food in Australia. To the French, the ancient *blanc manger* – white food – was a highly prized pudding of almond milk. It was considered to be very difficult to make because its essential qualities were that it be perfectly smooth and perfectly white. British cooks adopted the dish long ago, but in their hands *blancmange* was never exalted. By Victorian times almost any plain milk pudding, including nursery and sickroom horrors, was allowed the name. Occasionally it was made with milk extracted from sweet almonds but more often from cows' milk and 'flavouring' (among which lemon peel and bay leaf would have been the happier choices). Australian examples included both milk and almond milk versions, and were set variously with isinglass, gelatine, cornflour, ground rice, arrowroot and egg yolks.[9] Puddings made with egg yolks would, of course, fail miserably the test of whiteness. That shortfall was sometimes faced boldly by calling the product *jaunemange*; often it was simply ignored. Amy Schauer carried the dish as far from the original as it might be taken: she made a chocolate cornflour custard, set it in a mould and called it *chocolate blanc mange*.[10]

The Italian influence was evident in Australia even at Federation in the form of pasta (generally referred to as *macaroni*, regardless of shape), tomato sauce and a few other Italian preparations which had earlier been incorporated into British cookery. Some of the dishes *à l'italienne* came to the British via French cooks before they were exported to Australia, and much was lost in the translation. It was not until the post-war migrations of the late 1940s and '50s that Australians were able to learn first hand of the Italian way with food.

Italian soup, according to the *Art of Living*, was made of tomatoes, macaroni and 'cheese rind' layered in a tureen, covered with the water or pot boilings in which the macaroni had been cooked. Dried cheese was thought to have a slight sharpness vaguely reminiscent of Italian cheeses such as parmesan. The Schauer version was simply clear soup with boiled macaroni or vermicelli, served with grated cheese. She also gave a recipe for *clear soup and egg garnish*, a consommé with beaten egg stirred in, that could have been an anglicised *stracciatella*.

Hannah Maclurcan's recipe for *rosetti* showed not only the difficulty of getting the foreign name right, but also the sad result of trying to reproduce a dish using British methods in place of those not understood. It is easy to see how a British cook with some left-overs on hand sought to imitate the creamy, moist *risotto*, rich with the flavour of the boiling stock ladled a little at a time into the rice as it cooked, by mixing left-over gravy into left-over boiled rice.

Amy Schauer's *macaroni a la italienne* was not only bad French but bad Italian. It was a dish which 'may be made when plenty of good gravy is at hand' by boiling macaroni into a solid mass, shaping it as cutlets, pouring the gravy all over it and garnishing the result with cauliflower and little bunches of grated coconut. 'This is an excellent dish for luncheon or second course, or it may be served in the place of an entree,' she said – though modern readers may dispute all three. Isabel Ross did a better job: hers was of boiled pasta layered with a fairly respectable sauce of meat stock and tomatoes – including even 'a morsel of grated garlic' – and parmesan cheese.

Italian ways with vegetables were barely recognised. *The Art of Living* suggested *Italian cabbage*, a solid mass of boiled chopped cabbage recooked with a little dry cheese and butter. A gratin of stewed celery and cheese went under the name of *celery au parmesan* or *celery à l'italienne*.[11]

Heroic efforts

Killing days on country stations have been mentioned as times of anxiety and great activity. On the scale of domestic kitchens the quantities to be dealt with were sometimes vast.

There was an understandable preference for curing methods that rubbed the pickling mixture into the surface of the meat rather than those which required the meat's complete immersion. The Presbyterian recipe for cured ham gave a pickling mixture of one pound of bay salt, two ounces of saltpetre, half a pound of common salt and one ounce of black pepper. After four days of rubbing this mixture into the meat, one and a half pounds of treacle were added and the meat allowed to lie in the mixture for a month. This recipe was for a modest ham weighing 15 pounds.

Jean Rutledge was more serious. Her first recipe for curing bacon and hams began 'for a pig weighing 150 lbs., take 20 lbs. of salt, 12 lbs. brown sugar, ½ lb. of saltpetre, ¼ lb. of carbonate of soda.' A pig of this weight would cure in three weeks; larger animals took longer. She also gave a spicier mix: 'for every 140 lbs. of pork make a mixture of 1 lb. each of mustard, black pepper, and ground allspice, 6 lbs. of brown sugar, and ½ lb. saltpetre'; this was applied after some days of rubbing with salt and saltpetre.

The method of pickling by immersion is illustrated by Zara Aronson's recipe for an American pickle for pork, beef or tongues, 'an old tried recipe and simply invaluable to people living in the country'. A solution was made of seven pounds of salt, ten ounces of saltpetre and one pound of raw sugar in eight quarts of cold spring water, and the meat was kept immersed in it. This pickle would 'keep good from three to four months, according to the quality of provisions preserved in it'.

On country stations where large numbers had to be fed, the cook would favour large joints of meat, cooked without too much fuss, and stews. There are few references in cookery books to the art of feeding large numbers, which introduces an element of surprise to Zara Aronson's recipe for *Irish stew*: 'six pounds of breasts or scrags of mutton... fourteen pounds of potatoes... six pounds of onions.' Clearly, this is intended for feeding hungry workers at minimum cost. Recognising that something better would be wanted for the family, she also gave 'another mode – smaller quantities' which was rather more generous with the meat and relied less on potatoes.

Another curiosity was Harriet Wicken's *cheap soup for the poor*, made from a plain stock of bones (thirty gallons of it), split peas, carrots, turnips, onions, and a relatively modest fourteen pounds of leg of beef. 'Th is an excellent soup if carefully made, and can be sold to th poor, if desired, for about 1d. a quart.' Such a recipe may hav been useful to those engaged in charitable works anc assuming that the suggested price was no more than the cos a great comfort to the poor, but the inclusion in the book (this one recipe is hard to understand. A soup kitchen, it seem was literally that.

Households blessed with a vegetable garden or a few fruit trees had to face the question of what to do with a surfeit of produce. Cabbage could be pickled in brine to make sauerkraut, but was not widely popular. Red cabbage, onions, cucumbers and sometimes other vegetables were pickled in vinegar for relishes. Chutneys and mustard pickles were popular and recipes abounded. Lemons, limes and eggs were pickled in vinegar. Eggs were also preserved by other means, including immersing them in brine, lime water or water glass (sodium silicate), or coating them with vaseline and storing in boxes of bran. Plums and, sometimes peaches, were preserved in sugar syrup and vinegar to be eaten with cold meat. Vegetable bottling was known, but does not seem to have been popular. A surfeit of vegetables probably meant an overabundance of carrot pudding, carrot tart, pumpkin pie, potato pudding, potato fritters, sweet potato soufflé, potato scones or even a compote of tomatoes for dessert.

Many different methods were tried for preserving fruit for winter use. The most popular ones were boiling it in sugar syrup or sterilising it in bottles which were later sealed with wax. The Fowler's Vacola craze with its clever sealing lids had not yet begun.[12] An abundance of fruit often meant making jam in heroic quantities. The Presbyterian recipe for *citron melon jam*, for example, called for 21 pounds each of melon and sugar and three pounds of preserved ginger.

Jam from anything

Jams and preserves occupied an important place in the larder and were used more widely than they are now. They were not simply a source of sweetness or a spread for the breakfast toast, but often a feature of cakes, tarts and puddings. Although commercial jams (and pickles for that matter) were readily available, the home-made ones were generally thought to be superior in flavour and goodness.

Few opportunities to make a pot of jam were passed by and enterprising cooks would have a go at making it from almost any fruit or vegetable. If the produce seemed unsuitable – perhaps it lacked distinctive flavour, was low in pectin or simply went mushy when boiled – then there was usually something else that could be put with it to make good the deficiency. And if jam was too absurd a use even to contemplate, then a pickle, chutney or relish might still have been possible.

Apricot, black currant, blackberry, cherry, cumquat, fig, gooseberry, grape, mulberry, orange, passionfruit, peach, plum, quince, raspberry, red currant and strawberry might be expected. They were all there. A few that might not have been expected were apple and lemon, barberry, citron, melon and ginger, melon and pineapple, pear, pineapple, rose hip, rosella and shaddock (also known as *pomelo*). More interesting still were carrot, coconut, gramma, mango, pawpaw, prickly pear, rhubarb (look for rhubarb and ginger at country markets), rockmelon, tomato, tomato and pineapple (pleasant, but inclined to be runny), green tomato, vegetable marrow and ginger, and even walnut. A few decades later the irrepressible ladies of the CWA took the grand prize: they made a jam from the dreaded choko.[13] I wonder what they used it for?

Mrs Sophie Corrie

Preserving fruit and making jams, pickles and confectionery were not just ways of using up surpluses and keeping the pantry full. Like cake making, they acquired the status of a culinary art. Amy Schauer and Margaret Pearson produced separate books on the subject.

Mrs Sophie Corrie, of Colo Vale, New South Wales, was one of many women who took her art into the Agricultural Show circuit and actively sought recognition for it. For many years she exhibited her preserves, pickles and candies, building up an impressive record of 700 prizes, including 500 firsts.

> More tempting, luscious-looking preserves could not be imagined. That someone has such an industry particularly at heart is gratifying, and Mrs Corrie is to be congratulated upon her earnest efforts in promoting what is essentially a womanly occupation, and for endeavouring to make it an avenue for employment for her sex. As an exhibitor this lady ranks high.
>
> – *The Evening News*[14]

In the early 1890s she published a little book on the subject and kept it in print through at least half a dozen editions. It dealt with preserving, jams, jellies, marmalades, conserves (rather like jams, but retaining the fruit whole or in large pieces), and crystallised fruit. A small selection of pickles and condiments in the early editions was later dropped.

Mrs Corrie's book was not notable for its variety or novelty, rather for her emphasis on technique. For preserving fruits she preferred cans to the more popular bottles, claiming that it was the exclusion of air, rather that the presence of sugar, that prevented fermentation of preserved fruit. The truth was both simpler and more complex. A French food processor, Nicolas Appert, had shown in the early nineteenth century that food could be preserved in glass jars by a combination of controlled heat treatment and effective sealing. His method was little different from that still used for home-bottled fruit. However, the method was not well understood. Appert, and those who followed him, placed too much emphasis on the exclusion of air. What was necessary was the exclusion of micro-organisms.

George Peacock was one of the early fruit preservers in Australia and founded the company which became Henry Jones (IXL) Limited. He began to can jam in Hobart in 1861 and later extended his operations to Sydney. His method was to boil the jam, pack it by hand into open cans, then solder on the tops after the contents had cooled overnight. This method subjected the jam to contamination from airborne micro-organisms, leaving the high sugar content and airtight seal as the only real protection. His method of preserving fruit was to pack it into cans, top them up with condensate, solder on the lids, then heat the cans for a predetermined time. The process was completed by extracting air from the cans, which could have been achieved by allowing a small hole to remain in the lid and soldering it closed after heating was complete, or by piercing the can and resealing it. This final step probably did more harm than good.[15]

Doing without

At the other extreme, cooks in remote locations could expect to have to do without many ingredients that might otherwise have been taken for granted. Even in towns, adjustments had to be made from time to time as seasonal variations pushed prices up. Cookery books gave eggless versions of common recipes and marked them for ease of reference. For example, Zara Aronson gave two versions of *baked rice pudding*, one sub-titled 'with eggs', the other 'without eggs... My own recipe. Very good.' Others gave recipes for plum pudding, plain cake and rock cakes 'without eggs'. We have already noted the use of dripping. When fresh milk supplies dried up, the cakes, biscuits and pastry were moistened with water; there does not seem to have been much reliance on powdered or condensed milk. If cooks could not devise some way of 'making do' with what ingredients were on hand – by adapting, substituting, or imitating – then they had to do without. Cheese and cheese dishes would be off the menu for a while, so would milk puddings – and suet puddings with treacle or jam sauce, jellies and fruit compotes would appear even more frequently than usual.

There was a distinction to be drawn between 'plain cookery' and 'plain food'. The former, as we have seen, meant mastery of the basics. But many people enjoyed plainly cooked food. Although cooks needed little instruction on how to do a plain job on vegetables and meat, writers felt compelled to pass on simple recipes for plain dishes. Examples from Isabel Ross included *plain onion soup (maigre)* made with water instead of stock; and poured over toast without the usual sprinkling of cheese. Her *plain brown sauce* was of brown stock thickened with a simple brown roux. Her *plain white sauce* was of milk thickened with white roux; the only flavouring was salt and pepper. It could be turned into *oyster sauce (plain)* by adding blanched oysters, but this was a mere shadow of what she thought an oyster sauce really should be.

> ### OYSTER SAUCE
> *(Isabel Ross)*
>
> Blanch and beard three dozen oysters, lifting them out of their liquor with a skimmer to free them from particles of shell or sand. Add them to a good, white sauce made hot, adding the oysters just before serving. Or the sauce can be made as follows:– Put into a small saucepan two ounces of butter with two ounces of flour, fry without discolouring; add half a pint of milk, a gill of fish stock, and a gill of cream. Cook well, adding a little of the oyster liquor carefully strained. Just before serving add a few spoonfuls of rich, raw cream. Make the sauce hot, and pour over the oysters with a squeeze of lemon juice if liked.

The discipline of plainness was often applied to puddings. Jean Rutledge's *plain suet pudding* was made of flour, suet, salt, baking powder and water. Sweetness and flavour came with the sauce. Harriet Wicken didn't bother with the baking powder, but suggested that egg and milk would be 'a great improvement' – few would argue with her. She did not mention what sauce should be served with it.

The *Goulburn* book gave six recipes for *plum pudding*. The first was respectably rich with butter, eggs, dried fruit, almonds, spice and brandy. The second was a little less rich, and omitted the almonds and spice. The third, 'without eggs' had still less fruit and offered a choice of suet or butter. The fourth, *drought plum pudding*, used all flour (no bread crumbs), little sugar, the barest minimum of butter, and no eggs. The 'plain' version used flour, suet, brown sugar, a minimum of fruit, a single egg, and no spice or brandy. The sixth recipe was for *sago plum pudding*, a steamed pudding of sago, bread crumbs and raisins.

Biscuits, cakes and buns also came in plain versions. *Plain cake* meant little or no fruit, perhaps almond or lemon essence, easy to make, and probably no icing or decoration. Sometimes it also meant economy of butter and eggs or use of dripping.

PLAIN CAKE
(Goulburn Cookery Book)

One dessertspoonful butter, 1 cup sugar, 1 cup flour, 1½ teaspoonsful baking powder, 2 eggs, ½ cup milk; melt the butter, then add the sugar, flour and baking powder; beat the eggs, and mix them with the milk and a few drops of essence of lemon. Stir all together and bake in a moderate oven.

GOOD PLAIN CAKE
(Schauer Cookery Book)

½ lb. dripping, 1½ lb. flour, 1 lb. fruit, ½ lb sugar, 4 eggs, ¼ lb. candied peel, 1 full cup of milk, 2 teaspoons baking powder, pinch salt.

Beat dripping and sugar to a cream, add eggs one by one, and beat each thoroughly into the mixture; sift the flour, baking powder and salt together; add fruit and candied peel; mix alternately with the milk; bake 3 hours (or in 2 tins 2 hours) in a moderate oven.

Waste not, want not

Economy in the kitchen was a virtue next to godliness; cooks and mistresses were urged to study it even in good times. In hard times the practice of economy became a matter of greatest importance. Cookery books gave 'economical' versions of many dishes which were, at their best, plain. The obvious measures of domestic economy – purchase of only inexpensive ingredients, avoidance of all waste, use of left-overs – were recognised or advocated in most cookery books. Soup was a highly suitable food for the poor. Meat could be made to go further by making it into fritters, *toad in the hole* or a savoury pudding or pie, or by stewing it with cheap vegetables and dumplings. Even an omelette could be stretched with milk and bread crumbs.[16] Puddings were not necessarily dispensed with; they simply became plainer.

When mere economy was not enough, there was no need to mince words. The Presbyterian book gave a *cheap family white soup* of veal knuckle and ham. It also had *cheap cake* and *cheap icing* (sugar, water and lemon juice, boiled). Amy Schauer offered a steamed *cheap pudding* with suet and an egg. However, her recipe for *cheap ice creams*, which were made on milk and many eggs, ignored the fact that eggs were often as scarce as cream.

If 'hard up' one would hope for an occasional *poor man's dish* of reheated meat with its *poor man's sauce*, or would look forward to *poor man's pie* of minced cold cooked beef, potatoes and boiled eggs.[17] There was *poor man's goose* – a truly humble dish of sheep's heart and liver, potatoes and onions – or perhaps one would be content with a *vegetable goose* of bread, suet, onions and sage that was, in effect, the stuffing without the goose.[18] If one could afford the comfort of a pudding it would have to be *half-pay pudding*, a boiled suet pudding with a little dried fruit, or the *poor woman's pudding*.[19] Neither included eggs; the really poor went without eggs in their puddings. If fortunes declined still further one would be thankful for a thin *retrenchment stew* of beef leg, onion and carrot.[20]

POOR WOMAN'S PUDDING
(*Goulburn Cookery Book*)

Three cups of flour, 1½ cups of brown sugar, ½ cup currants, 2 tablespoons of dripping, 1 tablespoon of carbonate of soda, a little spice and salt, 1 cup of boiling water.

Mix the flour, soda, sugar, currants, and spice together. Dissolve the dripping in a cup of boiling water, and add to the dry ingredients. Tie loosely in a floured cloth, and boil for 3 hours. Serve with sauce.

Common property

Recipes and household hints were freely circulated and freely copied. It was coin for social intercourse and served a very practical purpose. Mina Rawson explained it this way:

> Ladies in the bush who are in the habit of cooking regularly, either for pleasure or from necessity, are constantly finding out little hints and dodges that would be very useful to all situated in like manner, for often one runs out of certain things in the bush, and then it is either a case of discovery or inventing a substitute; or else doing without till

the drays come from town. I have often thought what a good plan it would be to exchange hints with each other through some newspaper. Some years ago I belonged to a society of this kind, but it was merely among personal friends, and we exchanged recipes by letter. Anyone who discovered or invented a new dish or cake at once made it known to the others; and in this way each was benefited by the cleverness of the whole number.[21]

Among writers and compilers of cookery books there was not much concern for intellectual property rights. Leafing through their work one notices recipes so similar that either one must be an adaptation of the other or both must be adaptations of a third. Sometimes there was no adaptation and it is obvious that one or both were unacknowledged copies. The source may not have been a book; it may have been a newspaper, magazine or even a common correspondent. Books compiled from contributed recipes must have included many copied or adapted recipes.

An interesting example was *Aunt Nellie's pudding*, found in the Presbyterian book. Aunt Nellie was typical of late nineteenth century suet puddings, and no lightweight, relying for buoyancy on a very high fat content and long boiling rather than any rising agent. A few years later Zara Aronson, who I suspect borrowed or copied most of her material, gave exactly the same recipe under the name *My favourite pudding*. It was not that Zara's aunt was Presbyterian; both books borrowed the recipe from Mrs Beeton – and where did she get it?[22] Mrs Beeton was a gatherer, not an inventor of recipes.

AUNT NELLIE'S PUDDING

Chop finely ½ lb. suet, mix with it ½ lb. treacle, the rind and juice of 1 lemon, a few strips of candied peel, 3 tablespoonsful cream, and 2 well-beaten eggs. Beat the pudding well; put into a buttered basin; tie down with a cloth, and boil 4 hours.

Useful hints

Kitchen and household hints were invented, adapted, shared, traded, copied and recorded like recipes. General household references like the *Enquiry Book* tried to give wide coverage to the many little problems or tasks for which some obscure item of knowledge might be just the thing. Cookery books were also logical places for them. Most gave small, quite random selections tucked away in a chapter on 'odds and ends' or 'little things worth knowing', ranging from mending broken china to advice on how to make the oil lamp of your bicycle burn brighter (Mrs Maclurcan).

KITCHEN HINTS
From the Presbyterian Cookery book

> Fresh fruit dipped in boiled sugar and let dry makes a pretty garnish for sweet dishes.
>
> To cut new bread first dip the knife into boiling water. Repeat when cool.
>
> Put about the size of an egg of bread crumbs tied in muslin in with the cabbage when cooking. Cabbage cooked like this may be used in any way. The bread absorbs all the bitter juices, and the cabbages are digested quite easily. The bread crumbs also absorb almost all the smell of the cabbage while cooking.[23]
>
> Cakes will be much lighter if mixed with the hand than if a spoon or knife be used.
>
> Remember that sauce for boiled fish should be thicker than that which is for broiled or fried fish.

From the Goulburn Cookery Book

> TO PRESERVE EGGS IN LIME WATER
>
> Three gallons of boiling water, 1 quart of lime, 1 oz. of cream of tartar, ½ lb. of salt.
>
> Pour the boiling water over the lime, and leave for two days, stirring now and then. Then pour the water off without any of the lime, and mix the salt and cream of tartar into the lime water. It is then ready for use. Put the eggs in each day as they are laid. Be very careful that none of them are cracked.
>
> *(Recipes were also given for preserving eggs in water-glass or rubbed with vaseline and buried in bran.)*
>
> CLARIFIED FAT
>
> Two pounds of mixed fat, ½ pint of water.
>
> Cut the fat into ½-inch squares; remove all lean. Place the fat in a saucepan with ½ pint of cold water, cover closely, and boil gently for 1 hour. Stir occasionally with an iron spoon. Remove the lid, and boil until all water is evaporated. Allow it to cool, and strain into a basin. Press the pieces to squeeze out the fat.

> CARAMEL FOR COLOURING
>
> Put ¼ lb. of sugar into a saucepan, and let it get very brown. Pour over it ¼ pint of water, and stir till it boils and all the sugar is dissolved. Strain, and, when cold, put into a wide-mouthed bottle. Cork well, and keep for colouring soup, gravy, &c.

MEASURES AND WEIGHTS
(*XXth Century Cookery*)
Four teaspoonfuls equal one tablespoonful (liquid).
Four tablespoonfuls equal one wineglassful or half a gill.
Two wineglassfuls equal one gill, or half a cup.
Two gills equal one coffeecupful, or sixteen tablespoonfuls.
Two coffeecupfuls equal one pint.
Two pints equal one quart.
Four quarts equal one gallon.
Two tablespoonfuls equal one ounce (liquid).
One tablespoonful of salt equals one ounce.
Sixteen ounces equal one pound, or a pint of liquid.
Four coffeecupfuls of sifted flour equal one pound.
One quart of unsifted flour equals one pound.
Eight or ten ordinary-sized eggs equal one pound.
One pint of white granulated sugar equals one pound.
Two coffeecupfuls of powdered sugar equal one pound.
One coffeecupful of cold butter, pressed down, equals half a pound.
One tablespoonful of soft butter, well-rounded, equals one ounce.
An ordinary tumblerful equals one coffeecupful, or half a pint.
About twenty-five drops of any thin liquid will fill a common-sized teaspoon.
One pint of finely chopped meat, packed solidly, equals one pound.

Cottage industry

One of the late offerings to the Federation kitchen was the *Keeyuga Cookery Book* by Henrietta McGowan of Victoria.[23] Described by its publishers as

'The Australian Mrs. Beeton' and 'The Australian Unbeaten', it indeed gives a good account of its subject from the introduction 'Meals make the man' to the final chapters of practicalities ('Sundries', 'Waste not, want not' and 'Things worth knowing'). More interesting than the recipes – which largely confirm what has been found in the books that went before it – and its rich collection of advertisements is what it shows of the times. The author marked out three particular areas of practicality for her special contribution to the household literature.

Reversing the order in which she introduced them, the first was that class of women who sold foodstuffs for a living. 'If a woman can make good jams, good marmalade, good preserves, good pickles, good sauces, good cakes, and good sweets she has always a good living at her fingertips.' The idea was not to compete with the factories, but to specialise in the many items such as fruit honeys, melon marmalades and mixed jams which the factories left alone. The market was big hotels, residential flats and boarding houses.

The outdoor life

A section on camp life and weekend cookery would come as no surprise in a contemporary book, but in 1911 it was novel. 'Every year sees immense increase in the ranks of the week-enders. The variety of their habitations is no greater than the variety of themselves. From a tent or two to a perfectly appointed cottage and from one galvanised iron room to some rambling old house, may the week-ender be found.' She went on to lay down the laws of successful camping: order and system as well as simplicity were absolutely essential. She recommended a 'proper hanging meat safe' of perforated zinc covered with wet hessian for storing perishable food. Since 'any fine day may bring a crowd of visitors with well sharpened appetites, while bad weather may mean waste of good food', she recommended a fair supply of tinned food, making it clear that she did not advocate the use of 'tinned stuff' generally. Cooking could be done on a makeshift stove made from an oil drum or on a portable kerosene stove. And she thought it would not offend the proprieties at a weekender to serve a stew or curry direct from the earthenware crock in which it had been slow-cooked.

Bachelor women

The final practicality sheds light on an aspect of Australia's social history which is often overlooked. From the arrival of the first fleet until well into the twentieth century, men outnumbered women. In 1861 there were 138 men for every 100 women; at Federation the ratio was still 110:100. Both the imbalance of numbers and the social pressures for keeping up the birthrate

170   A FRIEND IN THE KITCHEN

ensured that women of most ages who were willing to marry had little difficulty finding husbands, whether or not they enjoyed the result.

However, there was always a significant number of women who did not marry and raise families. Denied the status 'Mrs', they occupied an uncertain position in society. Whether they were factory workers or teachers, the wage structure which discriminated against all women condemned many of these female bachelors to live at levels of economy well below their station in life in cheap flats, rooms or, later, hostels.[25]

So Mrs McGowan addressed a few pages to 'the host of women and not a few men' who lived without the comforts of a household. It soon became clear, however, that bachelor men were not her concern. She approached the subject delicately:

> The average individual living in rooms is very apt to suffer from ignorance of how to do for herself. She may be young, and either a student of some sort or she may be a much older woman who circumstances or inclination has made dependent on her own exertions for her physical comfort. We very frequently hear the expression "She has given up her home and gone into rooms." The lucky few who find in rooms, or even one room, a very happy home, are always inclined to smile at the subtle irony contained in this remark. The unhappy fact remains, however, that the bachelor woman's "diggings" are often no abode of bliss and the tendency of the bachelor woman herself to "go to pieces" through her inability to feed herself properly is a very distressing one. A very little knowledge and the strict maintenance of a little system can convert the menage of any intelligent individual into something in which she can take pride as well as pleasure.

It was 'essentially bad' for a bachelor woman always to eat alone, and to have to take all her meals out was a dismal prospect.

> When you can only afford something under ninepence for a substantial meal, you cannot, in justice, take exception to quality or the company you have to dine with. When you compare the lot of a women, or of two women, sitting in a depressing little restaurant eating a cheap meal, eating in quite unlovely and often unpleasant surroundings, a meal that costs them at least a shilling, with the lot of a woman in her own home, you are naturally sorry for her who dines out.

The remedy was to fit up one's room with a bachelor's kitchen and to ask a friend home occasionally. (The friend, of course, was female.)

Two wooden 'kerosene cases' screwed together, given a coat of paint and fitted with a roller blind to the front made a simple cupboard. The two internal shelf spaces were lined with newspaper; the top was covered with linoleum to make a workbench and a few nails were driven into the outside to provide hangers for utensils. The essential utensils were a small kettle, two small saucepans, a frypan, mincer, grater, colander and two cheap casseroles which could double as table dishes. A canvas cooler or some makeshift equivalent would do for keeping perishable food. Cooking was done on a kerosene burner or in a small 'Davies oven' – a cheap metal box with internal shelf which could be placed over the burner. The entire kitchen outfit could be had for 'rather less than £2', soon recovered from money otherwise spent in restaurants.

The cookery regime was understandably simple and very economical, though Henrietta McGowan saw no reason why milk and cream should be regarded as luxuries. 'As a well-known woman doctor says, "Cream is much cheaper than cod-liver oil and quite as effective, and honey is quite as useful as malt extract."'

> The same pair of women in even the humblest room prettily if inexpensively furnished, at a neat table with a nicely shaded light are more likely to profit by a nourishing meal however simply it is served.

With these arrangements one need no longer feel sorry for the bachelor women of Australia.

CHAPTER 12

THE AWFUL TRUTH

Looking through the old books one finds a few dishes, whether born of fantasy or practicality, that seem simply awful. Such judgements must be made with care, for in matters of taste there are no absolutes and one may find plenty that are no better in modern books. Every one of these awful dishes met a need in some Federation kitchen and was thought pleasant or useful enough to be published for the benefit of others. We have already seen the results of cooks trying to incorporate in their repertoire foreign dishes that were not well known or understood, experimenting with unfamiliar ingredients or coming to terms with shortage of raw materials. It is worth looking at a few of the worst outcomes for what they show, not only of changing tastes in food but of the other imperatives that shaped what people wanted to eat, or were prepared to eat.

Here it is hard to avoid the curries.

Curry was a popular way of using up cold meat. It was often the last in the succession of made-dishes produced from the roast or boiled joint, so that what went into the curry may have been thought good for little else. There was always the suspicion that when it became necessary to disguise the tell-tale signs that meat was beginning to 'go off', the cook would turn to curry. But even when the meat was sweet the results were often wretched.

> ### CURRY OF COLD MEAT
> (*Schauer Cookery Book*)
>
> Take 1 oz. butter, 1 onion, fry them together; add an apple chopped, 1 tablespoon of curry powder, 1 dessertspoonful of plain flour; stir well and add slowly ½ a pint water or stock; boil 3 minutes; cool slightly; put in cold meat, cut small; add pepper and salt; heat meat through; serve on hot dish surrounded by wall of rice.

Chicken, fish, prawns, eggs and vegetables were treated no more sympathetically than the ageing roast. There seemed to be few items of food safe from curry: oysters, liver, pigeon, calf's head, tripe, asparagus, mushrooms and banana all received the treatment. It is hard to imagine how a sauce of onion, apple, common curry powder and stock was thought to benefit asparagus; it must stand among the worst treatments of the vegetable one is ever likely to encounter. The recipe was Hannah Maclurcan's and her *curried bananas* were just as bad: green bananas, desiccated coconut, milk, curry powder, Worcestershire sauce, anchovy sauce and cayenne, all thickened with an egg.

But consider her plan for the damnation of oysters:

CURRIED OYSTERS
(Mrs Maclurcan's Cookery Book)

2 or 3 doz. oysters; 1 large onion; 9 cloves; 1 piece ginger; 1 apple; Tablespoonful chutney and curry powder; Tablespoonful cocoanut; Lemon; Butter.

MODE.– Slice the onion very thin, put into the saucepan with the butter; when cooked add the ginger, cloves, apple and small piece of rind of lemon all chopped very fine; when these are cooked add the curry powder; now add the liquor off the oysters; if that is not enough add a little milk and the cocoanut; just before serving put in the oysters. Some people like a little garlic, which is an improvement, a very small piece about the size of a pea chopped up is sufficient.

Apple, it seems, was very nearly mandatory; spices – apart from commercially prepared curry powder – were optional. Coconut milk was not understood; many recipes substituted cow's milk and suggested that grated or desiccated coconut could be added. Her recipe for *beef curry (plain)* noted that either fresh or cooked beef would do and for liquid suggested either milk or 'strong beef gravy'.

Boiled rice was always served with a curry dish. In a few unhappy cases it was simply added to the curry itself, so that the lot could be dished up together. Perhaps this convenience combined with a need for strict economy to inspire Harriet Wicken's recipe for the simplest curry of all: boiled rice mixed with a sauce of gravy, butter and curry powder.

The Art of Living gave a dish of tomatoes which were stewed in a sauce of minced onion, apple, curry powder and milk. The *curried vegetables* were no better: a selection of boiled vegetables in a very basic white sauce spiked with curry powder. In Harriet Wicken's own book the sauce was a mixture of milk and gravy with the addition of a little minced onion and a flavouring of lemon juice. Her recipe for *a good curry* called for chops fried, then stewed in a sauce of gravy and milk with onion, apple, curry powder, desiccated coconut, sugar, lemon and flour. The dish included sliced tomatoes and potato.

Other horrors

In *The Art of Living* a dish of *cream toast* was made by pouring a very plain white sauce over toasted slices of bread. 'If a richer dish is desired, a little butter may be put on the toast'; in Mrs Wicken's own book, she suggested that 'a gill of cream is a great improvement'. The *suet pudding* was a simple stodge of flour, mashed potatoes, suet and water, boiled in a cloth. Its only virtue was versatility: it was 'delicious with roast meat, or it may be served as a sweet; jam sauce is nice poured around it.' Arguably the worst dish on offer in this book was its version of *hasty pudding*.

HASTY PUDDING
(*The Art of Living*)

1 pint Milk; 1 oz. Butter; 3 oz. Flour; 2 oz. Sugar.

Total cost – 4d. Time – 5 minutes.

Put the milk on the fire to boil, and when boiling stir in the flour quickly; it should be rather lumpy. Pour it into a dish, melt the butter and sugar, and pour it in the middle of the pudding. A little flavouring of grated lemon peel may be put into the milk, or jam served with the pudding.

Harriet Wicken's recipe for horseradish sauce was a mixture of horseradish, cream, flour and vinegar. It was not cooked, so the flour remained raw. The egg plant, one was told, 'may be cooked and served the same as choko, but does not require quite so long to cook.' I suppose that meant boiled.

Warm water paste was an oddity: a soft short pastry made with butter or dripping, baking powder and warm water instead of the usual cold. It was rolled out, cut in squares and baked in a hot oven. The result must have been somewhere between a very heavy scone and a rather biscuity pastry. There was no immediate suggestion of what to do with it and one cannot imagine many people undertaking to eat it without further inducement. However, another recipe offered a slight clue to its purpose: *apples, stewed - no. 2* were to be sent to table with 'plain pastry, baked in squares, or short cakes'. Would stewed apples be sufficient inducement?

Miss Cook's steamed mutton and rice has been given as an example of the better side of Federation cooking. The Presbyterians gave a less attractive recipe for mutton and rice, and Jean Rutledge liked it enough to copy it into her own book or, perhaps, both copied the recipe from a third source.

MUTTON AND RICE

Put a shoulder of mutton in a stewpan with two cups of cold water, with some sliced onion and a few pieces of lemon rind, pepper, salt, and grated nutmeg. Let it stew slowly 1 hour, then add ½ cup of rice, and a cup of milk (or more); just before serving add some chopped parsley. Time, 2 hours.

The Presbyterian *gooseberry fool* was an unhappy example of 'making do': a purée of stewed gooseberries mixed with some milk in which a little condensed milk had been dissolved. The recipe explained: 'condensed milk added to milk makes it more like cream, but a proportionately less quantity of sugar must be used. Of course cream is far superior.'[1] The same book gave a sauce that may very well have deserved Harriet Wicken's *suet pudding*:

SAUCE (2)
(for steamed puddings.)

One tablespoon arrowroot, ¼ pint water, a dessertspoonful sugar, and colour with red currant jelly or cochineal.

An even poorer version of it was taught in schools as *pink sauce*.[2] For a cold sweet, the following may be as unpleasant as any:

SAGO JELLY

One cup sago, 2 cups water, boiled with a lump of citric or tartaric acid till a jelly, sweeten to taste with sugar (about 1½ tablespoonfuls), boil all together. Place in a mould till cold. Serve with whipped cream or jam.

Horrors from the *Goulburn Cookery Book* included ox palate diced, simmered in water or water and milk for eight hours, served with onion sauce or crumbed and fried. A fitting vegetable dish for it might be the celery simmered in water for two or three hours. Mrs Rutledge offered a dessert of *peaches au gratin*: tinned fruit baked with bread crumbs, a sauce of the peach syrup and a topping of more bread crumbs and butter. *Sago sauce* was made by simmering sago in water with lemon peel, then removing the lemon peel and adding lemon juice, sugar and wine (of unspecified type, presumably cooking sherry). She said this was 'a nice sauce with sago plum pudding'.

Zara Aronson claimed that her *entrée made of cold chicken* was 'a most delicious dish'. It was essentially a purée of cold cooked chicken and 'thin bread sauce' set with gelatine, shaped, crumbed and *fried*. The physics of frying jelly are not generally favourable.

Hannah Maclurcan's gave *mock whitebait*, a way of spoiling good fish without providing any reasonable substitute for whitebait, but it was surpassed in awfulness by her *whitebait à la française*, using real whitebait cooked in white sauce and served on toast.

Her recipe for *cheese soufflé* was an example of a short-cut not worth taking. It did not begin with a white sauce, as did the classic French soufflé; instead, the egg yolks, flour and cheese (no butter) were worked to a paste then mixed with the egg whites and milk. The amount of stirring needed must have been about the same; the only real differences were the absence of heat, butter and, I would guess, success. One of her worst desserts was *iced sago pudding*: sago boiled in milk, mixed with beaten eggs and sugar, frozen in moulds. But I award the wooden spoon for the following, from the chapter on pastry, pies and puddings:

VERMICELLI PORRIDGE
(*Mrs Maclurcan's Cookery Book*)

Bring the milk to the boil, shake in the vermicelli, stirring until all is mixed; give it half an hour's cooking with frequent stirring; add a pinch of salt; turn on to small hot plates; sift sugar over and eat with hot or cold milk. If an egg be added, a still greater delicacy is obtained.

An interesting recipe of Isabel Ross was *horly of oysters*. Good oysters were blanched, slit, stuffed with a mixture of glaze, parsley, onion and cayenne pepper, then skewered, crumbed and fried. To those who consider the highest state of the oyster to be freshly opened, unwashed and uncooked, this is surely an abomination.

Amy Schauer also did unpleasant things with oysters. She devilled them, curried them, crumbed and fried them, battered and fried them, stuffed them with macaroni into tomatoes, and even served them in tomato sauce. She made cutlets of minced oysters and cooked veal, stretched with bread crumbs and bound with egg. She was equally brutal with caviar, giving it the devil treatment by heating it with meat extract, pepper, lemon juice and curry powder or simply serving it hot on fried bread (and it was Russian caviar, not lumpfish roe).

In a more economical vein, her little *sausage loaves* were small shapes of sausage mince and mashed potato sprinkled profusely with vermicelli and deep fried. And she gave the most unappealing of recipes I have seen for *savoury mince*: 'put ½ a lb of minced steak in a saucepan; cook about 10 minutes; add 1 tablespoon of flour; boil up again; add salt, pepper, squeeze of lemon juice.' Her *lemon filling* was painfully plain – lemon juice, sugar and water, thickened with cornflour – yet in my copy it was marked as a favourite.

LOUISA PUDDING
(*Schauer Cookery Book*)

Spread fresh bread with red jam; fold into sandwich. Cut into dice; place in a glass dish, pour ½ pint boiling milk over it. Make a good boiled custard; sweeten and pour over; flavour with vanilla. Garnish with white of egg stiffly beaten, sweetened, flavoured with vanilla and a small part coloured pale pink. Stick with almonds cut in halves.

Good reasons for not getting sick

At first glance it may seem that discussion of home medicine and nursing should have been included in the previous chapter as one of the great practicalities of Federation household management. However, there are good reasons for putting it here.

Through much of the nineteenth century Australia was not a healthy place to live. Sanitation was generally very poor and infectious diseases such as typhoid, diphtheria, tuberculosis and gastro-enteritis spread rapidly. Drainage and waste management and the purity of water and milk supplies were particular problems. The growth of towns made the establishment of hospitals possible, but they were often located on the outskirts for fear of epidemic, and staffed by what were regarded as the dregs of the health professions. Childbirth was a risky business, especially in the country, where attendance of a midwife or doctor was not always possible. Child mortality rates were alarmingly high.

Doctors and quacks

The medical profession was held in low regard and to many people the quacks and charlatans were no worse. Writing in 1891, Edward Kinglake observed:

> Though it is open to unqualified persons to practice medicine to their own sweet will, there are sharp distinctions between them and those who are duly qualified. The funny thing about it all is that with the sole exception of prestige and social position (for which they care nothing) all the advantages are on the side of the quacks.
>
> A diplomaed individual who registers his name on the list of the qualified, has the courtesy of the medical fraternity at once extended to him, and henceforth must follow the rules of their etiquette. The only other advantage (?) he reaps is his liability to be cast in damages at law if a jury should decide that he has not used sufficient skill or care in the treatment of any case.
>
> It is no use suing a quack. The answer is, why did you employ him? You know he is unqualified.[3]

Kinglake noted that one curious result of the state of the law in New South Wales was that any person could give a death certificate. The certificate had only to state whether the person signing was qualified or not. He observed that the given causes of death were often curious:

> "Fits" is very commonly set down as the cause of death. "Worms in the Bowels," "Want of Breath," "Weakness," "Debility," there are a few more; as for the "Fevers," "Inflammations," "Colds," &c., without any more specific indications, their name is legion. One infant was certified of coming to an untimely end through the instrumentality of a cat. "Breath drawn by a cat" was the entry on the certificate, I believe. I should like to know the end of that particular puss. I suspect it was a tragic one, and that he was the innocent victim of a silly superstition.[4]

Kinglake found Australia so well supplied with doctors, most of whom seemed to do very well, that 'one would not pronounce Australia a particularly healthy place.'

On the other hand, Australian folk lore contains plenty of evidence of scarcity of medical services, especially in the bush, and of appalling suffering that sometimes resulted from lack of timely or competent treatment. Even among qualified doctors, the state of knowledge and practice of many was such that people were often prepared to take their chances with 'bush cures', home remedies and patent medicines.

Home remedies

There were plenty of home remedies in circulation. Understandably, the country books were generally first to give them. Mina Rawson's *Enquiry Book* gave detailed directions for hygiene in the sick-room and for dealing with common ailments, followed by a wide range of 'simple remedies' for such things as flesh wounds ('every woman who expects to live in the bush or at a distance from a town and doctor, should learn how to put a stitch into a wound'), treating ingrowing toenails, ring worm, bunions, lice and throat infections.

Jean Rutledge gave a few home remedies to cover the essentials: her *cure for diarrhœa* was a mixture of laudanum, peppermint oil and brandy (whatever effect the cure may have had on the bowels, it would have at least made the patient a whole lot happier).[5] She also recommended *senna and prune medicine* for the alternative affliction; common vinegar for hiccoughs – 'this simple remedy has never been known to fail'; and a *cure for drunkenness* (a 'highly recommended' compound of iron sulphate, magnesia, peppermint water and spirits of nutmeg that would probably be more effective as a deterrent than as a cure).

In the city, the Presbyterian women took several decades to get together an organised body of home remedies. The 'useful hints' chapter at the end of their first edition suggested that mosquito bites could be prevented by spraying with 'tincture of insect powder' and that bites and stings could be relieved with liquid ammonia, a mixture of 'toilet vinegar' and glycerine, or with 'the laundress's blue bag, damp.' For bleeding at the nose one should 'move the jaws vigorously as if in the act of mastication. In the case of a child give a wad of paper and make the patient chew it hard'.

Sickroom cookery

In times of illness people relied less on medicine and more on nature. Diet was thought to be a very important part of caring for the sick, especially at home. It therefore fell to the lot of most women, at one time or another, to nurse the sick and prepare food for them and most cookery books provided a selection of recipes suitable for people who were suffering illness, recovering from it, or enduring chronic poor health. Although Isabel Ross published an edition of her cookery book especially for nurses, I have here drawn mainly from the *Goulburn Cookery Book*, since it seems more representative of invalid cookery in ordinary households.

Invalid or sickroom cookery, as it was often called, was not based on any general notion that illnesses could be *cured* by diet. The object was to provide the most nourishing food that the patient could – or would – take. At the extreme, this meant easily administered preparations so plain that almost any digestive system could cope with them. They could have provided little nourishment and a person of healthy appetite would undoubtedly have found them revolting. However, they were valued in cases where any food intake at all was considered an important step towards recovery. Most of them resulted from long experience and a genuine desire to do the best for the patient.

> ### BEEF-TEA
>
> Take a juicy slice of the top side of the round. Cut it finely on a board, removing skin and fat. Put it into a stone jar with its own weight of water; put the lid on the jar, and tie paper over it. Let it soak for an hour. Place it on the hob for 3 hours, and then for ½ an hour in the oven, or standing in a saucepan of boiling water. When cold, skim, and heat up as required. Good beef-tea should never be boiled. It ought not to jelly.[6]

Beef tea was one of the great stand-bys of the sickroom and considered to be full of 'goodness'; it was often ordered in cases of severe fever.

Peptonising was advocated by several cookery writers. Amie Monro explained it thus:

Pre-digested or Peptonised Foods

In severe illnesses the patient is often not able to digest food of any kind without some assistance. This is owing to lack of the digestive juices; the gastric or pancreatic juices are deficient, and this is sometimes a serious condition. But certain foods can be digested outside the body, and the patient may be tided over a critical period. Thus it is easy to make milk, beef tea, gruel, etc., perfectly digestible. Any chemist will supply the materials, of which there are several kinds.

The food may either be **peptonised** by the aid of peptonising powder or **pancreatised** by the assistance of liquor pancreaticus.

"Pancreatic extract" is another name for a similar article.

The more generally used medium is peptonising powder. This is sold in small glass tubes, with complete instructions for use, so that the most inexperienced can prepare the foods.

Bread jelly (water and bread boiled, then strained) was thought to be useful for babies who were unable to digest milk. There were various preparations of arrowroot or cornflour. The plainest was simply water thickened with arrowroot and flavoured with lemon; if the patient could take it, the lemon was replaced with wine. Others were made with milk or water and a little blackcurrant jam. More substantial nourishment – still assuming the patient was unable to fight back – could be provided by a thin gruel of oatmeal or by diced bread in hot milk.

> ### BARLEY WATER
> (*Goulburn Cookery Book*)
>
> One ounce of pearl barley, 1 cup of cold water, 1 quart of boiling water, a small piece of very thinly peeled lemon rind.
>
> Wash the barley, and put in a saucepan with the cup of cold water. Put on the lid, and let the barley boil for 10 minutes. Pour the water off, and add the lemon rind and a quart of water. Boil gently till it is reduced to half the quantity, and then remove the lemon peel. Carefully pour the water off the barley, sweeten to taste, and serve a small quantity at a time. The juice of the lemon is a great improvement to this.

Fluid intake was supplied by such preparations as *barley water, rice water, hot milk and soda water*, and *toast water* (as its name suggests, a strained infusion of toast and water). Lemonade – a weak mixture of lemon juice and water or soda water – was often given. Among the drinks most likely to provoke a swift recovery were *albumenised milk* (milk and egg white, sweetened and flavoured 'to taste') and *milk and suet* (mutton suet and milk boiled, with sugar and cinnamon), both given by Isabel Ross. Or this:

> ### BAKED MILK
> (*Presbyterian Cookery Book*)
>
> This is very nourishing for invalids. Put some milk into a stone jar. Tie it down with paper, and put in a moderate oven for 8 or 10 hours till it has become the consistency of cream.

A good patient might have been rewarded with a hot *egg flip*, a warm drink of 'good Australian wine', water, egg yolk and sugar.[7]

A large part of invalid cookery was concerned with providing simple, nourishing food that made no unreasonable demands on the digestive system – in other words, plain cookery at its best. Amie Monro explained that 'pork, and often veal, the richer kinds of fish, and all kinds of pastry, must be quite put aside. Dry frying is out of the question, and, generally speaking, baking also.' Stomach irritants such as pepper or some spices were avoided, so were excessive fats.

The range of dishes had to be wide enough to cater for fussy eaters and those used to better things than plain cookery, to stimulate jaded appetites and to provide variety for long-term patients. Many recipes were therefore simplified versions of common dishes. For example, Jean Rutledge gave invalid recipes for barley cream soup, chicken broth, mutton broth, fish cakes, fish soufflé and oysters scalloped, fricasséed or baked. (Yes, sick persons could sometimes be tempted to take an oyster, although Isabel Ross warned that 'if subjected to prolonged heat [they] are unfit for invalids' – or, one might add, for anyone else.) There was also steamed whiting, boiled or grilled chicken and grilled or stewed chop. Fish and white meats were generally considered to be more suitable because of their easy digestibility.

Sweets included steamed batter pudding, an invalid version of *canary pudding*, bread and butter pudding, vanilla soufflé, stewed apple, *blancmange* and a tapioca custard pudding. Some of the plainer dishes of the standard repertoire were also regarded as suitable for invalids and often so labelled in the books.

Persuading the patient to eat – despite the fare sometimes on offer – was an important step towards recovery. Mrs Wicken's advice was:

> Remember to have everything very hot and well served...Punctuality is a very important virtue in the sick-room. Always have the meals ready exactly at the time they are expected. Nothing is more trying to an invalid than waiting, and the appetite often vanishes before the food arrives. As a rule, never ask the patient what he would like; so few can bear this. Rather bring a tempting, tasty little meal as a surprise. It will often be eaten and enjoyed, when, if talked about beforehand, it would be refused.

Invalid cookery could be either comforting or repulsive and it was important that the plainness of the dish be matched to the state of mind of the patient as well as to dietary needs. A well flavoured chicken broth, a scallop of oysters, a pigeon stew and a nice bread and butter custard might be a fair reward for unwanted illness. However, too many meals of brains or tripe, too much sago and too much *milk and suet* would soon provoke rebellion in the sickroom – but if these responses hastened departure from it and reduced the likelihood of return, who should question the wisdom of the Federation housekeeper?

CHAPTER 13

Breakfast or Lunch?

Were rissoles served at breakfast, luncheon or dinner? The search for Federation cookery does not stop with discovery of recipes; how the dishes were used is equally important. Important, that is, to families who cared about 'doing things properly'. The culture of the table included a vast body of customs and understandings about the kinds of food that were normal or proper for each occasion. Unfortunately, they were never written down systematically.

For one answer to the rissole problem we could turn to that great authority on Victorian eating, Mrs Beeton (or, rather, to the 1892 book published in her name). Rissoles of cold fish and potatoes were suggested, among other things, for Tuesday family breakfasts in summer; 'of any cold meat' for Saturdays; and of cold fish or tinned salmon for Wednesdays. Economical breakfasts on Wednesdays (summer or winter) could include rissoles made from tinned meats or 'any scraps left'. Rissoles were for breakfast.

A family luncheon in summer might include chicken rissoles on Tuesdays, 'patties made from any scraps of cold meat' on Wednesdays and rissoles from cold fish and potatoes on Fridays. In winter there might be rissoles of cold meat or poultry (both with mashed potatoes) on Wednesdays. Small and inexpensive luncheons could include rissoles of cold meat on Mondays. Clearly, they were equally suitable for breakfast or luncheon.

Family dinners in summer could also include them, made of cold meat, at least every second Tuesday. In winter, fish rissoles might be served at suppers for guests. Family suppers might include the cold meat kind every second Monday. Rissoles were for breakfast, luncheon, dinner or supper. They were certainly versatile little bundles, perhaps an extreme case of versatility, but they illustrate nicely that the formal rules about what made up a family meal in Federation times were not as rigid as may be supposed.

A dainty dish of oyster patties in little puff pastry cases might have appeared before dinner as *hors dœuvre*, after dinner as a savoury, at a reception, or even as a luncheon entrée. According to Mrs Beeton, fried soles might be found at breakfast, luncheon, or dinner; so might haddock. A hash or salmi of game or poultry would not be out of place at any meal except tea.

Our reluctance to confine dishes to exclusive uses allows us to innovate and to compromise. It fuels the best of cooking and the worst of cooking. It stimulates creativity and frustrates tidiness. Food is taken when we need it, when we want it, when it is convenient or when habit conditions us to expect it. The formal pattern of meals – breakfast, morning tea, luncheon, afternoon tea, dinner and supper – were probably no more rigidly observed in Federation times than they are now. In many working class families dinner replaced luncheon; tea or supper replaced dinner; high tea was the evening meal on Sundays. Some meals had distinctive dishes (porridge and tea cakes for example); some dishes, like a roast joint, defined the meal. Many dishes, like the humble rissole, had no fixed place, they simply went where they were wanted.

Mrs Beeton's scheme

In her 1892 book Mrs Beeton set out quite detailed menus for breakfast, luncheon, dinner, tea and supper, catering for formal parties of ten or twelve, for everyday family use and for economical family use. There was also a picnic, 'a troublesome luncheon to provide'. The Beeton scheme can fairly be taken as a model of the approved way of doing things in Australia, with allowances for the rather heavier meat consumption here.

The suggestions for breakfast began with a complaint. 'Amongst English people as a rule, breakfast, as a meal, does not hold a sufficiently important place; and with some it means, in reality, no meal at all, unless we reckon the proverbial "cup of tea" to form one.' The book argued for more variety ('it is no unusual thing to hear of people having eggs and bacon *every* morning') and for more attention to be given to the setting and decoration of breakfast tables. Suggestions were given for 'family' and 'economical' breakfasts for each day of the week, summer and winter separately. By way of example, Wednesday family breakfasts were:

> [In summer] Tea, milk, bread, toast, butter, hot buttered scones, beef croquettes, ham and egg toast, and fresh fruit.

[In winter] Cocoa, tea, hot and cold milk, bread, muffins, butter, rissoles made from any cold fish or from tinned salmon, grilled bacon, boiled eggs.

Economical breakfasts for Wednesdays were:

[In summer] Coffee, hot milk, porridge, buttered toast, rissoles made from cold meat (any scraps left), any fresh fruit.

[In winter] Cocoa, hot milk, bread, butter, rissoles made from tinned meats or any scraps.

On luncheon, Beeton said:

> Under the above name come a very great variety of meals; for we have no other name for the one that comes between breakfast and dinner. It may be a crust of bread and butter or cheese, or an elaborate meal of four or five courses; it is still "luncheon." Also it may take place at any time. The lower classes lunch between 10 and 11; the upper, some three or four hours later; but in one thing both rich and poor alike agree, that it should be of all meals the most informal.

The suggestions for Wednesday luncheons were:

[In summer] Cold lamb (or any other cold joint), mint sauce, patties made from any scraps of cold meat, salad. – Cake, preserves. – Bread, butter, cheese, biscuits.

[In winter] Macaroni soup, rissoles of cold meat, or poultry, and potatoes. – Mince pies, jelly. – Bread, butter, cheese, biscuits.

A 'small and economical' luncheon on Wednesday (regardless of season) could be 'any kind of inexpensive soup' followed by plain cake, then bread, butter and cheese.

Beeton did not give much advice on the timing and nature of dinner ('our chief meal'), noting that 'more than they do at present, these two things should depend less upon our means and appetites than our work and the lives we lead. Were this the case fewer of us would have to suffer from what may almost be called a national complaint, that of indigestion.' This concern seems to have been directed towards the many people who were '*obliged* to take their principal meal of the day in the very midst of their work, when they have not sufficient time to digest it properly before the business of the day be resumed.' Much more attention was given to laying the table, table decorations and various ways of folding serviettes for 'dinner parties in ordinary middle-class households'. Two menus for family dinners were given for each day of the week for each season. Here are the first Wednesday suggestions for each season:

> [Spring] Roast chickens, ham, steak pie, potatoes, greens. – Sweet omelette.
>
> [Summer] Spring soup. – Hashed lamb, veal cutlets, peas, potatoes. – Cheese salad.
>
> [Autumn] Fish pie. – Boiled beef, carrots, turnips, potatoes, small suet dumplings. – Cheese and tomatoes.
>
> [Winter] Soup made from liquor from beef bones and turkey – Croquettes of turkey, cold beef, salad, fried potatoes – Plain plum pudding.

By the late Victorian era tea was more ceremony than meal:

> Except in the nursery or in large homely families, the old-fashioned "tea" has ceased to exist. We are not now bidden to partake of tea-cakes, hot buttered toast, new laid eggs, and such delicacies at 5 o'clock in the afternoon; we can only then expect the ordinary "at home" tea in tiny cups with its accompanying thin bread and butter; and this in many houses which cannot lay claim to be fashionable ones.
>
> It is so easy now to have a "reception" one day in the week at the trifling cost of a little tea and bread and butter, that those who are not rich enough to give good dinners or suppers to their friends, gladly take to this mild form of entertainment.

We should not be misled by these comments into thinking that 'thin bread and butter' was the only nourishment served for 'at home' teas. The suggested menu for such an occasion in the summer months was:

> Cucumber, Foie Gras and Cress, and Anchovy and Salad Sandwiches. Bread and Butter, White and Brown.
> Rout cakes, Madeira cake, Pound cake, Petits fours.

> Ices, Raspberry and Cherry.
> Strawberries and cream.
> Tea, Coffee.
> Claret and Champagne Cup.

High tea was a more homely affair. The following summer menu was offered as a guide:

> Mayonnaise of salmon.
> Cold dishes: Tongue, Veal and Ham Pie.
> Cucumber. Salad.
> Compôte of Fruit [sic], Jelly. Cream.
> Fresh fruit.
> Tea. Coffee. Wine.

Like 'at home' tea, supper was a meal of uncertain status. Beeton argued that it was an acceptable alternative to dinner for those with few servants who wished to entertain their friends without the formality and expense of a fashionable dinner, and could even replace that meal. 'Dinner in fashionable circles is at eight; why should not some of us who do not belong to them enjoy an equivalent meal at the same hour with impunity?' This plea was presumably made as much on behalf of the guest who might receive few, if any, invitations to 'fashionable' dinners as to the host who could not afford to give them.

In relation to food, the chief consideration was to avoid heaviness. A model menu for a summer supper with guests was:

> Lobsters.
> Mayonnaise of chicken.
> Cold Lamb.
> Salad, Cucumber.
> Mint sauce.
> Raspberry cream.
> Fruit tart.
> Custard.
> Fruit. Cake.
> Claret. Sherry.

A family supper might include 'Fish pie made from cold fish, any cold meat, salad, cake, cheese, &c. – Wine or beer' or 'Pie made from cold beef with dripping crust, baked potatoes, cheese, bread, butter, biscuits. – Wine or beer.'

The working classes

By providing so many model menus Mrs Beeton and those who revised her work clearly implied that in many households the finer points of kitchen and table were being overlooked (through ignorance) or ignored (through carelessness). The same conclusion can be drawn from most other cookery books of the time.

Mrs Beeton had addressed herself to middle class families. She emphasised the virtue of economy and gave plenty of advice on how to achieve it, but it was the economy of comfort, not of poverty.

The poor people of Victorian England – of whom there were, as we know, many – were also not left without advice. Many cheap cookery and household books were produced towards the end of the century by well meaning, well off writers anxious to reform the health, hygiene and morals of the working classes. From their advice we can glean a little about the eating habits of the masses. *The People's Housekeeper* of 1876 was such a book.

It acknowledged that many artisans began work well before other members of their households roused themselves for breakfast, and proposed (in some detail) a scheme by which the worker could make a cup of coffee with the aid of a small spirit lamp. Everything would be set up the night before. The worker needed no culinary skill and would have the coffee ready in minutes. It would be taken with a slice of bread and butter and was recommended as a more appropriate stimulus than a swig of spirits.

Those who did not have to rise so early should take a proper breakfast of meat, bacon or eggs and some bread and butter. Oatmeal porridge was also recommended. The working classes were accustomed to taking their main meal, dinner, in the middle of the day, followed in the late afternoon by tea, the meal which 16 years later Beeton said had 'ceased to exist.' If tea were taken about four o'clock, as recommended, something more would be needed before bed-time. Supper was the most pleasant meal of the day, for the children were in bed and the worker had the whole night to enjoy before the next day's labour. It was to be a light meal, since 'a mass of undigested food in the stomach produces dreams and broken rest'; say, a cup of cocoa with a little bread and butter, a small quantity of broth, some bread and cheese, a morsel of cold fish or an egg boiled or poached.

The Australian breakfast

Jean Rutledge included the following in 'a list of dishes suitable for breakfast, in addition to those in the Breakfast Section': *collops, croquettes, cutlets, baked curry, rice cutlets, grilled steak, mutton scallops, mutton steak, potato sausages, rissoles, scotch eggs, timbarlow, fish – fried, curried* and *grilled* presented as *balls,* cakes, cutlets, hash, kromeskies, patties, rolls, kedgeree, oyster croquettes, salmon balls, or salmon en papelote. The 'breakfast section' was actually headed 'breakfast and luncheon dishes', with no distinction made between the two, but concentrated on things like *bacon and eggs, bubble and squeak, devilled bones,* and *tomatoes on toast.* Apart from a few outside possibilities such as omelettes, *meat pancakes* and *scallops of forcemeat and oysters,* it is hard to see a smart luncheon emerging from the list. In the country it seems that luncheons were generally homely affairs.

Hannah Maclurcan's list of breakfast dishes included: *porridge or boiled rice, scrambled eggs, devilled bones, eggs and bacon, poached eggs and anchovy toast, minced beef with a little ham and poached eggs, fried fish, omelette, grilled chop or steak, cold steak pie, chicken croquettes, mutton cutlets,* kidneys minced on toast, grilled or devilled, *liver and bacon, hashed mutton, grilled ham, grilled bacon, baked eggs, grilled fish, grilled haddock, salmon rissoles, buttered eggs* and *devilled sardines.* This list was followed by recipes for porridge, boiled rice and *potato nest* ('a nice breakfast dish'). Egg recipes were given in another chapter.

Mrs Rawson on lunch and after

Mina Rawson offered no menus, but gave some general advice on luncheons and afternoon teas. For her the art of giving luncheons lay in being able to turn on a 'dainty' meal for a modest outlay and on decorating the table prettily (without, of course, over-dressing it, which would be 'a fault in the other extreme'). If wine were not served, there should be decanters of lemon and raspberry syrup. In her account the first course often consisted of sliced cucumbers followed by oysters. Then came game, an entrée and a good salad. 'For dessert there is great scope for the cook, as all sorts of cold puddings are allowable – blanc-manges, gelatine puddings, jellies, custards and creams.' Finally, coffee was served in tiny cups with cheese and fruit.

For a 'fashionable afternoon tea', according to Mrs Rawson, *Russian tea* was generally preferred. This was Ceylon tea poured over sugar, lemon and a little rum. (The rum could be omitted if not liked, but she thought it greatly improved the flavour.) She suggested serving rolled bread and butter and sandwiches of ham paste, potted ham, tongue, chicken or anchovy. Salads were 'allowable nowadays at afternoon teas'; egg, oyster or chicken were recommended, and should be served with brown bread and biscuits. Small cakes were served, along with candied fruits and other unspecified 'delicate tit-bits'. Wine, cordial and claret cup or champagne cup were also to be available.

Whatever the delights of tea, it is the next meal that offered the greatest interest. We turn to aristology.

CHAPTER 14

DINNER FEDERATION-STYLE

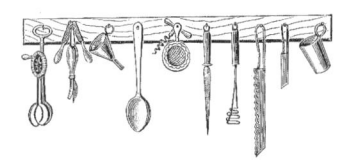

Our exploration of dining in Australia starts with Edward Abbott. He claimed this honour by going first to print on the topic and by his choice of pen name, an Australian aristologist. Although he wrote in the early Victorian period, more than 30 years before Federation, his comments about meals and menus, stoutly defensive of English tradition, set out for us a picture of where the early Australian *upper crust* was coming from.

For him only two meals were worth considering – breakfast (the meal of *friendship*) and dinner (the meal of *etiquette*).

In Victorian times an important transition was taking place in the manner of serving formal dinners. The old style, *service à la française*, was adapted from the French manner of serving grand dinners. Put simply,[1] a dinner was divided into several courses, or *services*, each of which consisted of a number of dishes all placed on the table at once in a formal pattern. The table was cleared between each service. Dishes placed at the ends of the table might be removed during the service and replaced by others of a different type. For example, if the first course were soup and fish, as was customary, the soup tureens might be taken away mid-course and replaced by substantial fish dishes, adding to the smaller fish dishes already on the table. The new dishes were called *removes*, since the new dish removed the old (in the same sense that one sentry relieving another from duty was called the *relief*).

The second course was mainly or exclusively meat and could be divided into *removes* – roasts and other larger, plainer dishes – and *entrées* – smaller, fussier dishes such as fricassées and vol-au-vents. There were also *hors d'œuvres* (side-dishes). As the system evolved, the entrées moved to a separate course between the first and second; modern practice is to serve the hors d'œuvres as appetisers before the meal.

The third course was of game, removed by puddings, and other sweet dishes. The meal finished with desserts and ices, which often amounted to a separate *dessert* course made up of elegant displays of fresh, candied and preserved fruit as well as various iced confections. Isabella Beeton mentioned that 'Zests are sometimes served at the close of the dessert; such as anchovy toasts or biscuits.'[2] These 'zests' became the 'savouries' of Federation dining.

A word on 'desserts' and 'sweets' may be in order. In formal dining 'dessert' was the last course of the meal, the final flourish. 'Sweets' were a class of dishes, not a course at dinner. Not all dishes served at dessert were sweet, and not all sweet dishes in a meal were served at the dessert course. Nowadays the two terms have become almost synonymous in Australia, as savoury dishes have all but disappeared from the final course and sweet dishes are rarely served earlier.

An example of *service à la française* is a menu quoted by Abbott. The meal is not English, but French (hosted by a certain Count D'Orsay), but it is the one that Abbott chose to hold up as an example of good dining. He did not say if his own accustomed mode of dining was similar.

FIRST SERVICE.

SOUPS: Spring, Queen, turtle.
  Turbot (lobster and Dutch sauce),
  Salmon (Tartar fashion, that is, with a *sauce piquante*
     – acid sauce),
  Gurnet (Cardinal fashion),
  Cod fritters,
  Whitebait.
REMOVES: Fillet of beef (in the Neapolitan fashion),
  Turkey, flavoured with shallots,
  Macaroni, in a high silver dish,
  Haunch of venison.
ENTREES: Chicken rissoles,
  Oyster patties, lamb cutlets,
  A thick soup of mushrooms,
  Lamb cutlets dressed with asparagus tips,
  Veal fricandeau, with sorrel,
  Sweetbreads, pierced with thin strips of bacon fat, and
     tomato sauce,
  Pigeon cutlets (Dunell fashion),
  A mixture of vegetables and minced pheasants,
  Duckling fillets (Bigarrade fashion)
  Richelieu sausages,
  Pulled fowl, with truffles,
  Raised mutton pie.
SIDE DISHES: Round of beef, ham, salade.

SECOND COURSE.

ROASTS: Capon, quails, turkey poults, green goose.
SIDE DISHES: Asparagus, haricot beans in the French fashion,
   Lobster salad,
   Mixed jelly (omnium gatherum jelly)
   Plovers' eggs in jelly
   Russian Charlotte
   Maraschino jelly
   Marble cream
   Basket of pastry
   Rhubarb tart (light pastry)
   Apricot tart (close or solid pastry)
   Basket of meringues (called, vulgarly, sugar eggs)
   Dressed crab,
   Salad au jelatine (we fancy this must be a misprint for
      salade en jalantine. Galantine is a fashion of
      arranging salad or poultry with herbs and jelly),
   Mushrooms, with herbs.
REMOVES: Vanilla soufflé (*i.e.*, beaten up – whipped)
   Nesselrode pudding,
   Adelaide sandwiches,
   Fondu (melted cheese).
(*Pièces moditers* are the ornamental articles of confectionery.)[3]

Whether this menu was Abbott's perception of how the 'upper ten thousand' should dine or simply one that fed his private fantasy, it is difficult to reconcile with the ambition he set forth in his 'introductory preface':

> My book will combine the advantages of Mrs Acton's work with the *crême de la crême* of the cheapest of Soyer's productions... Mrs Acton's work is excellent of its kind. It is only faulty in being so elaborate, so that it is not within the compass of persons of moderate means; and that is one of the reasons that induced me to enter the culinary field on this occasion.[4]

Swinish rule

At the time of Abbott's writing *service à la russe* was quite new and was beginning to replace the old service in the more fashionable households.[5] It was less rich, less magnificent, but had the great advantage that the entire dinner could be planned and managed so that all the dishes which should be eaten hot were indeed hot. It largely did away with useless ornamentation and asserted the importance of the food above that of mere display. Every dish was a focus of attention, and was judged more on its culinary merits than on its contribution to an overall display. The food was carved in advance and arranged in a correct and attractive manner, whether diners helped themselves or were served. This drastic simplification of the table did not, by any means, require pomp and circumstance to be sacrificed. It did not take long for new rituals and expectations to replace the old ones; dining *à la russe* could be a very elegant experience.

Abbott was not quite ready for this new fashion:

> The strict etiquette of a Russian dinner is, that the guests are seated, and the master and mistress of the feast remain standing – it being their business to wait on the company, and to see that the servants do their duty. Nothing can escape their observation: your plate is never empty, and your glass always full; you are literally crammed, according to swinish rule. This mode requires first-rate servants, and plenty of them.

The reference to 'swinish rule' should be taken as referring not so much to the amount eaten by each guest as to the passive role of the diners. There is no reason to suppose that diners faced with the groaning tables of *service à la française* were any more restrained than those whose every whim, including a discrete signal that no more was required, would be gratified by a band of servants.

Abbott gave no menu for a dinner *à la russe*. Nor had he much to say about luncheons and suppers because he considered them 'unnecessary and unwholesome'.

The third main form of service, the *buffet*, originated in the lavish displays of choice dishes set out on multi-tiered tables in restaurants. This service was considered suitable only for suppers and large receptions, including ballroom suppers and wedding luncheons; it had no role at dinner. Guests would come to the table – which was often magnificently laid out – and be served by a butler. It was not the free-for-all event that the modern *buffet* or *smörgåsbord* has become.

Whatever mode of service was adopted, the number of dishes provided at even a small dinner party must have made dining lightly – without causing offence – quite out of the question. A good dinner – especially *à la française* – seems, against prevailing sensibilities of the times, to have been a very male affair. The gross displays of roast meat, preferably whole animals or large parts of them; tasty sauces and relishes; high game from the hunt; and the solid, filling pies and puddings were hardly compatible with the delicate sensibilities of Victorian ladies. A lady of refinement of the time might well prefer the delicate or sophisticated concoctions, the made-dishes that showed a degree of creativity as well as kitchen skill. She might prefer fricassées, rissoles and vol-au-vents in which the substance of the animal is there, but diced or minced, and modestly veiled in sauce or decently clothed in pastry. She might rather dine before a vase of flowers than a haunch of venison.

The withdrawal of the ladies to allow the men to indulge in a further round of drinking was the ultimate assertion of male domination of the occasion.

In the end, I think the women won the contest – but by a narrow margin, and not until art deco ushered in the era of daintiness.

GENERAL RULES ON TABLE ETIQUETTE

It is rude and awkward to elevate your elbows and move your arms at the table, so as to incommode those on either side of you.

Whenever one or both hands are unoccupied, they should be kept below the table, and not pushed upon the table and into prominence.

Never lay your hand, or play with your fingers, upon the table. Do not toy with your knife, fork or spoon, make crumbs of your bread, or draw imaginary lines upon the table cloth.

Never lean back in your chair, nor sit too near or too far from the table.

A knife should never, on any account, be put into the mouth. Many people, even well-bred in other respects, seem to regard this as an unnecessary regulation; but when we consider that it is a rule of etiquette, and that its violation causes surprise and disgust to many people, it is wisest to observe it.

Never, if possible, cough or sneeze at the table.

Never use a napkin in place of a handkerchief for wiping the forehead, face or nose.

Refrain from making a noise when eating, or supping from a spoon, and from smacking the lips or breathing heavily while masticating food, as they are the marks of ill-breeding. The lips should be kept closed in eating as much as possible.

Eat neither too fast or too slow.

Do not find fault with the food.

If by chance anything unpleasant is found in the food, such as a hair in the bread or a fly in the coffee, remove it without remark. Even though your appetite be spoiled, it is well not to prejudice others.

Be careful to remove the bones of fish before eating. If a bone inadvertently should get into the mouth, the lips must be covered with a napkin before removing it. Cherry stones and grape skins should be removed from the mouth as unobtrusively as possible, and deposited on the side of the plate.

Strive to keep the cloth as clean as possible, and use the edge of the plate or a side dish for potato skins and other refuse.

At home fold your napkin when you are done with it and place it in your ring. If you are visiting, leave your napkin unfolded beside your plate.

Do not leave the table before the rest of the family or guests, without asking the head, or host, to excuse you, except at a hotel or boarding-house.

REGARDING SERVICE

If a plate is handed to you at table, keep it yourself instead of passing it to a neighbour.

If the guests pass the dishes to one another, instead of being helped by a servant, you should always help yourself from the dish, if you desire it at all, before passing it on to the next.

The host or hostess should not insist upon guests partaking of particular dishes; nor ask persons more than once, nor put anything in their plates which they have declined. It is ill-bred to urge a person to eat of anything after he has declined.

The old-fashioned habit of abstaining from taking the last piece upon the plate is no longer observed. It is to be supposed that the vacancy can be supplied, if necessary.

Tea or coffee should never be poured into a saucer to cool, but sipped from the cup.

If a person wishes to be served with more tea or coffee, he should place his spoon in his saucer. If he has had sufficient, let it remain in the cup.

When the plate of each course is set before you, with the knife and fork upon it, remove the knife and fork at once. This matter should be carefully attended to, as the serving of an entire course is delayed by neglecting to remove them.

Greediness should not be indulged in. Indecision must be avoided. Do not take up one piece and lay it down in favour of another, or hesitate.

When a dish is offered you, accept or refuse at once, and allow the waiter to pass on. A gentleman will see that the lady whom he has escorted to the table is helped to all she wishes, but it is officiousness to offer to help other ladies who have escorts.

You are at liberty to refuse a dish that you do not wish to eat. If any course is set down before you that you do not wish, do not touch it. Never play with food, nor mince your bread, nor handle the glass and silver near you unnecessarily.

Never allow the servant, or the one who pours, to fill your glass with wine that you do not wish to drink. You can check him by touching the rim of your glass.

If you have occasion to speak to a servant, wait until you can catch his eye, and then ask in a low tone for what you want.

Never reprove the waiter for negligence or improper conduct; that is the business of the host.

REGARDING DINNER

Always make use of the butter-knife, sugar-spoon and salt-spoon, instead of using your knife, spoon or fingers.

Bread is broken at dinner. Vegetables are eaten with a fork.

Asparagus may be taken up with the fingers, if preferred. Olives and artichokes are so eaten.

Fruit is eaten with silver knives and forks. Never bite fruit. An apple, peach or pear should be peeled with a knife, and all fruit should be broken or cut.

Pastry should be eaten with a fork. Everything that can be cut without a knife should be eaten with the fork alone. Pudding may be eaten with a fork or spoon.[6]

Miss Schauer and the Parish Tea

The Schauer Cookery Book had little to say about menus or the rules of dining. However, the few comments – jumbled though they were – are interesting because they suggest that *service à la française* was being taught as late as 1909, at least in Queensland. Perhaps it was still considered proper among the more conservative diners even though practicality demanded drastic reduction from the scale of menu held up by Abbott.

> A menu consists of savoury soup, fish, entree, roasts, sweet pudding, cheese, and dessert.
> *Menu for six persons.* One soup, one fish, two entrees, one roast, two sweets, cheese and dessert.
> *For twelve persons.* One soup, two fish, two entrees, three roasts, four sweets, cheese, and dessert.

Later editions brought the Schauer book into step with fashion. In 1931 its advice on 'an informal dinner' was:

> Hors d'oeuvre.
> Soup or Fish. Have both if you are giving a big dinner; but one is enough for an informal function.
> Entrée. Little patties or a nice made-dish.
> Joint. A loin of mutton is a very nice thing to give.
> Two vegetables. Potatoes and peas, celery, asparagus, or whatever is in season at the time.
> Sweets. Give a choice, as some people like plainer things than others.
> Cheese and Biscuits.
> Dessert and Coffee.[7]

The institution of the semi-formal 'parish tea' as it was still being practiced in some places in the 1950s and '60s owed much to the French style of service. The idea was to place on the table at once many plates of various kinds of food so arranged that each (seated) guest would have ready access to a representative sample. The dishes could be put out in three courses – savouries and sandwiches; main dishes; cakes, pies and tarts – or all at once in a single course.

This modified *service à la française*, in which parishioners could participate by each 'bringing a plate' had many benefits. The meal could be provided at no cost to the parish (which need not prevent a small 'donation' being sought of participants). Because the 'plate' was of normal family proportions, each cook would operate within her area of competence, bringing one of the dishes she made best: there were few risks of wholesale culinary disaster, though one might learn to avoid certain dishes identified with cooks of indifferent talent. Variety was assured to everyone. Finally, there was always useful symbolism in the act of sharing a meal, as the priest or parson was not slow to point out.

Mrs Wicken's English-style menus

In 1888 Harriet Wicken gave 30 dinner menu suggestions: six for dinners of seven courses and a dozen each for dinners with guests and family dinners. Not surprisingly, their style was similar to many of those in Beeton. She was apparently well satisfied with them, for she kept them virtually unchanged in subsequent editions. One of her seven-course menus was:

> Prawn savoury. Oysters.
> Clear Soup. Tapioca Cream.
> Fried Whiting. Boiled Cod and Béchamel Sauce.
> Roast Turkey. Braised Fillet of Beef.
> Cutlets à la St James. Veal Cutlets.
> Lemon Jelly. Boiled Cabinet Pudding.
> Anchovy Toast. Parmesan d'artois.[8]
> Ices and Dessert.

As a general rule, she suggested that potatoes and two plain vegetables in season should be served with the roast. Dressed vegetables should be served as a separate course occasionally. There was no mention of the mode of service, but this menu must have been *à la russe*.

Her dinners with guests were much less pretentious. Here is the first of them; again the vegetables are to be assumed:

> Clear Soup.
> Fried Garfish and French Melted Butter.
> Quarter of Lamb.
> Boiled Chicken and Egg Sauce.
> Lemon Jelly. Queen of Puddings.
> Cheese Soufflé.

And for a family dinner:

> Fried Bream and Melted Butter.
> Roast leg of Mutton.
> Blanc Mange and Stewed Fruit.

The 12 family menus made little use of left-overs. The proper places for using up remains were breakfast and luncheon.

Mrs Maclurcan's menus

As befitted a hotel-keeper, Hannah Maclurcan took menus seriously. She gave six dinner menus for six or eight persons, six for 15 to 20 persons (including two 'special menus') and a dinner and three suppers for 50 to 100 persons. At a more homely level there were menus for 21 'economical dinners for every day in the week'. All menus were for *service à la russe*.

Hannah Maclurcan's suppers were as elaborate as her large dinner. Each required more than 30 dishes and followed much the same menu structure. The only important difference was that service at supper was likely to be less formal.

Her two 'special menus' would have tested the endurance of servants and guests alike. Here is the less pretentious of them, as she gave it:

>HORS D'ŒUVRES.
>Caviare.
>
>SOUP.
>Clear Soup.
>
>FISH.
>Fillets of Soles au Beurre.
>
>ENTRÉE.
>Larded Sweetbreads and Green Peas.
>
>SAVOURY.
>Anchovy Canapès.
>
>JOINTS.
>Roast Lamb and Mint Sauce.
>Fillet of Beef.
>
>POULTRY.
>Roast Chicken and Rolled Ham.
>
>SAVOURY.
>Prawns à la Française.
>
>SWEETS, ETC.
>Pears in Jelly Verney Pudding.[9]
>Iced Sago Pudding. Sweet Omelette.
>
>Cheese Straws.
>Olives. Almonds, etc.
>
>Coffee.

Both menus involved ten separate courses, in some of which guests were offered a choice; there was no expectation that each guest would taste each dish. As with Harriet Wicken's menus, it should be assumed that potatoes and plain vegetables were served with the joints.

The more ordinary menus for six or eight persons were scarcely less lavish, and represented very fine dining; for example

> Oysters.
> Turtle Soup.
> Baked Barramundi.
> Beef Olives.
> Chicken Cream.
> Roast Fillet of Beef Larded.
> Roast Turkey and Bread Sauce.
> Asparagus on Toast.
> Angels' Food. Cherries in Jelly.
> Fruit in Season.
> Olives and Devilled Almonds.

Mrs Maclurcan's family dinners were plain, but satisfying. A typical Wednesday example:

> Small Boiled Leg of Mutton and Caper Sauce.
> Boiled Potatoes. Carrots and Turnips.
> Devilled Sardines.
> Boiled Apple Pudding.

The following day's dinner would include mutton broth made with the liquor in which the mutton had been boiled, and cold leg of mutton with potato salad.

In the next week, Tuesday would feature boiled corned beef, and Wednesday would bring:

> Pea Soup, made from the liquor of the Beef.
> Cold Beef and Potato Salad.
> Blancmange and jam.

The beef not yet exhausted, there would be a dry hash made from the remains of it to begin dinner on Thursday.

Another way

Most of the Federation cookery books had nothing to say on menus. Nor should the schemes laid out by Harriet Wicken and Hannah Maclurcan be taken too seriously. Neither writer pretended to describe common practice; their menus were no more than recommendations or ideas. Their interest for us is that they give some understanding of what Australians were taught to regard as a 'smart' dinner or supper.

The scheme of courses at a formal dinner – hors d'œuvre, soup, fish, entrée, joint, poultry or game, sweet, savoury, dessert – was scaled down as necessary for lesser occasions. For example, a family dinner with guests might start with tomato, pea or potato soup. Then would come fish, fried fillets or boiled fish with a garnished white sauce or an entrée of olives or possibly rissoles or cutlets, nicely sauced and garnished. The joint would probably be a leg or shoulder of mutton served with gravy. Roast lamb with mint sauce or a piece of beef or veal braised would also be popular choices. There would be boiled or baked potatoes and boiled cabbage or beans or peas. If the occasion warranted it, there could be a vegetable made-dish of tomatoes stuffed with a mince mixture or cauliflower *au gratin*.

There would be two sweets – one hot, one cold. The hot one would be a boiled or steamed suet and treacle pudding or a steamed cabinet pudding; in either case with custard sauce. The cold pudding would be lemon sponge or blancmange, both suitable for those who prefer plainer sweets. The savoury would be anchovy toast or, just possibly, oysters rolled in bacon and grilled.

An intimate week-day family dinner would have an eye to economy. Generally there would have been no more than two or three courses: soup or fish; an entrée or joint or poultry (with vegetables); a sweet or dessert (perhaps cheese, fruit and a savoury). The soup could be lamb broth or mulligatawny with boiled rice. If there were a fish dish it could well be one of remains – say, fish pie. A joint would be corned or fresh beef boiled; with the remains visiting the table for the next two meals. But a made-dish (an entrée, in fact) would probably be more practical – rissoles or a hash or pie to use up some remaining beef, mutton or poultry. The sweet, if there were one, could be a rice pudding (this was a real favourite), an omelette soufflé with jam, an orange jelly pudding (much the same idea as *lemon sponge*) or a fruit salad. Or there could be dessert of cheese, biscuits and fruit instead.

The last word

According to Richard Twopenny, who was generally unimpressed with the standard of Australian food and cooking, reality was well short of any of any ideals. He said that even the upper classes contented themselves with very plain daily fare:

> The dinner consists of beef or mutton, roast or boiled, potatoes and greens, bread-and-butter pudding, and cheese. The details change, but the type is always the same – what his wife calls 'a good plain English dinner, none of your unwholesome French kickshaws,' which are reserved for company.

MULLIGATAWNY SOUP (No. 2)
(Goulburn Cookery Book)

Two quarts of stock, 1 apple, 1 onion, 1 carrot, ½ a turnip, 1 stalk of celery, 1 oz. flour, 1 oz. butter.

Slice up the apple, onion, and carrot, and fry them in the butter. Sprinkle over the curry powder and flour, and brown also; pour over the boiling stock, and stir till it boils up. Simmer gently for an hour and a half; rub through a sieve, return to the saucepan, bring to boiling point. Squeeze in the juice of ½ a lemon. Send to table with boiled rice. Chicken or veal stock is best for this soup, and small cubes of cooked chicken or veal may be served in it.

BAKED FISH
(Goulburn Cookery Book)

One fish, 1 oz. of butter, juice of half a lemon, ½ a teaspoon of chopped parsley, salt.

Put the fish on a baking-dish, squeeze a few drops of lemon juice over it, and sprinkle the salt and parsley; add the butter in little bits, cover with buttered paper, and bake from 20 to 30 minutes. Parsley sauce may be served with it, or it may be garnished with cut lemon and parsley and served with oiled butter. The fish may be filleted, and then cooked in this way. The fish may be stuffed with breadcrumbs, parsley, and a tiny bit of onion, if liked.

ROAST FOWL
(Schauer Cookery Book)

Truss fowl neatly, put into a baking tin with heated fat, and if a young bird roast ¾ of an hour, for an old bird allow about 1½ hours for roasting. Make gravy as for goose. Serve with bread sauce.

BREAD SAUCE

Two ounces breadcrumbs, small piece of onion, 1 oz. butter, ½ pint milk, and one blade of mace.

Boil the milk and steep the onions and mace in it, by the side of the fire for 15 minutes; strain, return milk to the saucepan, add crumbs and beat well with a fork, leave with the lid on for 5 minutes; add butter and serve; season with salt and pepper.

ROAST SADDLE OF MUTTON
(Isabel Ross)

Let the meat hang as long as weather permits in a cool larder. Trim it, take off the thin, transparent skin and the superfluous fat. Bind the meat to keep it in proper shape; rub it over with dripping, and cover with greased paper. Baste well and very often. About a quarter of an hour before taking it up remove the paper and let the joint brown nicely, allowing from fifteen to twenty minutes, if the meat is liked much done, for each pound of meat. That time would, however, overcook it according to many tastes. One hour and a half to one hour and three-quarters for a saddle weighing about ten pounds would in a general way be sufficient, remembering that much fat will keep the meat underneath it from cooking, and that individual taste must to a certain extent regulate the time. Serve with clear, rich gravy and red currant jelly.

CAULIFLOWER AU GRATIN.
(*Kingswood Cookery Book*)

1 Cauliflower; 2 ozs. Parmesan Cheese; ½ pt. White Sauce.

Boil the cauliflower, until tender, in salt and water; cut away the green leaves and press all the water out with a cloth; place on the dish in which it is to be served; make a pint of white sauce and put into it half the cheese; pour this over the cauliflower and sprinkle the dry cheese on the top; place it in front of the fire, or in the oven, for a few minutes to brown; it is then ready to serve.

RICE PUDDING (WITH EGGS)
(*XXth Century Cookery*)

Wash well two handfuls of rice, and cook in nearly a quart of milk, sweetened to taste, and add the thin rind of one lemon cut in one piece, and a small stick of cinnamon. Let the rice boil very slowly until it has absorbed all the milk. Turn it out into a basin, and when cold, remove the lemon rind and cinnamon; then stir into it the yolks of four eggs and one whole egg, beaten up; add a little candied citron, cut into small pieces, and mix it well in; butter and sprinkle with breadcrumbs a plain tin mould, put the mixture into it, and bake in a quick oven for about half an hour. The method of knowing when the pudding is done is to stick a bright trussing needle into it, which will come out clean when the pudding is cooked.

BAKED RICE PUDDING (WITHOUT EGGS)
'My own Recipe. Very Good.'

Take half a teacupful of rice, put in a pie-dish with three ounces of sugar, three small lumps of butter, and three cups of new milk; bake in a slow oven for two and a half to three hours; send to table with caster sugar strewn over.

ORANGE SPONGE
(Goulburn Cookery Book)

One pint of orange juice, ½ pint of water, ¾ of an ounce of gelatine (8 sheets), ¼ lb. of sugar, the grated peel of 3 oranges, 3 eggs.

Grate the peel of 3 oranges, and squeeze the juice of 10 or 12, or enough to fill a pint measure. Put into a saucepan with the grated peel and sugar, and boil for a few minutes; add the gelatine, which must be soaked in the ½ pint of water. Beat the yolks of the eggs, and pour the liquor gently on to them. Return to the saucepan, and let it just thicken, but be sure it does not boil. Pour into a basin, and, when beginning to set, add the stiffly-beaten whites of the eggs. Pour into a mould, which has been dipped in cold water, and turn out when set.

DEVILLED ALMONDS.
(Presbyterian Cookery Book)

Blanch ½ lb. Jordan almonds, and dry them thoroughly; put them into a frying pan with 2 oz. butter made very hot; fry gently till a light brown, then drain on a sieve before the fire; sprinkle with salt and a little cayenne.

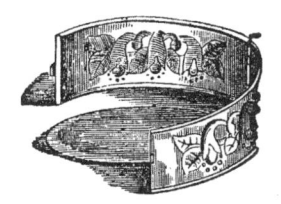

CHAPTER 15

SWEEPING UP THE CRUMBS

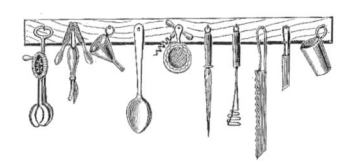

We may argue from sherry to cognac about the character of Federation cookery and not settle the question. It would be hard enough to distinguish with certainty between fact and folklore, between what great-grandma actually cooked and what grandma *said* her mother cooked. We would have to shake off the tendency to assume that what we eat now and how we cook it are suitable standards against which to judge the food and cookery of another age. We would probably be driven into the great twin errors of such debates: generality and particularity (the first being to take refuge in vagueness; the second, to be seduced by stereotypes and neat simplifications). We would theorise, as others already have done, on the influences of geographic isolation and the convict system but would be left with the question: were these (and many other factors which are often overlooked) the driving forces or merely the *context* in which Australian cookery developed? The purpose of this book has been more to rediscover Federation cookery than to theorise about it, but we have browsed through quite enough material to venture some conclusions.

Where did it come from?

To say that it was brought from Britain in the first fleet and developed according to Australia's needs would be too simple. For a start, most of what came to Australia was strictly English, rather than British. The flag was planted in the name of Great Britain; Scots and Irish were well represented among the white settlers and convicts, but the colony was planned to meet English needs and managed according to English ideas and English direction.[1] To the Scots and Irish the English were unwelcome overlords, or worse. To the early German immigrants the colonies were populated not by British, but by English, Scottish and Irish. For nearly 100 years the idea of *Britishness* had little relevance to the majority of the population— ironically, not until native-born white Australians began to outnumber immigrants. For the most part, the roots of Australian cookery are therefore found in England.

It is not too fanciful to think of English cookery as a vast cauldron that had simmered over the collective fires of castle, house, cottage and hovel since antiquity. Into it went also the home cooking of Romans, Celts, Vikings, Saxons and the many other peoples who had contact with the island. All these ingredients, and many more, were blended together in centuries of slow cooking.

The cities were the centres of trade and commerce in England and it was mainly through them that English cookery gained its spice: of French, Italian, German, Middle Eastern and other foreign ways with food, brought back as novelties to the courts and great houses and slowly adapted to local tastes till they were barely recognisable. Traffic between England and France was a special case: many 'English' dishes can be traced back to France; even the humble rissole was once French.

Another special case were the many so-called Indian dishes which found their way into the kitchen repertoires of the middle- and upper-class households. The British Raj went to astonishing lengths to recreate its home cooking in a country where the climate was unsuitable, the ingredients were mostly unavailable and the local cooks untrained for it. At the same time, with typical imperial arrogance, it engaged the local foods and techniques and repatriated to Britain that bizarre body of 'Anglo-Indian'[2] dishes which, having achieved respectability in Britain, was ready for transportation to the colonies.

The cooking of Scotland followed a somewhat similar pattern, blending into the ancient Celtic culture the influences of Viking raiders, the *auld alliance* with France (especially noticeable in the many dishes whose names and preparation are corruptions of old French ones), the long contest with the Dutch herring fleets for Scotland's off-shore resources and the harsh subsistence diet of the crofters and other highland peasants. Game and salmon poaching helped to ensure that knowledge of the more luxurious foods was not entirely confined to the middle and upper classes. In Ireland perhaps the most remarkable feature of peasant food was the extreme dependence on potatoes, as a result of which the art of cooking was virtually lost to a large part of the population.

Although Australian kitchens and eating patterns were founded along lines dictated by the English masters and workers, Scots migrants of the mid nineteenth century – free settlers and merchants – brought many dishes with them and Scottish cookery was probably the second most important national influence. (Here it is difficult to separate the direct influence of migration from the indirect contribution of the many dishes that had already been incorporated into English cookery.) As Twopenny pointed out, the Irish peasant girls who came to Australia and sought domestic employment had nothing to offer as cooks and had to be taught English ways. In any case, there was no reason for Irish potato farmers and Scots crofters to persevere with their accustomed subsistence diets here: the monotony of mutton, salt beef, potatoes, cabbage, bread and tea was vastly superior.

The census figures for country of birth give sufficient confirmation of the main ethnic sources of Federation cookery. In 1891 the recorded population was a little over three million people, of which about two-thirds had been born in Australia.[3] The number of Aboriginal people (not counted in the census) was about 100 000 and declining. The largest migrant groups were English (457 000), Irish (229 000), Scots (125 000), Germans (45 000) and Chinese (36 000).

The German influence is easy enough to find in the cookery books – sauerkraut, dumplings, bread puddings, yeast cakes and various other specialties. The Chinese immigrants made virtually no mark on Federation cookery, though they became famous for their market gardens and some were employed as cooks. Quong Tart's scones and the Presbyterian Cookery Book's recipe for *Chinaman's pastry* were about the extent of it. Chinese cookery did not begin to gain general acceptance by Australians until the 1950s.

Quite apart from the foreign dishes which made their way to Australia via England, other countries were represented in the books in small numbers. It was fashionable for cookery writers to be able to offer new recipes from overseas sources. However, while such embellishments added interest, few of them ever became significant in the body of cookery.

What happened to it?

The elements of colonial cookery – English with a little Scottish and traces of German – were subjected to a wave of new influences. At the risk of oversimplification, we could trace the development of Federation cookery through four main stages: its founding traditions, the exigencies of survival, its colonial adaptation and its romancing. (Forward from Federation one might look for evidence of a period of national maturity before the serious onset of internationalisation. Whether it would be found is a question wide open to debate.)

Having already identified the founding traditions, we look briefly at the influence of each of the other stages.

The colonists in Australia were rather more successful in preserving their imported traditions than the Raj had been in India. Embarrassing though it may be to contemporary republican sentiments, the dominating feature of Federation cookery was not how Australian it had become, or even how much it had been influenced by Australia, but how English it had remained.

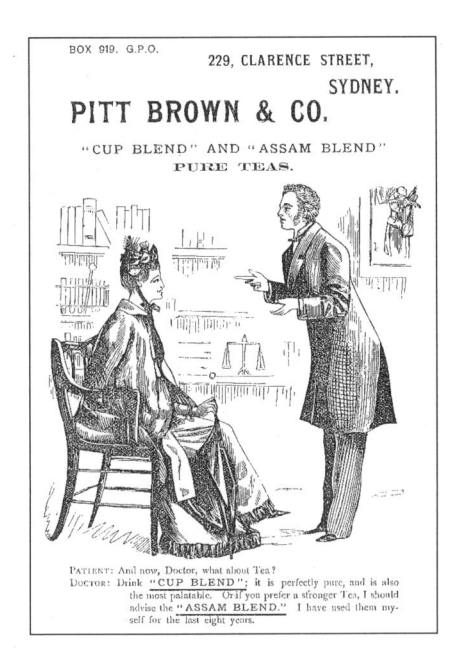

> BOX 919. G.P.O.
>
> 229, CLARENCE STREET,
> SYDNEY.
>
> ## PITT BROWN & CO.
>
> "CUP BLEND" AND "ASSAM BLEND"
> PURE TEAS.
>
> PATIENT: And now, Doctor, what about Tea?
> DOCTOR: Drink "CUP BLEND"; it is perfectly pure, and is also the most palatable. Or if you prefer a stronger Tea, I should advise the "ASSAM BLEND." I have used them myself for the last eight years.

The main reason for this was that, except on a relatively small scale on remote country stations, the Aboriginal people were not recruited and trained for domestic service in large numbers and their food traditions never went into the modern Australian cauldron; nor did the abundance of native food resources generally relieve the hardships of the survival years.

Another feature of the survival period – the convict influence – can also be discounted as relatively minor. The convict regime was geographically confined; its greatest impact was in New South Wales and Tasmania. The subsistence rations fed to convicts did not set the pattern for the colonies and many ex-convicts prospered; some came to live as well as middle-class merchants and professionals. Whatever numbers may have continued with something like convict food – because they knew or could afford no better – were quickly swamped by free settlers who were certainly expecting better.

In short, the survival period did little to disturb the essential Englishness of Federation food and cooking, though it left its mark clearly enough in the dominance of meat, flour and tea.

Although explorers and pioneers found a few native animals and birds useful for supplementary food, they ate the native fruits and vegetables only in desperation and the survival diet of meat, damper and billy tea was consolidated as a colonial tradition. Wealthier colonists, anxious not to be deprived of the amusements of the old country, were quick to explore the possibilities of native game (and quick to import the familiar varieties). We have seen what Edward Abbott had to say of native game and fish. Settlers in the bush turned to Aboriginal knowledge of native foods and bush cookery to relieve the monotony of salt meat, flour, treacle and the few vegetables they grew; Mina Rawson's advice that 'whatever the blacks eat the whites may safely try' was sound, but the two never developed symbiosis on a large enough scale for Aboriginal ways to have a lasting impact or to spread into urban society. Instead, the British remained as British as their circumstances would allow and developed a dependency on portable and storable food that some would argue became a lasting characteristic of Australian eating habits.[4]

The period of colonial adaptation was merely a gradual mutation of homely dishes as cooks trying to remain true to England nevertheless lost sight of the originals. Most of the dishes were not socially important enough to be kept pure against the home standard; they remained easily recognisable, but gradually moved down paths not necessarily equivalent to those which they would take in Britain. The main forces for difference were the relative abundance of meat, uncertainties of supply, the development of a colonial society and the shortage of competent cooks. The difference in climate was a minor factor.

The adaptation process was led by Australian households rather than by the reformers and teachers. The idealism that carried Federation forward can be seen clearly enough; it was in the air. Was not Philip Muskett's reformist tirade driven by the ideal of creating a little Southern Europe in Australia – only a year or two before Mary Gilmore despaired of it and directed her sail to Paraguay, to create Utopia there? Surely it was idealism that inspired the Presbyterian women to raise funds for home missions and led Mary McLean to take the benefits of education to the natives of India. It inspired Harriet Wicken's vision of the cosy kitchen and of the day when emancipated woman would have 'more leisure to cultivate her intellect'. There was idealism, too, in the vision of Zara Aronson and Ina Strickland, who looked above the male politics of nationalism and saw that out of the sordid and brutal beginnings of colonialism could rise a common wealth of taste and refinement centred on happy homes.

Translating ideals into reality was another matter. Among the teachers Ramsay Whiteside, Annie Fawcett Story, Margaret Pearson and Harriet Wicken were reformers in their way. They saw the need for the people to be taught how to cook but they were not so visionary about *what* people should cook. The style and standard had been set by the National Training School for Cookery, London. It was plain, English and strictly economical; anything better was 'high class'. They responded to the more obvious needs for local adaptation, but even in its own day much of their teaching must have seemed conservative. It is now clear that, in culinary terms, the reformers and teachers were backward-looking. Many of Jean Rutledge's dishes were 'old familiar friends'; her concern was that they be made accurately. Henrietta McGowan responded to changing social needs, yet she acknowledged that much of the food she presented was old.[5] Mina Rawson was a champion of active adaptation, but her influence was slight. The Presbyterians and Mary Gilmore made no claims to culinary leadership, but played an important role in collecting the experience of ordinary households and circulating it as the people's alternative to the teachers. Only Zara Aronson tried to ride the new wave.

In a sense they were right. The first concerns of ordinary households were with the daily practicalities of supply and storage rather than with ideals and novelty. In nineteenth century Australia the rural population was still expanding as city-based industry grew; in effect, city and country competed for labour at the dockside as each shipload of migrants arrived. Since it was quickly becoming an urbanised country heavily dependent on rural industry, it also faced a need for rapid development of distribution and other services, but the vast distances and urban sprawl changed the nature of the task. Here the essential problem was not concentration, but dispersion; the distance factor ensured that the early reliance on portable and storable food remained.

The development of social class structures also helped to divert the course of adaptation. Entry to the upper classes was gained more through wealth and influence than through birth, family and education. Those who 'made it' were a mixed lot, but at the risk of stereotyping one can identify among them two groups of extremes according to their eating habits.

First, there were people of 'breeding' – not necessarily of the old aristocracy, but sufficient to have a good knowledge and appreciation of food. They understood reasonably well fashionable British cookery and took a lively interest in the best that could be imported from other countries. They constituted the tiny body of Australian aristologists.

The second – and much larger – group were the newly rich whose money exceeded their taste. Twopenny satirised them as the Muttonwools and grubbers at table. Having been bred to mutton, damper and billy tea their contributions were quantity and ostentation. They kept Australian cookery English and made stodge respectable. They wanted salmon, jugged hare and cabinet pudding but often settled for tinned salmon, jugged wallaby and bread pudding. They did much to make it egalitarian by bringing their lower and middle-class tastes to their more expensive tables. In a way, they reversed the tradition of Britain, where for centuries poaching had enabled intrepid (or hungry) peasants to share the pleasures of upper class tables.

The weight of influence was on the side of the Muttonwools. The middle classes, whose social position was less dependent on displays of wealth, settled for good plain cookery more or less as defined by the departments of public instruction, but as the supply of servants dried up they had to adopt new ways. By the turn of the century rather less than ten per cent of households still had servants and the proportion was declining rapidly. Throughout the late nineteenth century working women withdrew from the domestic service market in favour of factory work and other occupations; this left a large and influential group of middle class women, quite untrained in culinary skills, with no choice but to do their own cooking. We can assume that they did their best to maintain their established standards of living and to do so they led the push for short cuts through the traditional recipes and for the use of processed food, with predictable results.

The working classes also contributed to the egalitarian nature of Australian cookery. Poor migrants to Australia were overwhelmed by the variety, quality and cheapness of food they found here. At first they took no trouble with it, finding mutton and damper the food of paradise. Gradually they widened their interests in food, but their tastes remained simple: good food was plentiful, inexpensive and tasty. Made-sauces were pretentious, but gravy was good. There was no objection to bottled sauces, and a splash of Worcestershire or anchovy could do wonders for many savoury dishes. There was no great concern for how things should be done or what should be served with what – except, perhaps on Sundays. If it pleased, it was good.

It can hardly be said that a national body of cookery is ever 'finished', but there was a final process of garnishing at work just before the point at which we may stop the calendar and call it 'Federation'. It was the romancing of Australian cookery.

Romancing

Romancing took three forms. The first was the celebration of sweetness. We have seen the great Australian fondness for biscuits, cakes, puddings, jams and home-made sweets, decorated lavishly and given romantic and fanciful names. In the midst of practicality and the harsh reality of life, sweetness provided retreat into a realm of fantasy. Even in survival mode there was the comfort of a crude flour dumpling swimming in golden syrup (*cocky's joy*, in fact).[6]

The second was the enrichment of English cookery with novelty. The middle-class fashion leaders, mainly though the magazines and quality newspapers, fed fashion-conscious Australians a steady diet of interesting and novel dishes, generally imported from non-British sources. French, American, German and Jewish were the most popular. Their efforts to bring new dainties to Australian households reflected Australia's attempts to catch up culturally with the rest of the European world and to find a place on the international stage – the same nationalistic imperatives that drove the great international exhibitions. Many decades of Federation passed before Australia ceased to think and talk about Britain as the mother country, but it was from this source, supplemented by the ethnic cooking sucked in with the waves of twentieth century migration, that our more cosmopolitan cookery of the 1990s was formed.

Finally, the food of survival was itself romanced. Popular celebration of Australian folklore – which generally means rediscovering, reinventing (or should that be 're-enacting?') and romancing the convict era, the gold rushes and white pioneers in bush and outback – is not just a recent phenomenon. Much of Australia was explored and settled during the great romantic era of literature and art that came of age with Wordsworth, Byron and others and gave us the music of Schubert and Schumann and, later, Brahms. It was an age of dreams and visions inspired of idealism. Australia was not merely a harsh and inhospitable land, a fitting place to transport convicts, it was a land of promise and opportunity. Fortunes had been made and could be made. Success in commerce, on the land or at almost any occupation could raise a family's status in the colonies to a level to which it could never aspire in Britain. So explorers set off in search of the inland ocean, gold diggers staked out their claims, farmers cleared their land, graziers mustered their animals. And before the period of dreaming had quite ended, Edward Curr had taken on the name of Rolf Boldrewood and given us *The Squatter's Dream* and *Robbery Under Arms* and Andrew Barton Paterson, a Sydney solicitor whose connection with the bush went little further than his early childhood and family oral history, created the folklore of *Clancy of the Overflow* and *The Man from Snowy River*.

Bush food never became the daily fare of average Australians. But, as we shall see, damper and billy tea became icons of a romantic life that city-dwellers would dream about (and perhaps still dream about as they mount their four-wheel-drives to ride from suburban house to office or factory). The *Worker Cook Book* explained how to make an excellent rabbit stew in a treacle tin; probably half its readers were city folk. And Henrietta McGowan found romance in the poverty of spinsterhood.

What was it like?

We should start by distinguishing the food of Federation from the manner in which it was cooked and presented. The stereotype of meat, flour, sugar and tea was well deserved. These were the basic rations for the bush and the foundation of town cookery. As Morison observed, meat dominated. It was so plentiful that there hardly seemed a need to make much of the offal and less attractive cuts, yet liver, kidneys, tripe and macho dishes such as baked bullock heart and boiled calf or sheep head had strong followings.

Enthusiasm for meat was not matched by enthusiasm for vegetables. Plain vegetables such as potatoes, cabbage, carrots and some greens were widely accepted, but few of the others, now common and even then known well enough, appeared regularly on the table. Besides being consumed as bread in its various forms, flour featured in puddings and pastry, both of which generally assumed greater importance in daily meals than they do now. Milk and jellied puddings were also popular. Cakes were an important part of household cookery.

There were some favourite ingredients: anchovies, cheese and bacon were popular for 'savoury' dishes. With the exceptions of the ubiquitous parsley and of nutmeg, cloves and perhaps one or two others, herbs and spices were used less frequently and in less variety than now. Most people were afraid of garlic. Onion, though widely used, was treated with caution; perhaps it was also more strongly flavoured than modern varieties. Tomato was more important as a flavouring agent than as a vegetable. Tomato sauce – usually home-made – was much liked. The most popular fruits for dessert use were apples, lemons, oranges, plums and apricots. Almonds, walnuts and pistachios were the favourite nuts; peanuts were thought to have too strong a taste for most purposes. Coconut was often freshly grated.

Cooking methods emphasised baking (the late-nineteenth century replacement for the open-fire roasting of earlier times), braising, stewing, boiling and pan-frying. Meat was generally cooked in large pieces or joints rather than in individual serves. If baked it was preferred rare, in imitation of the roast meat of old England. Pork was an exception; it was always well cooked. Stewing by the slow-cooking method (in tightly sealed 'jug' or 'jar') produced some wonderfully flavoursome dishes.

Sauces, a vital part of Federation meat cookery, were thickened by stirring the liquid into a roux made by cooking flour and butter together and were of three main types: white, brown and *melted butter*. Compound sauces were made by adding flavouring, colouring and garnishing ingredients. Bland sauces – parsley, caper, onion etc – were preferred for strongly flavoured meat, especially boiled mutton and corned beef. Blander meat often attracted stronger sauces – mint sauce with roast lamb; tangy apple sauce with roast pork; tomato sauce and grilled bacon rolls with roast veal. Roast fowls, more strongly flavoured then than are the battery-bred things we now tolerate, were usually served with bread sauce and gravy, while white sauces gently flavoured with oysters, celery or boiled eggs went well with boiled fowls. Cooked meat was thought to lose flavour when reheated; hashes therefore had their sauces enhanced with condiments, wine, lemon peel or whatever.

Vegetables were boiled until they were well and truly cooked. This practice now seems unenlightened, but it was more likely to have been a practical way of improving the digestibility of vegetables that were generally tougher and more fibrous (and probably more strongly flavoured) than modern commercial varieties. Potatoes stood head and shoulders above all other vegetables in popularity and good cooks took them seriously. For daily fare vegetables were likely to be served plain or tossed in a little butter. *Melted butter* or a white sauce turned them into 'dressed vegetables'.

Federation diners wanted substantial, filling sweets and boiled or steamed puddings were very popular. They were generally made with suet shortening but, if reasonable care was taken, did not have to be stodgy, providing they were eaten hot. Baked puddings were popular, particularly milk-and-egg puddings and those featuring apples and cereals (rice, sago and tapioca). Many puddings were designed to use up scraps of stale bread. Cold puddings emphasised jelly in various forms.

The contrast of bland sauce with strong meat, strong sauce with mild meat carried through to sweet dishes. Even plain suet pudding – unsweetened, unflavoured – was acceptable to many if it came with a rich, lively sauce made of jam, treacle, golden syrup or lemon. Custard went with almost any pudding, but its purpose was nearly always to provide contrast of colour, texture or flavour.

For company, the style was elegant and showy. Dishes were arranged and garnished elaborately, with an emphasis on geometric pattern and colour. Artificial colouring was considered normal. In the fading idealism of the romantic era the highest goal of presentation was still to coax the food into perfect shapes and colours.

While it is fashionable to dismiss Federation cookery as stodgy, glutinous and dull, to do so is not good history. The main problem – apart from the intrusion of stereotypes and personal preferences – is to define the standard. A search of more than 10 000 recipes has produced examples of excellent eating and miserable eating (every bit as bad as one might now buy from a 'fast food' outlet). Choosing a point somewhere in the middle, such as the popular *Schauer Cookery Book*, can only be a very rough approximation, but would suggest that most households had access to quality fresh ingredients and to recipes for good, plain food with plenty of ideas for variations, using up left-overs and catering for special occasions.

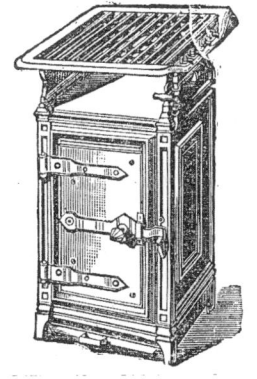

How well they used the recipes was another matter. Then, as now, there were cooks who, through ignorance or lack of time or effort, taught their households how unpalatable good ingredients could become, prompting cookery writers to pass beyond helpful advice to stern warnings on such matters as boiling, saucing and presentation. Hence Jean Rutledge pointed out 'what a difference there is in meat *boiled* and meat *simmered*.' And Henrietta McGowan warned that 'a stew boiled is a stew spoiled'. The capacity of cooks to make good dishes badly has changed little in the past 100 years.

The declining availability of domestic help, the 'coming out' of women, improving systems for food processing and distribution and the growing power of the advertising industry to change patterns of domestic consumption were all coming together in a new force that was both to ease the drudgery of cookery and at the same time to work against good cookery: its name was convenience. Arrowroot and cornflour were soon to push flour aside as a thickening agent – especially in the form of custard powder for thickening boiled custards, where their innocence of eggs removed the risk of curdling. Pre-mixed baking powders quickly became popular, though self-raising flour took longer to catch on because Federation cooks generally took considerable pride in the texture of their cakes and did not readily compromise it. Gelatine quickly replaced calf's foot jelly and commercially flavoured jelly powders were already beginning to degrade jellied puddings.

Progress in kitchen equipment, particularly gas and electric cookers, mixing devices and well-controlled ovens gradually removed much of the drudgery and risk from Federation cookery. Except for the replacement of roasting and grilling by baking and broiling, the steadily increasing stream of new and improved gadgets generally benefited the quality of cooking.

A common criticism of Federation food is its lack of variety, a predictable result of the adaptation process working on traditions which mostly came from a single country. The hundreds of soups were all variations on just two basic themes: texture and the presence or absence of meat. Half a dozen or so basic methods served the whole body of meat cookery; similarly, most of the puddings and sweets were conctructed from only a handful of ideas. However, one of the great challenges of Federation cookery was to turn sameness into refinement by the creation of an array of subtly different dishes from a limited variety of ingredients and techniques.

Another criticism is the prevailing preference for hot food throughout the year, regardless of season. There was little interest in vegetables; even salads were mostly made from cooked vegetables. However, the preference for hot food was founded in good sense: in the absence of refrigeration (and, in many households, even an ice-chest), eating most food freshly cooked or reheated was one of the more sensible health practices of the age.

The icons

One may look in old books for a few celebrated dishes that have become so embedded in the popular lore of Australian cookery (whether deservedly or not) that we may call them icons.

Scones and sponge cakes, while well represented, are British.

Despite its importance to Australian food history, damper was rarely mentioned in early cookery books. Edward Abbott was an exception; describing 'colonial damper' he said:

> This bush fare is simply composed of flour and water, with a little salt, made into flat round pieces on bark, and baked in the ashes. All old colonists are experts in making damper. "Tea, damper, and mutton," is a colonial institution, as the weary bushman is fully aware of.

Damper is generally thought to have been an adaptation of Irish soda bread, though the combination of flour, water and heat is so ancient and basic it hardly seems necessary to find an origin for it. While there is no doubt that it was common survival food, its value as a 'colonial institution' was still under debate thirty years after Abbott. Lamenting the absence of any Australian national dish, Philip Muskett wrote in 1894:

> Although tea and damper instinctively arise in the mind when the matter is referred to, yet I take it that we would all repel such an accusation if levelled against us. Does the Australian, moreover, away from his native land perpetuate his patriotism by oft partaking of this pastoral fare? Certainly not.

Mina Rawson started to give a recipe for it in her *Enquiry Book* but allowed herself to become sidetracked into a rambling, though historically interesting, discussion of baking soda and baking powder.

> **A Damper** is very easily made, but still it requires a certain amount of knowledge to make it, and more than all to bake it. Now-a-days, most men travelling carry baking powder, but years ago I have often been amused when bushmen have asked me for a small quantity of soda for their dampers. I have argued with them that soda alone could be of no use, save to give a most unpleasant flavour, that they must have acid to counteract it; but it was to no purpose. They always used a pinch of soda, and, right or wrong, they preferred keeping to the old custom. In everything, be it bread, cake, or pudding, when soda is used half the quantity of acid should be added, or else sour milk, which, of course, comes to the same thing, as the acidity of the milk acts upon the soda. Anyone who gives the matter a moment's thought will understand

why it is, but let me illustrate it more plainly. Dissolve a little soda in water, and then add a wee pinch of acid. It fizzes. Just the same effervescence takes place in the cake or damper as in the tumbler , and it is the air bubbles, caused by it, that make the cake, pudding, &c., rise or swell, and become light...

A decade later Ina Strickland found in damper a symbol of Australian unity and so gave directions in her *Commonwealth Cookery Book* for both *Australian damper* and *Federal damper*. The first was true to tradition except for being baked in a camp oven rather than directly in the ashes. The second recipe, like one which later appeared in the 1937 *Coronation Cookery Book*, turned both damper and Federation into romantic ideals: it was an urbanised version made from self-raising flour and milk, baked in an oven. A farmhouse version eventually appeared in the Presbyterian book in 1950: self-raising flour, water and salt mixed to a stiff dough and cooked in hot ashes in a camp oven or a brick oven. But these were curiosities; damper was survival food and the knowledge of how to make it belonged to bush lore, not the body of recipes for respectable cookery.

Zara Aronson gave the only formal recipe for billy tea that I have found in Federation books. It was stirred with a stick and had no trace of a gumleaf.

The meat pie has a history much longer than that of white settlement in Australia.[7] The particular thing now known as the Australian meat pie probably began as it has remained – a commercial product. It has never been a significant part of our household cookery tradition, and bears little resemblance to the meat pies described in Federation recipes, some of which were excellent.

The pavlova does not belong to Federation cookery; it came much later. Lamingtons had their origin in the Federation period but, again, their popularity came later. Queensland's *Schauer Cookery Book* gave a recipe for *Lamington cake*, a plain slab cake spread with chocolate icing and sprinkled with coconut, presumably named after Lord Lamington, appointed Governor of Queensland in 1896. Very similar recipes appeared in New South Wales and Victoria about the same time.[8] In 1916 a Western Australian book gave, under the same name, the small squares with which we are now familiar.[9] It has been said that the chocolate and coconut coating was intended to keep the delicate Victoria sponge from drying out in the hot climate.

Australians whose roots on this continent go back to Federation might expect to find some favourite or hated dishes from their individual family traditions. Savoury mince, sweet curry, condensed milk salad dressing, gramma pie, stewed rhubarb and the dreaded choko are all there. But while their origins may lie a hundred years ago, or more, these dishes are not real Federation food. Their popularity came later; they belong to the traditions of people still living. Good luck with your own list.

APPENDIX 1

WHO'S WHO

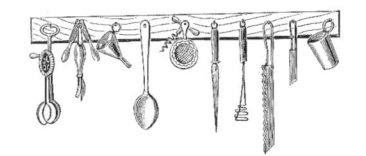

Here is a list, in chronological order, of some of the culinary VIPs who contributed to Australian Federation cookery. Those in Britain were, of course, remote but each had a role in developing dishes that became part of the Australian heritage.

THE BRITISH HERITAGE

QUEEN HENRIETTA MARIA, widow of Charles I who was beheaded in 1649. To her is attributed *The Compleat Cook and Queens Delight* (first published 1655).

ROBERT MAY. Author of *The Accomplisht Cook*, the first full-scale English cookery book (first published 1660).

ELIZABETH SMITH. Author of *The Compleat Housewife* (first published 1728 or earlier).

CHARLES CARTER. Author of *The Complete Practical Cook* (1730).

HANNA GLASSE. Author of *The Art of Cookery, made Plain and Easy* (1747).

ELIZABETH RAFFALD. Author of *The Experienced English Housekeeper* (first published 1769).

MARGARET DODS (Scotland). Fictional character in Sir Walter Scott's novel *St. Ronan's Well*. Meg Dods, inn-keeper, presided over the table of the Cleikum Club in the Border country of Scotland. To many she was as real as the charming *Cook and Housewife's Manual* published in her name in 1826.

ELIZA ACTON. Author of *Modern Cookery for Private Families* (1845).

ISABELLA BEETON. Compiler of *Beeton's Book of Household Management* (1861). Later revisions and Mrs Beeton books were by other authors.

MARIE JENNY SUGG. Author of *The Art of Cooking by Gas* (1890).

ARTHUR GAY PAYNE. Author and compiler of books on food in late Victorian period. Edited the *Shilling Cookery* (1900) and a *Dictionary of Cookery* for Cassell, London. One of his books was published by Cole's Book Arcade, Melbourne (*Cole's Popular Cookery*, 189-).

AGNES MARSHALL. Operated a cookery school in late Victorian period; author of *Mrs A. B. Marshall's Cookery Book* and *Larger Cookery Book of Extra Recipes*.

CHARLES HERMAN SENN. Author of *The New Century Cookery Book* (1901).

THE AUSTRALIANS

EDWARD ABBOTT (Hobart). Parliamentarian; author of the first Australian cookery book *The English and Australian Cookery Book* (1864). He wrote under the name *An Australian Aristologist*.

ALFRED J WILKINSON (Melbourne). Chef of the Athenæum Club; author of (arguably) the second Australian cookery book *The Australian Cook* (1876).

Ramsay Whiteside (Sydney). First cookery teacher in the New South Wales public school system (1882-5).

Harriet Wicken (England – Melbourne – Sydney – Perth). Lecturer in domestic economy at Sydney Technical College and later at Perth High School; author of *The Kingswood Cookery Book* (English edition 1885; Australian editions from 1888) and several other cookery books.

Annie Fawcett Story (Sydney – Melbourne). Cookery teacher at Sydney Technical College and Fort Street Model School. 'Directress of Cookery' in the Department of Public Instruction until 1895, when she moved to Victoria. Obtained a similar position there in 1898.

Margaret Pearson (England – Melbourne). Teacher in cookery; author of *Australian Cookery recipes for the people* (c. 1888).

Philip Muskett (Sydney). Medical practitioner and author of *The Art of Living in Australia* (1894) and various books on health.

Mina Rawson (Queensland). Author of *The Australian Enquiry Book of Household and General Information* (1894) and *The Antipodean Cookery Book and Kitchen Companion* (1895) and similar books.

Mrs George (M.) MacInnes for the Presbyterian Women's Missionary Association (New South Wales). Compiler of *Cookery Book of Good and Tried Receipts* (1895).

Hannah Maclurcan (Townsville – Sydney). Proprietor of the Queen's Hotel, Townsville and later the Wentworth Hotel, Sydney; author of *Mrs Maclurcan's Cookery Book* (1897 and later).

Mrs Forster (Jean) Rutledge (Bungendore, New South Wales). Author of *The Goulburn Cookery Book* (1899).

Mrs Theo. (E. M.) Winning (Moree, New South Wales). Author of *The Household Manual* (1899) and *The Australian Housewife's Guide to Domestic Economy* (1902 and earlier).

Mrs F B (Zara) Aronson (Sydney). Newspaper columnist (writing under the name Thalia) and author of *XXth Century Cooking and Home Decoration* (1900).

Fanny Fawcett Story (Sydney). Teacher of domestic economy and cookery, Sydney Technical College and author of *Australian Economic Cookery Book and Housewife's Companion* (1900).

Isabel Ross (Melbourne). Cookery demonstrator for Metropolitan Gas Company and author of *Cookery Class Recipes* (c. 1900 and later).

Ina Strickland. Author of *The Commonwealth Cookery Book* (1904).

Amy Schauer (Brisbane). Teacher of cookery and domestic arts at the Brisbane Technical College and author of *The Schauer Cookery Book* (1909) and *Fruit Preserving and Confectionery*.

Henrietta Walker née McGowan (Melbourne). Journalist and author of the *Keeyuga Cookery Book* (1911).

Amie Monro (Sydney). In charge of the Domestic Cookery department, Sydney Technical College and author of *The Practical Australian Cookery* (1913 and earlier).

Dame Mary Gilmore (Sydney). Journalist, poet, political activist, editor of the Women's Page of the *Australian Worker* newspaper. Compiled the *Worker Cook Book* (1915 and earlier).

Emily Futter (Melbourne). Author of *Australian Home Cookery* (c. 1924).

APPENDIX 2

WHAT'S WHAT

The most popular dishes of Federation cookery are listed below. It is based on a search of more than ten thousand recipes in fourteen Australian books published between 1888 and 1914. The three hundred and one dishes listed below are those which were included in at least half the books. They accounted for about forty two per cent of all recipes. Altogether, there were about fifteen hundred dishes which could be found in at least two books. The list gives a sense of what 'ordinary' cookery was like, but does not, of course, illustrate the variety of recipes in circulation or necessarily the most interesting dishes.

SAVOURIES

Anchovy savoury: anchovies on little rounds of fried bread, garnished in some way. Hot or cold.
Anchovy toast: toasted bread topped with an anchovy paste. Cold.
Cheese biscuits: savoury biscuits made with cheese pastry.
Cheese straws: cheese pastry rolled out and cut into thin straws, baked, and served threaded through rings also made of cheese pastry.
Fondu: something between a baked cheese pudding and a cheese soufflé.
Oyster fritters: oysters dipped in batter and deep fried.
Oysters and bacon: oysters rolled in bacon, baked, served on hot buttered toast. Known as *angels on horseback* or *little pigs in blankets*.
Scotch woodcock: toast spread with anchovy paste or a relish, piled with creamy scrambled eggs – or simply a pile of anchovy toast and *white sauce*.
Welsh rarebit: stewed or toasted cheese with toasted bread. Sometimes called *rabbit*.

SOUPS

Artichoke soup: purée or cream soup of Jerusalem artichokes.
Barley soup: a purée of barley boiled in well-flavoured stock, finished with cream or egg yolk.
Carrot soup: a purée of carrots, sometimes with other vegetables for added flavour.
Celery soup: a smooth thickened soup of celery with cream or milk.
Chicken soup: usually a special soup of good chicken stock thickened with cream and egg yolks.
Clear soup or Consommé: a good stock of meat, bones and vegetables clarified and garnished.
Fish soup: various types, including clear soups of small pieces of fish boiled in stock with a few sliced vegetables (*water souchet*) and elegant cream or purée soups.

Fish stock: whole fish or the head and trimmings, simmered in water, usually with vegetables, then strained.

Julienne soup: consommé garnished with vegetables cut into fine strips.

Kidney soup: a thickened or puréed soup of ox kidney fried and simmered in water or stock with vegetables.

Lentil soup: a thin purée of lentils and other vegetables. Usually 'maigre' (meatless).

Macaroni soup: consommé with pieces of boiled macaroni, served with grated Parmesan cheese. There was also a thickened 'white' version with milk and stock.

Mulligatawny: a clear soup or purée flavoured with curry powder, often garnished with chicken or rabbit pieces, always served with boiled rice.

Mutton broth: neck of mutton and vegetables and pearl barley simmered with water.

Onion soup: onions sliced, fried brown and simmered in stock (*brown onion soup*) or simmered in butter, then milk, sieved and thickened (*white onion soup*).

Ox tail soup: ox tail pieces fried, simmered in stock with vegetables and herbs, strained, thickened and garnished with the best of the meat.

Oyster soup: a white milk or cream soup with oysters.

Oyster stew: oysters made hot in a thickened cream sauce.

Pea soup: a purée of split peas and other vegetables made more or less rich according to taste. A purée of green peas was also made.

Potato soup: generally a purée of potatoes, onions or leeks, and perhaps celery in white stock or water, finished with milk or cream.

Rice soup: a purée of rice cooked in white stock, finished with milk or cream. Sometimes vegetables were included.

Sago soup: similar to *rice soup*.

Scotch broth: in Australia, this was much the same as *mutton broth*.

Stock: most books gave a range of meat stocks such as *white* (veal etc), beef, chicken and *economical* (any trimmings).

Tapioca cream: made by boiling tapioca in white stock until clear. Often finished with cream and egg yolk.

Tomato soup: a purée of tomatoes cooked in their own juices or with stock, sometimes with vegetables and a little ham or bacon, filled out with stock or milk and thickened if necessary. The most popular Federation soup.

Vegetable soup: a garnished consommé; a thick soup of diced vegetables in stock; a purée of vegetables and stock; or a 'maigre' soup for meatless days, made with milk instead of stock.

SEAFOOD

Baked fish: whole fish sprinkled with lemon juice and parsley, dotted with butter and baked. Served plain or garnished with lemon, often with a sauce. Sometimes stuffed.

Boiled fish: not really 'boiled', but poached. Usually served with a sauce such as egg, oyster, parsley, *hollandaise* or *melted butter* (with anchovy).

Curried fish: fish pieces cooked or reheated in a *curry sauce* (typically of onions, curry powder, white stock, milk and lemon juice) and served surrounded by a wall of boiled rice.

Fish and potato pie: a fish mixture such as left-over boiled fish and *white sauce* topped with potato purée browned in the oven.

Fish and white sauce: a popular combination rather than a single dish. Included both elegant made-dishes and simple invalid preparations.

Fish cakes: left-over or tinned fish and mashed potato or thick *white sauce*, shaped, crumbed and fried. *Fish croquettes, fish cutlets* and *fish rissoles* were different only in shape and name.

Fish pudding: various made-dishes ranging from boiled suet crust filled with seasoned fish pieces, *white sauce* and other additions to steamed or baked puddings of flaked fish, *white sauce*, bread crumbs, eggs, etc.

Fish scallops: cooked fish and *white sauce* topped with bread crumbs, dotted with butter and baked in scallop shells.

Fried fish: whole fish or fillets crumbed and deep fried.

Grilled fish: split, marinated and grilled quickly on a hot gridiron before a clear fire or under a gas grill.

Kedgeree: a breakfast dish of boiled rice, flaked cooked fish, boiled eggs and butter, occasionally with a sprinkling of curry powder.

Oyster scallops: oysters in a creamy *white sauce* under a crust of buttered bread crumbs, served in scallop shells.

Oysters and white sauce: oysters and a thick *white sauce* made with the liquor from the oysters and milk or cream. Served on toast.

Salmon cakes: fish cakes made with tinned salmon.

Salt fish (dried): usually cod. It required long soaking in water. It was then boiled, garnished and served with sauce, or used for made-dishes.

Stewed fish: various recipes. A popular version, generally regarded as Jewish, included sliced onions, ginger, treacle, spices and vinegar or lemon and was served cold, with its sauce.

EGGS

Anchovy stuffed eggs: boiled eggs, topped, hollowed and filled with the yolks mashed to a smooth paste with anchovy fillets, butter and cayenne. Served standing upright on croûtons of fried bread, nicely garnished, or warm with a rich *white sauce*.

Baked eggs: a basic Federation method for cooking eggs. Each was first broken into a thickly buttered mould, seasoned, and topped with a little butter, cream or grated cheese.

Boiled eggs: these were taken seriously and instructions were sometimes quite detailed.

Curried eggs: boiled eggs in a *curry sauce*.

Egg and tomato: a common breakfast combination. Poached or fried eggs were served on toast with a *tomato sauce* or the tomatoes were fried, then set with eggs.

Egg sandwich: dainty sandwiches of egg and watercress or lettuce, for tea.

Omelette: made by the basic French method.

Omelette soufflée: a savoury omelette for which the egg whites were beaten to a stiff froth. When set, the top was browned under a salamander.

Scrambled eggs: eggs beaten lightly with a little milk and seasoning, poured into bubbling butter and stirred until set in a feathery mass.

MEAT DISHES

Boiled meat: a popular method of cooking large pieces of meat; the only satisfactory method for corned beef or pickled pork. It was not 'boiled', but simmered.

Roast meat: cooked by radiant heat before a fire. Oven-baked meat was also often called 'roast'.

Beef and veal

Beef olives: thin slices of beef rolled with a seasoned stuffing and simmered in rich gravy.

Beef stew: beef steak and onions stewed, sometimes with other additions such as vegetables, mushrooms or pickled walnuts.

Boiled calf's head: soaked and cleaned, boiled with vegetables, herbs etc., laid out on a platter with tongue and brains (cooked separately) and garnished. Served with egg, parsley, melted butter or brain sauce.

Grilled beef steak: done on a hot gridiron, rubbed with a piece of suet to prevent the meat from sticking, over a clear fire. Served with *maître d'hôtel butter*.

Ox tail stew: a rich stew of tail joints with onion, carrots, turnips, celery, herbs and spices in beef stock. Served with boiled rice or sippets of toasted bread.

Scotch collops: thin squares of beef and sliced onions fried in butter, simmered in gravy and served with sippets of fried bread.

Veal cutlet: neat pieces cut from the leg or fillet, crumbed, fried and served with a sauce – say, of tomato.

Lamb and mutton

Grilled lamb or mutton chop: one of the great stand-bys of Australian cookery. Same method as for *grilled beef steak*.

Haricot mutton: a fairly plain stew of mutton chops (or other cheap cuts) with onions, carrots and turnips.

Hot pot: a baked dish of pieces of neck mutton layered with sliced, parboiled potatoes, quartered lamb kidneys and seasonings.

Irish stew: the famous dish of mutton chops ('scrag end' would do) layered with sliced potatoes and onions, gently simmered.

Mutton pie: made in various forms including small patties, raised pies and mutton chops baked under pastry.

Lamb cutlet: a popular cut of meat taken from the neck, usually crumbed and fried, but presented in many different ways.

Sheep head: boiled and presented in much the same way as *calf head* (with *parsley sauce*) or as a stew, fricassée, sauté or scallop.

Stewed chop: usually a plain stew with onion and perhaps a few herbs. It could make a tasty meal – or a dreadful one.

Poultry

Boiled fowl: a full-flavoured farmyard fowl simmered in water with onion, herbs and perhaps carrot and celery. Served with a rich, creamy sauce.

Boiled turkey: cooked in the same way as *boiled fowl* and served with *oyster sauce* and stuffing or *celery sauce* and sausage stuffing.

Chicken aspic: diced chicken set in aspic in a fancy mould with ham or tongue, sliced boiled eggs, beetroot and other vegetables, and garnished with salad and shapes of coloured aspic. Also simpler versions.

Chicken croquettes: minced chicken bound with thick *white sauce*, shaped, crumbed and deep fried. Also made of fish, cold meat, egg etc.

Chicken salad: an arrangement of cold cooked chicken, lettuce and other salad vegetables. Usually dressed with mayonnaise.

Chicken sauté: chicken pieces floured, browned in hot butter, cooked slowly with various additions and dished up with some sauce.

Curried chicken: cooked meat heated in a sauce of onion, diced apple, lemon juice and rind, desiccated coconut, curry powder, cloves and milk. Served with boiled rice.

Fricassée of chicken: chicken pieces in a *white sauce*, sometimes with mushrooms.

Roast fowl: trussed, stuffed with a seasoned mixture of bread crumbs, suet, bacon and veal and oven baked. Served with *bread sauce* and gravy.

Roast turkey: oven baked and served with all the festive trimmings: chestnut stuffing, roast potatoes, fried sausages, bacon rolls, *bread sauce* and brown gravy. Boiled ham, tongue or pork usually went with it.

Game

Jugged hare: a fragrant stew of hare cooked slowly in a closed 'stew jar'. Served with savoury *forcemeat balls*.

Roast quail: roasted plain and served on croûtons of toast or fried bread.

Stewed rabbit: usually a plain dish with an onion and a few herbs for flavouring.

Pies and puddings

Beef steak and kidney pie: a shallow pie of beefsteak and kidney pieces baked under puff pastry.

Beef steak and kidney pudding: a savoury stew of beefsteak and veal kidney cooked slowly in a case of suet pastry (boiled in a basin).

Beef steak pie: usually *beef olives* baked under a puff pastry crust. Cold beef steak pie (with boiled eggs and jellied stock) was also popular.

Cornish pasty: the Australian version was a mixture of diced beef steak, potatoes and onions enclosed in short pastry.

Macaroni and meat pudding: a baked dish of macaroni, cold meat and tomatoes or a steamed pudding of macaroni, minced cooked meat, eggs and milk or stock.

Pigeon pie: beefsteak, pigeons, boiled eggs and sometimes ham, baked under puff pastry. Hot or cold.

Rabbit pie: rabbit, ham or bacon, boiled eggs and sometimes forcemeat balls, baked under puff pastry. Hot or cold.

Savoury balls or dumplings: balls of seasoned suet paste boiled with a stew. The dumplings could replace potatoes.

Sea pie: a meat stew made with a suet crust steamed on top (in the saucepan). Also known as *sailor's pie*.

Shepherd's pie: left-over cooked meat minced with gravy, topped with mashed potato and browned in the oven. Also known as *cottage pie* or, with potato lining the dish as well as forming the top 'crust', *potato pie*.

Toad in the hole: beef steak, chops, pieces of cooked meat or sausages baked in *Yorkshire pudding* batter.

Veal and ham pie: a cold pie of pieces of veal and ham, hard-boiled eggs and sometimes forcemeat balls, cooked in gravy under the pastry.

Yorkshire pudding: plain batter pudding baked under the roast to catch the drippings, or as individual puddings.

Kidney, liver etc

Kidney toast: a breakfast dish of kidneys cooked in butter and served on hot buttered toast.

Liver and bacon: a breakfast dish of fried bacon and lamb or calf liver, usually with gravy.

Stewed kidneys: diced, lightly fried, then stewed in gravy. Suitable for older and more strongly flavoured kidneys.

Stewed sweetbreads: soaked, skinned, blanched, pressed, then stewed in any suitable gravy.

Tripe and onions: boiled tripe pieces served in a *white sauce* flavoured with onions.

Tripe and tomatoes: prepared tripe stewed in a sauce of onions and tomatoes, thickened with cornflour.

Cold meat cookery
Brawn: boiled meat set in its own jellied stock, usually flavoured with onion, herbs and spices. Often used for coarser meats.
Cold meat reheated: the remains of a joint covered with mashed potatoes, warmed up for another meal.
Croquettes of cold meat: cooked meat minced, bound with a stiff savoury sauce or mashed potatoes, then shaped, crumbed and fried.
Curry of cold meat: any meat stewed in a *curry sauce*, generally of onion, apple, curry powder and additions such as desiccated coconut or tomato.
Dry curry: much the same as *curry of cold meat* except that it was cooked to dryness.
Hash: almost any kind of cooked meat cut into small slices and reheated very gently in a well flavoured sauce.
Kromeskies: small cork-shaped croquettes of cold meat or fish wrapped in bacon, dipped in batter, deep fried.
Meat fritters: slices off the cold joint battered (or simply crumbed) and fried. A breakfast dish.
Meat loaf: a savoury dish made from minced cold meat, generally with egg and bread crumbs, boiled rice or mashed potatoes. Baked or steamed in a mould.
Rissoles: small round shapes of minced cooked meat, fried.

VEGETABLES, RICE AND MACARONI
Artichokes: globe artichokes were boiled and served with a sauce such as *poivrade* or *hollandaise*. Jerusalem artichokes were sometimes boiled and served with *white sauce*.
Asparagus: tied in bundles, boiled and served with *hollandaise sauce*, *melted butter*, or even *white sauce*.
French beans: boiled and served plain, tossed in butter, or with a sauce such as *white sauce*, *veloute sauce* or *melted butter*.
Beetroot: boiled and served hot, often with *white sauce* or soaked in vinegar for salads.
Cabbage: boiled. Sometimes stewed, scalloped or sauced for a change.
Carrots: plain boiled, stewed slowly in butter and stock or parboiled and glazed in butter with a little sugar.
Cauliflower: boiled; often served with *melted butter* or *white sauce*.
Cauliflower au gratin: boiled cauliflower coated with *white sauce*, Parmesan cheese and bread crumbs, browned.
Haricot beans: boiled and dressed with butter, chopped parsley and lemon juice.
Macaroni and tomato: boiled macaroni mixed or layered with *tomato sauce*. Served as a vegetable or as a separate dish, with grated cheese.
Macaroni cheese: boiled macaroni dressed with grated cheese and butter (or *cheese sauce*), browned under a salamander.
Onions: boiled or blanched, then simmered in stock or milk and served with *white sauce*. Occasionally baked.
Peas: boiled and tossed in butter. Fresh mint and a littler sugar were often added.
Potato: the technique for boiling potatoes varied according to their age and intended use.
Potato chips: in Federation times, a rather special dish.
Potato croquettes: seasoned mashed potatoes shaped, crumbed and fried.
Potatoes mashed: a popular form of presentation, usually thought worth a little trouble.
Potatoes sauté: parboiled potatoes tossed in hot dripping or butter.
Potato puffs: Baked potatoes hollowed, refilled with mashed potato lightened with whipped egg whites, and baked. Also known as *potato soufflé*.

Potato stuffed: baked potatoes hollowed out and filled with some kind of savoury mixture, then re-baked.
Rice: boiled. It was expected that each grain would be separate.
Savoury rice: rice cooked in stock with onions and sometimes ham. Served with grated cheese.
Spinach: boiled or steamed, chopped finely, finished with butter and cream or gravy and served with croûtons or sippets of toasted bread.
Tomato stuffed: filled with some savoury mixture such as minced ham, bread crumbs, herbs and butter, then baked.
Turnips: boiled and served in *white sauce*.
Vegetable curry: boiled (or boiled and fried) vegetables dressed in a (usually) plain *curry sauce*.
Vegetable marrow: boiled and served with *white sauce*.
Lettuce salad: lettuce leaves with *vinaigrette* ('French salad') or with *mayonnaise* or a *boiled salad dressing* and boiled egg garnish.
Potato salad: various arrangements of sliced boiled potatoes, salad dressing and garnishes such as boiled eggs and beetroot.
Tomato salad: tomatoes and *vinaigrette* or *mayonnaise*, garnished.
Vegetable salad: mixed cooked vegetables dressed with *mayonnaise* or *vinaigrette* and presented as attractively as possible.

SWEETS
Boiled and steamed puddings
Boiled pudding: there was a wide variety of puddings from plain to rich, boiled in a covered mould or in a pudding cloth. The most popular versions are mentioned separately.
Boiled apple pudding: sliced or diced apples (with sugar and grated lemon, nutmeg, cinnamon or cloves) encased in a layer of suet pastry, boiled in a pudding cloth.
Boiled bread pudding: various combinations of bread, egg custard and sometimes jam or fruit, boiled in a covered basin. Also boiled puddings using all or mainly bread crumbs in place of flour.
Cabinet pudding: a steamed pudding of sponge cake or fingers soaked and set in a custard of milk, eggs and sugar. There were many versions, ranging from plain to rich and elaborate presentations incorporating glacé cherries, angelica and macaroons.
Canary pudding: a light yellow pudding rich in butter and eggs, flavoured with lemon rind.
Date pudding: boiled or steamed suet pudding with bread crumbs, brown sugar and chopped dates.
Ginger pudding: either a boiled suet pudding or a lighter, steamed version. Usually with brown sugar, golden syrup or treacle.
Jam pudding: any boiled or steamed pudding flavoured or sweetened with jam.
Marmalade pudding: more popular than *jam pudding*.
Plum pudding: the familiar festive pudding, also made in plainer versions. Usually made with bread crumbs, flour, suet, brown sugar, raisins, currants and eggs, but with many variations.
Roly-poly: suet pastry rolled up with a sweet filling, tied in a cloth and boiled. Served with custard or sweet sauce.
Steamed pudding: a lighter alternative to boiled puddings, often with rising agents or whipped egg whites and less fat. Many versions.
Suet pudding: the basic form of boiled pudding. High suet content and long boiling could make it deceptively light.

Treacle pudding: boiled pudding, usually with suet, with treacle and orange or lemon juice, candied peel or spices for extra flavour.
Fig pudding: boiled pudding, usually with suet, featuring chopped dried figs.

Dumplings and fritters
Apple dumpling: individual puddings, each of a peeled apple, encased in suet pastry, boiled or baked.
Apple fritters: apple slices dipped in batter, then deep fried and sprinkled with fine sugar. Similar treatment was given to other fruits.
Bread fritters: bread slices dipped in milk, then in egg and fried.

Baked puddings and custards
Apple Charlotte: apple purée baked in a plain mould lined with slices of buttered bread until the crust was crisp and brown. Unmoulded and served hot.
Apple pudding: various baked puddings of apples and bread crumbs, layered. *Brown Betty* was an example.
Baked apple: apples cored, stuffed with butter, sugar, dates, spices, etc and baked whole. Served with cream or custard.
Baked batter pudding: plain sweet egg batter baked. Sometimes varied with dried fruit or jam.
Baked bread pudding: layers of thin buttered bread and dried fruit in a baked egg custard. Many variants.
Baked custard: a custard of eggs, milk, sugar and flavouring, baked slowly.
Baked rice pudding: two main versions: rice, milk and sugar baked slowly until thick, or a baked egg custard 'filled' with boiled rice. A similar pudding was made with sago.
Boiled custard: the best versions were thickened with egg yolks. Others used whole egg. Custard powder was also becoming popular.
Queen pudding: a fine bread pudding base spread with jam and topped with meringue.
Omelette soufflée: a sweetened omelette for which the egg yolks and whites were whipped separately. Sometimes filled with jam.

Cold puddings and jellies
Apple jelly pudding: two types were popular – a jellied apple purée, sometimes lightened with whipped cream or egg whites, and a fancy dish of cooked apples set in jelly.
Apple snow: a snowy white froth of apple purée of apples and whipped egg whites.
Blancmange: a plain milk or almond milk pudding set with gelatine, isinglass or cornflower.
Calf foot jelly: crystal clear jelly flavoured with lemons and sherry or white wine. The gelatine was obtained by boiling a calf foot. Sometimes used to mould fruit in elaborate arrangements.
Charlotte russe: a jellied milk or cream pudding set in a mould lined with sponge finger biscuits. Many variations.
Chocolate cream: a moulded pudding of chocolate, egg yolk custard and sometimes whipped cream, set with gelatine. Also made in simpler versions.
Custard jelly pudding: various moulded puddings based on egg yolk custard strengthened with gelatine. Usually decorated.
Fruit salad: any selection of sliced fruit with sugar or syrup Sometimes sherry, wine or brandy were included.
Junket: the well known pudding of milk set with an extract of rennet. Simple or elegant with rum or sherry, spices and a topping of whipped cream.

Lemon jelly: crystal clear jelly of water, white wine or sherry, loaf sugar, gelatine and lemons. Moulded plain or with fruit.
Lemon sponge: a lemon jelly pudding given a sponge-like texture by the incorporation of whipped egg whites and set in a mould.
Orange sponge: similar to lemon sponge.
Sponge cake pudding: a cold pudding made from sponge cakes, often incorporating jam or fruit, custard and sometimes wine.
Stewed apple: a simple sweet with boiled rice, custard or *blancmange* or the basis for an elaborate presentation dish.
Strawberry cream: a jellied pudding of stiffened strawberry purée and whipped cream, moulded.
Tapioca cream: a cold milk pudding incorporating tapioca. *Rice cream* was similar.
Trifle: a compound of sponge cake soaked with sherry and spread with jam, scattered with macaroons or ratafias, covered with egg yolk custard and usually topped with whipped cream.
Wine jelly: flavoured with port wine, claret or sherry.

BAKING
Biscuits and small cakes
Biscuits: there were many recipes for biscuits. Among those not quite popular enough to be listed separately were *kisses, bachelor's buttons, brandy snaps, coconut macaroons* and sponge, currant, ratafia, oat, cornflour and shortbread biscuits.
Buns: the many buns and cookies included *cornflour cakes, lemon cakes, raspberry buns* and *London buns*.
Coconut biscuits: sweet biscuits or cookies incorporating desiccated coconut.
Ginger biscuits: a wide variety of recipes and names such as *ginger nuts, ginger snaps* and *ginger wafers*. They usually included butter, brown sugar and treacle.
Lemon biscuits: plain rolled biscuits flavoured with lemon essence or grated lemon rind.
Meringues: small meringues filled with whipped cream or jam.
Oat cake: the traditional plain Scots oat cake of oatmeal, water and shortening.
Patty cakes: a variety of little cakes, either plain with a few currants or citrus peel, or extravagantly decorated.
Queen cakes: patty cakes rich with butter, eggs and currants. They became particular favourites.
Rock cakes: cookies baked in 'little rocky lumps' or 'rough heaps', usually including currants and candied peel.
Shortbread: the still-popular rich, sweet, buttery biscuit-type confection from Scotland.

Pastry
Apple pie: prepared apples baked either in a double crust of short pastry or under a single crust.
Banbury cakes: small flat cakes of flaky pastry filled with fruit mince, topped with sugar.
Cheese cakes: little tartlets, usually of puff pastry, with some kind of curd and egg yolk filling or, more likely, a rather distant imitation of it.
Cream puffs: choux pastry puffs filled with whipped cream – *profiteroles*, in fact.
Lemon meringue pie: the well known pie of lemon custard hidden between a short pastry base and a sweet meringue. Better known simply as *lemon pie*.
Puff pastry: the richest, lightest flaky pastry.
Flaky pastry: slightly less rich than *puff pastry*, and more easily made.

Rough puff pastry: a quickly made puff pastry for ordinary meat pies, sausage rolls etc.
Short pastry: the common, short-textured pastry, generally preferred for fruit tarts and pies.
Suet pastry: pastry made with suet (the thick layer of pure fat surrounding kidneys) as the shortening. Generally used for boiled puddings.

Cakes

Coffee cake: either a cake featuring coffee flavouring or a plainer cake intended to be taken with coffee.
Cornflour cake: plain, but soft and light in texture, made with cornflour or a mixture of it and wheat flour.
Currant cake: any cake – plain or rich – with currants.
Fruit cake: a large dark fruit cake for Christmas, wedding or birthday celebrations, usually encased in almond paste and *royal icing,* decorated elaborately. Light fruit cake for ordinary use.
Gingerbread: the most popular of cakes, generally made with butter and treacle or golden syrup.
Madeira cake: a rich, fine-textured butter cake sometimes flavoured with grated lemon or orange rind and topped with candied citrus peel.
Marble cake: made of chocolate and vanilla batters dropped in alternating spoonfuls or swirled together to produce a marble effect.
Orange cake: a whisked sponge or butter cake incorporating finely grated orange rind and, usually, orange juice. Normally with orange icing.
Plain cake: the stand-by of every kitchen. The name was often fancier than the cake.
Rainbow cake: a cake of chocolate, white and pink layers sandwiched with icing.
Seed cake: flavoured with caraway seeds. Usually a rich butter cake.
Snow cake: a very light, pure white cake made with whipped egg whites, but no yolks. Also called *angel cake, feather cake,* or simply *white cake.*
Sponge cake: the still-popular light, open textured cake featuring whisked eggs. There were several ways of making it.
Sponge roll: a sponge mixture baked in a large flat tin, spread with jam, then rolled up. Often called *Swiss roll.*
Sultana cake: either rich or plain, it featured sultanas.
Victoria sandwich: two light butter cakes sandwiched with jam. Also known as *Victoria sponge* or *jam sandwich.*

Bread

Bread: often home-made, usually with home-made liquid yeast.
Milk bread: bread made without yeast, but with a chemical rising agent, usually baking powder. Sometimes called *soda bread.*

Scones, teacakes and pancakes

Drop scones: scones or pancakes of batter dropped from a spoon onto a greased pan or girdle. There were many variants.
Pancakes: plain, rolled with lemon and sugar or *French,* thin cakes oven-baked on saucers or plates, spread with jam or preserves and folded over.
Scones: the only recipe certain to be found in any Federation book.
Tea cake: quite plain cake, quickly made, served hot with butter at afternoon tea.

Icing and sweet fillings
Boiled icing: thick sugar syrup beaten into stiffly whipped egg white.
Chocolate icing: a paste of chocolate melted with water, thickened with icing sugar.
Icing: common icing was made by beating together egg white, lemon juice and icing sugar.
Lemon cheese: a cooked compound of butter, sugar, eggs and lemon.
Mincemeat: a mixture of apples, suet, dried fruit, sugar, brandy, lemon juice and spice packed into jars to mature and later used to fill pies and tarts.
Royal icing: a mixture of icing sugar, egg white and lemon juice. Used for cake decoration.

MISCELLANEOUS
Pickles and chutneys
Pickled onions: tiny white onions pickled with vinegar and spices.
Tomato chutney: ripe tomatoes, apples, onions, raisins, brown sugar, vinegar, garlic, chillies and ginger, minced and boiled slowly. Many variations.

Savoury sauces
Anchovy sauce: white sauce or melted butter flavoured with bottled anchovy sauce and finished with lemon juice. Served with fish dishes.
Apple sauce: a purée of boiled apples finished with lemon juice, butter and sugar. For roast pork, goose or duck.
Aspic jelly: clear jelly of well flavoured meat stock.
Béchamel sauce: white sauce flavoured with herbs and vegetables such as onion, celery and carrot.
Bread sauce: milk thickened with bread crumbs and flavoured with onion and peppercorns. For roast fowl, turkey, some game birds and sucking pig.
Brown sauce: foundation sauce of stock thickened with roux, flavoured with vegetables browned in butter.
Caper sauce: any sauce that featured capers.
Curry sauce: any sauce with curry powder. Made with stock or milk, it usually included onion, often apple and sometimes other flavourings.
Egg sauce: white sauce or *melted butter* with chopped hard-boiled egg. For boiled dishes of fowl, fish, calf's head or celery.
Hollandaise sauce: butter beaten into egg yolk and lemon juice or flavoured vinegar over very gentle heat. Served with asparagus and some fish dishes. Also called *Dutch sauce*.
Maître d'hôtel sauce: white sauce finished with lemon juice, butter and chopped parsley. For grilled steak, baked or fried fish, calf's or sheep's head.
Mayonnaise sauce: a thick emulsion made by whisking oil and vinegar into raw egg yolk.
Melted butter (sauce): a common sauce of butter and water thickened with flour. Used for almost anything.
Mint sauce: a thin sauce of finely chopped mint steeped in vinegar and sugar, served with hot or cold roast lamb.
Onion sauce: white sauce with onions.
Oyster sauce: white sauce with oysters. For grilled beef steak, boiled or steamed fish, and boiled turkey.
Parsley sauce: white sauce finished with finely chopped parsley. For boiled fish, mutton, celery and parsnips.
Piquant sauce: usually *brown sauce* finished with vinegar, herbs, capers and chopped gherkins and served with dishes such as roast guinea fowl, grilled mutton breast and boiled ox tongue.

Prawn sauce: white sauce with prawns or *melted butter* sauce made with fish and prawn head stock; finished with lemon juice.
Salad dressing: various concoctions designed to substitute for mayonnaise.
Tartare sauce: mayonnaise with capers, chopped gherkins and sometimes herbs and mustard added. Served with grilled fish, kidney or spatchcock or with ox-tongue.
Tomato sauce: probably the most important sauce in Australian cookery; recipes abounded.
White sauce: a foundation sauce of milk thickened with white roux, often used by itself for vegetables and other dishes.

Sweet sauces
Custard sauce: the ubiquitous custard made as a pouring sauce.
Jam sauce: a pouring sauce for puddings.
Lemon sauce: a lemon flavoured syrup thickened with cornflour or egg yolk. Popular for many puddings.
Sabayon sauce: often called *German wine sauce*, it was made by whisking egg yolks, sherry and fine sugar over simmering water in a double saucepan.

Jams and preserves
Marmalade: the famous jam of bitter oranges.
Melon jam: made from any suitable melon, usually with lemon and often with ginger or another fruit for interest.
Quince jam or jelly: the jam, easier to make, seems to have been the more popular.
Tomato jam: usually with lemon. Ginger or pineapple were often added.

Confectionery
Toffee: the only home-made confectionery popular enough to be included. Others included *coconut ice* and fondant in various forms.

Drinks
Claret cup: claret, lemons, sugar and soda water with varying finishing touches. The only real alcoholic beverage common enough to warrant mention.
Coffee: the most common methods were 'English' (boiled) and 'French' (infused).
Ginger beer: a ginger-flavoured, mildly alcoholic home-made beverage. There was no standard recipe.
Lemonade: not bottled fizz, but a drink made with fresh lemons.
Lemon syrup: a lemon-flavoured sugar syrup that could be diluted with water as required. Usually made with citric or tartaric acid and lemon essence.
Tea: most cookery books gave directions for it.

Other preparations
Batter for frying: sometimes known as French batter.
Caramel: sugar heated until quite brown, then dissolved in little water. Used for colouring for soups, stews and gravies.
Clarified fat: pan drippings or excess fat cut from fresh meat and reclaimed for use as shortening.
Fried parsley: parsley deep-fried very briefly. Used for garnishes.
Pickle: various mixtures for curing meat. Both liquid and dry mixtures were used.
Porridge: a popular breakfast dish of oatmeal boiled in water.

Sage and onion stuffing: a mixture of sage, onions, bread crumbs etc. The customary stuffing for pork, geese and ducks.

Yeast: most books gave at least one recipe for capturing and 'growing' natural yeasts for bread-making. They were all liquid preparations.

INVALID AND SICKROOM COOKERY

Apple water: an infusion of apples made by pouring boiling water onto raw or roasted apples. Lemon and sugar were added.

Barley water: an extract of pearl barley in water, with lemon and sugar.

Beef jelly: a savoury jelly made from boiled meat and bones or by setting ordinary beef stock with gelatine.

Beef tea: an extract of beef. In various strengths, raw or cooked, as required.

Savoury custard: beef or chicken stock and beaten eggs, steamed.

Gruel: a thin porridge of groats or oatmeal made with milk, water or a mixture of both.

Milk drink: a variety of liquid preparations of milk. Examples included *baked milk* and *milk and suet*.

Toast water: an infusion of toast in water.

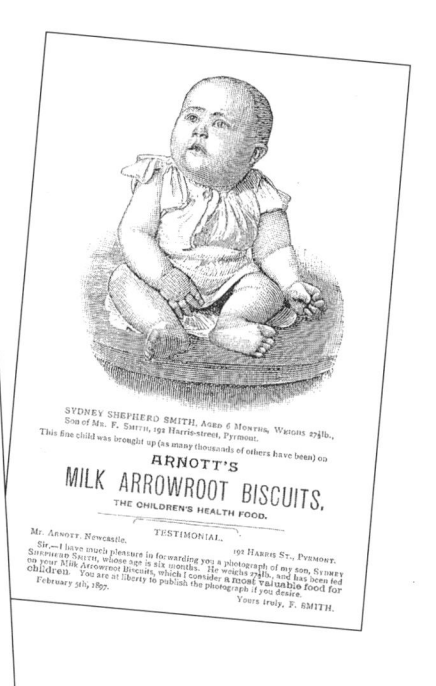

Notes

PRE-PRANDIAL
1. Tyrrell, 1952
2. Abbott, 1864 (the first published cookery book by an Australian author, now very rare).

CHAPTER 1
1. Rawson, 1895
2. Jewry, nd
3. Morison, 1867
4. Ada Cambridge, *Thirty Years in Australia*, London, 1903. Quoted in Teale, 1978
5. Gould, 1896
6. Twopenny, 1883
7. The first edition I have been able to locate was published in 1914. After mentioning its purpose as a school textbook the preface continues: 'It is hoped that the simple and economical recipes contained in this little book will also be of great practical value to all housewives, especially the more inexperienced ones.'
8. In the preface to her *Goulburn Cookery Book* (1899) Jean Rutledge says: 'Many of the dishes are old familiar friends, and it is often taken for granted that anyone can make them without instructions. Such is not the case.'
9. Knox, 1936, is a book of recipes contributed by 'prominent Australian hostesses' under the title *Something Different for Dinner*; Porter, 1949 *The Chef Suggests: Strange and exciting dishes with delicacies of the table for today and tomorrow* is another example.
10. *Don Dunstan's Cookbook*, 1976
11. War Chest Fund, 1917 *War Chest Cookery Book*. A revised edition was later issued as the *Kindergarten Cookery Book* in aid of the Kindergarten Union (Second edition 1924).
12. Disabled Men's Association of Australia *'All in One Recipe' Book and Household Guide*; and *Everyday and Everyway Recipe Book*, nd
13. PWMA, 1895. I believe the Victorian book was originally published in 1904 as *The P.W.M.U. Cookery Book*. The earliest edition I have been able to find is the *New P.W.M.U. Cookery Book*, 1931, CWA, 1937.
14. *Australian Dictionary of Biography*
15. Abbott, 1864

CHAPTER 2
1. *Australian Dictionary of Biography*

2. See Tyrrell, 1952. George Robertson also published *The Book of Diet* for Muskett in 1898.
3. Some authors (including Tyrrell, 1952, who should have known) list this book as 1893, taking the date from the preface. It is unlikely that a book completed in September, 1893 would have been published in London before the end of the same year. In any case, the date is established firmly enough by several of Muskett's later works, which include advertisements giving its date as 1894.
4. Tyrrell, 1952
5. Wicken, 1888
6. Wicken 1898
7. Recipes are regarded as 'typical' if they, or a similar recipe, can be found in at least half the common cookery books.
8. Johns, 1906; *Australian Dictionary of Biography*.

CHAPTER 3
1. Much of the educational history has been constructed by making detailed comparisons of secondary sources: Kyle, 1986; Morris, 1980; NSW Department of Education, 1980; Peacock, 1982. Original sources included Muskett, 1894; Wicken, sixth edition, nd.; Board of Technical Education of New South Wales *Report* for 1885, brochure for the *Melbourne Centennial Exhibition 1888*, *Calendar of Sydney Technical College for 1887*, *Report* for 1887; Technical Education Branch, 1909.
2. Quoted in Peacock, 1982.
3. NSW Educational Gazette 1 January 1897, reproduced in Peacock, 1892.
4. Quoted in Peacock, 1982.
5. National Training School, 1886. The school later moved to Buckingham Palace Road.
6. Ferguson's *Bibliography of Australia* listed publication of recipes given by Mrs Wicken at cookery classes in both locations. The Hobart publication was called a *Supplement to Kingswood Cookery Book*.
7. According to Peacock, 1982 '... one of the original group of teachers trained in 1894'. Amie Monro's second edition, the earliest I have seen, was published in 1909.
8. Sic. Technical Education Branch, 1909.
9. Wicken, 1891. In the 1888 edition she said that after living for some time in the colony she found 'that there were many recipes in it which were quite useless in Australia.
10. The Presbyterian book and *Mrs Maclurcan's Cookery Book*.
11. Good Housekeeping Institute, 1972; Allison, 1990 (which says that it is so named because of its shape).
12. *Illustrated Australian News*, 3 November 1875, quoted in Cannon, 1975.
13. *Illustrated Australian News,* 1 May 1891, quoted in Cannon, 1975.
14. Pearson, 1894. She also published an *Australian Book on Fruits*, dealing with canning, preserving, jellies, jams, puddings, summer sweets and drinks.
15. Peacock, 1982.
16. Originally published as the *Theory of Cookery* earlier in the same year.
17. Senn, 1901
18. Glasse, 1747, *Glossary*
19. Sugg, 1890.
20. It is autographed with the date 24-7-09.

CHAPTER 4
1. Much of the historical material is taken from *Centenary 1991*, distributed by the PMWA of NSW; *Jottings*, 1941 and early reports of the PWMA.

2. Many British settlers abused alcohol and opium, the latter in the form of *laudanum*.
3. *Jottings*, 1941
4. China was often referred to as the 'celestial empire'.
5. Annual Report, 1895
6. PWMA, 1902
7. Story, 1900; Monro made the same claim. However, recipes rarely specified mutton suet.
8. Schauer, 1909
9. Civil Service Store, 1899
10. Ross, 1907
11. Margaret Visser (1991) describes a formal European meal as a three-fold pattern of overture, climax and sweet final flourish.
12. This was a common expression, sometimes abbreviated to 'the upper ten'. The lower classes were sometimes described as 'the million'.
13. PWMA, 1895.
14. *Australian Dictionary of Biography*
15. Mrs W.M. Hughes, wife of the Prime Minister from late 1915 to early 1923, contributed three: cream puffs, a baked pudding of apples and custard, and 'a very good floor polish'.
16. Gilmore, c. 1915
17. 'Salting it back', the cook called it in a previous recipe.
18. Schauer, 1909
19. R.M. also contributed a recipe for suet dumplings boiled in treacle sauce.
20. The only other mention of *flappers* I have found in early Australian books was a fried version made of Granuma porridge. It was a promotional recipe (Inglis, 1896).

CHAPTER 5

1. *Australian Dictionary of Biography*
2. The first was offered as one 'written entirely for the colonies... and for those people who cannot afford to buy a Mrs Beeton or a Warne, but who can afford three shillings for this'. It was an ambitious price; the *Goulburn* and *Presbyterian* each cost only one.
3. Rawson, 1894
4. Rawson, 1895
5. Gollan, 1978 gave a good account of the development of the kitchen and kitchen equipment from colonial days to the twentieth century. I have therefore not dealt with the subject at any length here.
6. Rawson, 1894
7. Wicken, 1898
8. Rawson, 1895
9. Schauer, 1909
10. 'He was a bold man that first ate an Oyster' (Jonathan Swift 1667-1745).
11. Elsewhere she added paddymelon (a small scrub wallaby, not to be confused with the two fruits of the same name).
12. From the introduction by Helen Rutledge to the National Trust edition. The *Australian Dictionary of Biography* gave her name as Jane Ruth and her mother as Mary Emma.
13. Rutledge, 1937. Helen Rutledge noted in the fortieth edition that the thirty-sixth was published in 1936 and was the last with the old text: this can not be so, as my copy of the thirty sixth is the first *New Goulburn* and its preface is dated 1937.

14. Symons, 1982
15. Sic. Baking time should probably read 'from 1-1/4 to 2-1/4 hours'.
16. The same was said of *a good currant cake* and *a good plain cake*.
17. Gouffé was described by *Larousse Gastronomique* as one of the greatest chefs of the nineteenth century. Born in Paris 1807 and taught by Carême, he established a restaurant which became one of the most famous in Paris. He also published several cookery books. A similar test for oven temperature, but using flour sprinkled on a tray, was given in the Presbyterian book.
18. Forget the bananas! This pudding needs – and usually has – jam. Raspberry, blackberry or black currant are best.

CHAPTER 6
1. *Australian Etiquette*, 1886
2. Based on Martha Rutledge's article in Vol. 7 of the *Australian Dictionary of Biography* (pp. 101-2).
3. Wicken's *Australian Home, a Handbook of Domestic Economy*, and Rawson's *Australian Enquiry Book of Household and General Information*.
4. William, nd
5. Abbott, 1864
6. Local cookery competitions became a significant force in the circulation of recipes as the network of rural agricultural shows grew. Emily Futter's collection in the nineteen twenties included several recipes for *plum pudding*; one of which took first prize at the Braidwood and Cooma shows in 1907.
7. An advertisement in Futter, 1926 listed departments for grocery, provisions, cakes, wines and spirits, cigars and tobacco, confectionery, perfumery, drugs, china and glass, cutlery and silverplate, brassware, ironmongery, electrical, stationery, hand bags, hosiery and fancy goods. 'The Stores' also boasted an extensive mail order service for country customers.
8. Sic.
9. Mrs Aronson did not explain how a generous offering of fruit and a pint of jelly were *both* to be fitted into a pint mould.
10. This seems to have been a popular saying. The *Sydney Mail*, 7 December 1904, in a review of the *Goulburn Cookery Book* (first published some five years earlier), said: 'Of the making of cookery books there would appear to be no end, for yet another has arrived to swell the list.' Compare it also with the opening apology in Lady Hackett's *The Australian Household Guide*, 1916: 'Of the making of cookery books there is literally no end. They fall from the press "thick as autumnal leaves that strew the brooks in Vallombrosa [a resort near Florence]". '

CHAPTER 7
1. The following abridged account draws on the history published by the Wentworth Hotel's Managing Director, Charles Maclurcan in a small celebratory booklet in 1946. Additional material from Clune, 1961; Scott, 1958 and Maclehose, 1839. The Wentworth story is also told in Kennedy, 1991 (a book published to celebrate the twenty-fifth anniversary of its successor, the Sheraton Wentworth).
2. Radi, c. 1988 recorded that she was first married to one Robert Watson Wigham, was widowed, and married Donald Boulton Maclurcan in 1877. However, her account differs in several details from those generally accepted. For example, Maclurcan, 1946 gave his father's name as Donald Samuel.

3. Maclurcan, 1899
4. Quoted in Maclurcan, 1899
5. Ross, 1907
6. Freeman, 1989
7. Acton, 1865
8. Sugg, 1890

CHAPTER 8
1. Cannon, 1975
2. Broomham, 1987
3. Wilkinson, 1876. Ferguson's *Bibliography of Australia* lists an 1867 paperback publication of 24 pages by Edward Abbott entitled *Hebrew Cookery*. The recipes were apparently extracted from his *English and Australian Cookery Book* of 1864. It is open to argument whether a threepenny pamphlet that repeated material already published can fairly claim to be Australia's second cookery book. I believe Wilkinson should have the honour. The second claim rests on the belief that the earliest British book on gas cooking was Marie Sugg's *The Art of Cooking by Gas*, 1890.
4. Peacock, 1982
5. Broomham, 1987
6. Peacock, 1982
7. Peacock, 1982 commented, in relation to New South Wales, that 'As early as 1905 teachers commenced lectures and demonstrations to nurses. This work continued, with teachers lecturing from local hospitals in invalid cookery.'
8. Muskett, 1909
9. The correct name for this dish is *potage Bagration*.
10. Rutledge, 1899
11. Rawson, 1895
12. *Green and Gold Cookery Book*
13. Dods, 1829. Mistress Margaret Dods was a character in Sir Walter Scott's novel *St. Ronan's Well*. McNeill, 1929 claimed that the name Margaret Dods came from an inn keeper at Howgate and that the character was based on another inn keeper, one Miss Marian Ritchie of Peebles. St. Ronan's was at Innerleithen, in the county of Peebles. The cookery book published in the name of Meg Dods was said to be written by Mrs Isobel Christian Johnston, wife of an Edinburgh publisher and author of *Edinburgh Tales* and other works.
14. Carter, 1730
15. From the recipe for *croquettes of chicken*. It is hard to see how an extra egg yolk would help if the mixture is too thick.

CHAPTER 9
1. An edition of the *Commonsense Cookery Book* even advertised a competition, promising that '£1 a week for life will be assured to the housewife who collects the largest number of lids from the tins of Aunt Mary's Baking Powder before the 31st March, 1927.' The competition helped to establish the date of the edition.
2. See Farrer, 1980
3. Rawson, 1895
4. See Farrer, 1980

CHAPTER 10
1. PWMA, 1895
2. Maclurcan, 1909
3. Muskett, 1894
4. McGowan, 1911
5. Maclurcan, 1905
6. Examples are in Schauer, 1909; Rutledge, 1899 and McGowan, 1911 respectively. The *Commonsense Cookery Book* of 1926 explained them as 'fried scones'.
7. Isabella Beeton gave them as puff pastry rings filled with brightly coloured preserve.
8. Abbott, 1864
9. PWMA, 1895. Burton, 1993 commented that the British in India in the early nineteenth century 'liked bananas mashed with milk and sugar, in which they fancied a resemblance to strawberries and cream.'
10. Wicken, 1898. In a similar recipe in Muskett, 1894 she said that the sauce 'should be of a bright red colour'.
11. Eg Aronson, 1900; Ross, 1907; Monro, 1913; and Futter, 1924
12. Aronson, 1900
13. Muskett, 1894; Ross, 1907
14. Jean Rutledge called these *Little pigs in blankets*. To her, *Angels on horseback* were seasoned oysters just warmed through, placed on pieces of fried bacon and rounds of anchovy toast.

CHAPTER 11
1. Gilmore, c. 1915
2. Rutledge, 1899
3. Wicken, 1898; also *mock venison* in Aronson, 1900
4. PWMA, 1895. The recipe actually called for 'pork', but clearly pork fat was required. The error was never corrected in later editions.
5. Muskett, 1894
6. PWMA, 1895
7. Wicken, 1898. Compare this with the way her successor, Amie Monro, introduced the same subject a decade later in her own book: 'The question of what to do with cold meat is such an important one that I feel sure a few hints on this kind of cookery, together with some tasty dishes, will be acceptable.'
8. Payne, c. 1880
9. Isinglass is a jelly-forming substance made from the air bladders of fish. It was a forerunner to gelatine, which is made by boiling the bones and other parts of animals killed for the meat industry.
10. The Federation cooks were by no means the first to present 'white food' coloured. Raffald, 1782 included a *green blanc-mange of isinglass*. It was coloured with spinach juice and garnished with red and white flowers.
11. Wicken, 1898; Maclurcan, 1905
12. I have not attempted to trace the history of Fowlers Vacola. The 'vacuum method' of preserving fruit and vegetables seems to have been unknown to Federation cookery writers, although Fowler was well established in Australia by the early 1920s.
13. CWA, 1937
14. Quoted in Corrie, 1904
15. Farrer, 1980
16. Rawson, 1895

17. Muskett 1894; Wicken, 1898 and Ross, 1907; Maclurcan, 1905 respectively
18. Wicken, 1898 and Schauer, 1909; Rawson, 1895 respectively
19. PWMA, 1895 and Rutledge, 1899; Rutledge, 1899
20. Wicken, 1898
21. Rawson, 1894
22. *Aunt Nelly's pudding*, Beeton, 1861. The same pudding was included in *The Enquirer's Oracle; or What to do and How to do it*, published in Britain and Australia in the late nineteenth century. Quoted from the *Presbyterian Cookery Book*.
23. Smell was not the only objection. Henrietta McGowan advised that the water in which cabbage was cooked should be poured carefully down the sink. 'Cabbage water attracts meat flies by the thousand.'
24. 'Keeyuga' is explained as 'Western District broad-lip dialect' meaning 'within'.
25. For further information see, for example, Kingston, 1975.

CHAPTER 12

1. This miserable substitution was not an Australian invention. A British book (Payne, c. 1880) mentioned 'an admirable modern invention called Swiss milk, preserved in tins' and advised that 'when... you have any compound requiring cream and sugar, by using Swiss milk with ordinary milk you get an exactly similar result, at far less cost.'
2. The West Redfern Cookery School version was made of ½ pint water, 1 dessertspoon arrowroot, 1 dessertspoon sugar, 4 drops cochineal, juice of ½ lemon. It was to be served with *Urney pudding* or *lemon pudding*. The same school taught that *melted butter* could be made with milk.
3. Sic.
4. Wannan's *Folk Medicine* (1970) quoted a reference to an old English superstition that cats suck the breath of infants and so cause their death. Sometimes, it seems, they paid with their own lives.
5. Opium was the most widely used drug and was the basis of pain killers such as laudanum and chlorodyne. Its use led to widespread drug addiction.
6. Rutledge, 1899.
7. Ross, 1907

CHAPTER 14

1. For more information see Freeman, 1989; *Larousse Gastronomique*, 1961; Beeton, 1861.
2. Beeton, 1861
3. Sic.
4. See Acton, 1865; the second reference is probably to *The Shilling Cookery* by Alexis Soyer, published about 1855.
5. According to *Larousse Gastronomique*, 1961 it was popularised by Urbain Dubois about 1860. Beeton, 1861 included several *menus à la russe*.
6. From *Australian Etiquette*, 1885; edited and re-arranged.
7. Sic.
8. *D'artois parmesan* were tiny savouries of puff pastry layers sandwiched with a cheese mixture, cut in rounds and baked.
9. *Verney Pudding* was a steamed pudding with raspberry jam, probably originating from an old English family. The Presbyterian book gave a similar pudding under the name 'Olney or Urney'.

CHAPTER 15
1. See, for example, Denholm, 1979.
2. For a detailed analysis of Anglo-Indian cookery see Burton, 1993.
3. The Australian-born population outnumbered immigrants from about 1870.
4. Symons, 1982
5. 'Some of these recipes are over sixty years old, while others have stood the test of time much longer.'
6. Cannon, 1975 explains the term 'cocky' (cockatoo) as a 'small farmer who picked up a bare livelihood off the ground like birds pecking up grain.'
7. Something of its Australian history is given in Symons, 1982.
8. Monro, 1913 (fourth edition – I have not been able to establish when she first published the recipe); McGowan, 1911.
9. Hackett, 1916

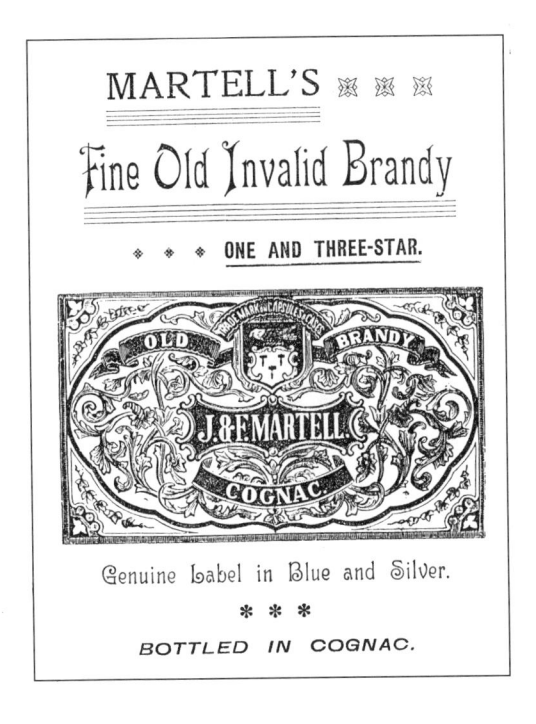

MARTELL'S

Fine Old Invalid Brandy

✦ ✦ ✦ ONE AND THREE-STAR.

Genuine Label in Blue and Silver.

✳ ✳ ✳

BOTTLED IN COGNAC.

References

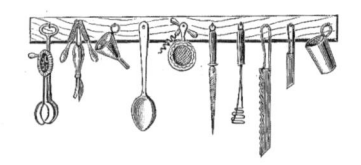

Abbott, Edward *The English and Australian Cookery Book: Cookery for the many, as well as for the "upper ten thousand." By an Australian Aristologist.* Sampson Low, Son, and Marston, London, 1864. (Most of the text, edited and re-arranged, is readily available in *The Colonial Cook Book: the recipes of a by-gone Australia*, published by Paul Hamlyn, Sydney, 1970.)

Acton, Eliza *Modern Cookery for Private Families, Reduced to a System of Easy Practice in a series of Carefully Tested Receipts.* First published by Longmans, London, 1845; final edition 1865, reproduced by Elek Books, London, 1966.

Allison, Sonia *The Cassell Food Dictionary.* Cassell, London, 1990.

Aronson, Mrs F B *XXth Century Cooking and Home Decoration.* William Brooks, Sydney 1900.

Aronson, Mrs Fred *Excell Cook Book containing 316 selected recipes. Also Many Short Articles on Practical Cookery. For all homes.* Junior Red Cross, Sydney, 1923.

Australian Dictionary of Biography. Melbourne University Press, 1986, 1988.

Australian Etiquette, or the Rules and Usages of the best society in the Australian Colonies together with their Sports, Pastimes, Games, and Amusements. Facsimile of 1886 edition published by J. M. Dent, 1980. First published by People's Publishing Company, Melbourne.

Beeton, Isabella *Beeton's Book of Household Management.* Facsimile of 1861 edition, Chancellor Press, London 1984.

[Beeton, Isabella] *Mrs Beeton's Cookery Book and household guide.* Ward, Lock, Bowden, London, 1892.

Board of Technical Education of New South Wales *Reports* 1885, 1887.

Board of Technical Education of New South Wales *Calendar of Sydney Technical College for 1887.*

Broomham, Rosemary *First Light: 150 years of gas.* Hale & Iremonger, Sydney, 1987.

Burton, David *The Raj at Table: A Culinary History of the British in India.* Faber and Faber, London, 1993.

Cannon, Michael *Australia in the Victorian Age* (Three volumes). Thomas Nelson Australia, Melbourne, 1975, 1978.

Carter, Charles *The Complete Practical Cook: or, a new system of the whole art and mystery of cookery.* Facsimile of 1730 edition. Prospect Books, London, 1984.

Cassell's New Dictionary of Cookery. Cassell, London, New York, Toronto and Melbourne, 1912.

Cassell's Shilling Cookery. Edited by A G Payne. Cassell, London, 1900.

Civil Service Store, Brisbane *The Twentieth Century Cookery Book*, 1899.

Clune, Frank *Saga of Sydney: The Birth, Growth and Maturity of the Mother City of Australia.* Subscribers' Edition, Sydney, 1961.
Colcord, Anna L *A Friend in the Kitchen: What to cook and how to cook it.* Echo, Limited, Victoria, 2nd edition 1898 (also later editions).
Complete Cookery Encyclopedia. Tudor edition. Octopus, London, 1973.
Corrie, Sophie *The Art of Canning, Bottling and Preserving Fruits.* William Brooks, Sydney, second edition 1898, fourth edition 1904, sixth edition 1913.
Country Women's Association of New South Wales *The Coronation Cookery Book.* Jessie Sawyer O.B.E. and Sarah Moore-Sims, eds, nd (1937).
Defoe, Daniel *A Tour through the Whole Island of Great Britain.* First published 1724-6, republished by Penguin Books, London, 1971 (reprinted in Penguin Classics, 1986).
Denholm, David *The Colonial Australians.* Penguin Books, Melbourne, 1979.
Disabled Men's Association of Australia *The "All in One" Recipe Book and Household Guide.* Veritas, Melbourne, nd (1920's).
Disabled Men's Association of Australia *The Everyday and Everyway Recipe Book.* Veritas Publishing Co., Melbourne, nd (c. 1926).
Dods, Margaret *The Cook and Housewife's Manual: a practical system of modern domestic cookery and family management.* Fourth edition, published by Oliver & Boyd, Edinburgh, 1829. Facsimile published by Rosters, London, 1988. Dods was a fictional character. According to F Marian McNeill (1929) the work was compiled by Mrs Isobel Christian Johnston.
Farrer, K T H *A Settlement Amply Supplied: Food Technology in Nineteenth Century Australia.* Melbourne University Press, Melbourne, 1980.
Freeman, Sarah *Mutton and Oysters: the Victorians and their food.* Victor Gollancz, London, 1989.
Futter, E *Australian Home Cookery.* George B Philip, Sydney, nd (c. 1924) and later.
Gilmore, Mary (ed) *The Worker Cook Book.* The Worker Trustees, Sydney, nd (c. 1915).
[Glasse, Hannah] *The Art of Cookery, made Plain and Easy by a Lady.* First published 1747, London. Facsimile edition Prospect Books, London, 1983.
Gollan, Anne *The Tradition of Australian Cooking.* Australian National University Press, Canberra, 1978.
Good Housekeeping Institute *Good Housekeeping World Cookery.* Universal Books, Sydney, 1972 (first published UK, c.1962).
Gould, Nat *Town and Bush: Stray Notes on Australia.* First published George Routledge, London, 1896. Facsimile edition Penguin Books, 1974.
Green and Gold Cookery Book. Rigby Limited, Adelaide, 27th edition 1960. (Originally issued c. 1923 by Combined Congregational and Baptist Churches of South Australia in aid of the King's College Fund).
Hackett, Lady Deborah *The Australian Household Guide.* E. S. Wigg, Perth, 1916.
James Inglis & Co., *The Housewife's Cookery Book of Economic Recipes, Shewing How to Provide an Excellent Table at a Small Expenditure.* Sydney, 1896.
Jewry, Mary *Warne's Model Cookery and Housekeeping Book, containing Complete Instructions in Household Management.* 'New edition.' Frederick Warne, London, nd (c. 1880-1900).
Johns's *Notable Australians and Who is Who in Australasia.* Fred Johns, Adelaide, 1906.
Kennedy, Buzz *Sydney's Own: 25 years of the Sheraton Wentworth.* Focus Books, Sydney, 1991.
Kidman, James (publisher) *James Kidman's Australian Cookery Book: a collection of practical recipes from the most eminent cooks of Australia.* Sydney, 1890.
Kinglake, Edward *The Australian at Home.* Leadenhall Press, London, c.1891.

Kingston, Beverley *My Wife, My Daughter, and Poor Mary Ann.* Thomas Nelson, Melbourne, 1975.

Knox, Barbara (ed) *Something Different for Dinner.* (By Australian hostesses). Angus & Robertson, Sydney, 1936.

Kyle, Noeline *Her Natural Destiny: the Education of Women in New South Wales.* New South Wales University Press, Sydney, 1986.

Larousse Gastronomique. Paul Hamlyn, London, 1961 (also revised edition, 1988).

McGowan (later Walker), Henrietta C *The Keeyuga Cookery Book.* Lothian, Melbourne, 1911.

Maclehose, James *Picture of Sydney and Strangers' Guide in N.S.W. for 1839.* Facsimile by John Ferguson, Sydney, 1977.

Maclurcan, Hannah *Mrs Maclurcan's Cookery Book, A collection of practical recipes specially suitable for Australia.* George Robertson, 3rd edition 1899 and 6th edition 1905. Also several later editions.

Maclurcan, Charles D *The story of the Wentworth Hotel and the historic site on which it is built.* Sydney, 1946.

McNeill, F Marian *The Scots Kitchen: its traditions and lore with old-time recipes.* Mayflower Books, Britain, 1974 (first published by Blackie, Britain, 1929).

May, Robert *The Accomplisht Cook, or the Whole Art and Mystery of Cookery.* Facsimile of 1685 edition. Prospect Books, UK, 1994. (First edition 1660.)

Monro, Amie M *The Practical Australian Cookery: A collection of up-to-date tried recipes for domestic and general use.* Dymock's Book Arcade, Sydney, fourth edition (revised and enlarged), 1913.

Moore's Australia Almanac and Country Directory. J. J. Moore, Sydney, 1895.

Moorhead, Arthur (editor) *The Australian Blue Book: A National Reference Book containing information on matters Australian from authoritative sources for all members of the community.* Blue Star, Sydney, 1942.

Morison, Reverend James (writing as 'a clergyman') *Australia as it is; or Facts and Features, Sketches and Incidents of Australian life with Notices of New Zealand by a Clergyman thirteen years resident in the interior of New South Wales.* Paul Flesch & Company, Melbourne and Sydney, 1867 (Republished by Charles E. Tuttle, Tokyo, 1967).

Morris, Clarice *'The School on the Hill': a Saga of Australian Life.* Morris Publishing, Sydney, 1980 (reprinted 1984).

Muskett, Philip E *The Art of Living in Australia (together with three hundred Australian cookery recipes and accessory kitchen information by Mrs H. Wicken, Lecturer on Cookery to the Technical College, Sydney).* Eyre and Spottiswoode, Sydney[?], nd (1894).

Muskett, Philip E *The Attainment of Health; and the Treatment of the Different Diseases by Means of Diet (including all the Dietaries necessary for the various maladies).* William Brooks, Sydney, Melbourne, Brisbane, Adelaide, Perth, Wellington, Hobart. Second edition, 1909.

[National Training School] *The Official Handbook for the National Training School for Cookery containing the lessons on cookery which constitute the ordinary course of instruction in the school with lists of utensils necessary, and lessons on cleaning utensils.* (Compiled by R. O. C.) Chapman & Hall, London, 1886.

New South Wales Department of Education *Sydney and the Bush.* Sydney, 1980.

Payne, A G *Choice Dishes at Small Cost.* Cassell, London, 1909.

Payne, A G *Common-sense papers on Cookery.* Cassell Petter & Galpin, London, nd (c. 1880).

Peacock, Jean *A History of Home Economics in New South Wales*. Home Economics Association of New South Wales, Sydney, 1982.
Pearson, Margaret J *Cookery Recipes for the People*. H. Hearne, Melbourne, 1894 (third edition).
Pell, Flora *Tested Cookery Dishes and valuable home hints*. Specialty Press, Melbourne, nd (c. 1916).
People's Housekeeper. A complete guide to comfort, economy, & health. Ward, Lock & Tyler, London, 1876.
Porter, John D *The Chef Suggests: Strange and exciting dishes with delicacies of the table for to-day and to-morrow*. National Press, 1949.
Presbyterian Women's Missionary Association (New South Wales) *Cookery Book of Good and Tried Receipts*. Original editor M MacInnes. S T Leigh & Co, Sydney, third edition 1896 (and subsequent revisions). Later known as Presbyterian Women's Missionary Union of New South Wales *The Presbyterian Cookery Book*. Angus and Robertson, Sydney, 1950 (and subsequent revisions).
Presbyterian Women's Missionary Association of N.S.W. *Jottings*. Robert Dey, Sydney, 1941.
Presbyterian Women's Missionary Union of New South Wales *Centenary 1991*. Unpublished monograph, 1991.
Presbyterian Women's Missionary Union of Victoria *The New P.W.M.U. Cookery Book*. Edited by A M Campbell. Brown, Prior, Melbourne, 1931.
Public School Cookery Teachers' Association of New South Wales *The Common-sense Cookery Book*. Angus & Robertson, Sydney, 1914.
Quong Tart, Margaret *The Life of Quong Tart; or, How a foreigner succeeded in a British community*. Sydney, 1911.
Radi, Heather (ed) *200 Australian Women: a Redress Anthology*. Women's Redress Press, c. 1988.
Raffald, Elizabeth *The Experienced English Housekeeper*. Facsimile of 1782 edition. E&W Books, London, 1970.
Rawson, Mina (Mrs Lance) *The Antipodean Cookery Book and Kitchen Companion*. First published by George Robertson, 1895; facsimile edition by Kangaroo Press Pty Ltd, Sydney, 1992.
Rawson, Mina (Mrs Lance) *The Australian Enquiry Book of Household and General Information: a practical guide for the cottage, villa, and bush home*. First published by Pater and Knapton, 1894; facsimile edition by Kangaroo Press, Sydney, 1984.
Ray, Elizabeth (editor) *The Best of Eliza Acton*. Longmans, Green, London, 1968; republished by Penguin Books, 1974.
Ross, Isabel *Cookery Class Recipes*. Specialty Press, Melbourne, second edition 1907.
Rutledge, Mrs Forster (Jean) *The Goulburn Cookery Book*. Facsimile of 2nd (1905) and 5th (1907) editions, National Trust of Australia, New South Wales, 1973. Also twentieth edition 1917 and twenty third 1918 published by Edwards, Dunlop & Co Limited, Sydney. From thirty-sixth edition (c.1937) known as *The New Goulburn Cookery Book*, edited by Mrs Walton (Thelma) McCarthy.
Schauer, A and M *The Schauer Cookery Book*. Edwards, Dunlop & Co Ltd, Brisbane and Sydney, nd (c. 1909). Later editions published by W. R. Smith & Paterson, Brisbane: *The Schauer Improved Cookery Book, Australian and Seventh Edition* (1931); *Schauer Australian Cookery Book* ninth edition (1946); and *Schauer Cookery Book* twelfth impression (1962). (The last was republished in facsimile by Weldon Publishing, NSW, 1992.)

Schauer, Amy *The Schauer Australian Fruit Preserving Recipe Book*. W. R. Smith & Paterson Pty Ltd, Brisbane, 1975. Facsimile published by Weldon Publishing, NSW, 1992.

Scott, Geoffrey *Sydney's Highways of History*. Georgian House, Melbourne, 1958.

Senn, Charles Herman *The New Century Cookery Book: Practical gastronomy and recherché cookery*. Spottiswoode, London 1901.

Simon, André L *The Wines, Vineyards & Vignerons of Australia*. Paul Hamlyn, Sydney etc, 1966 (reprinted 1970).

Simon, André L & Howe, Robin *Dictionary of Gastronomy*. André Deutsch, Sydney, 1978. (Revision of an earlier work under similar title by Simon.)

Story, Fanny Fawcett *Australian Economic Cookery Book and Housewife's Companion*. Kealy & Philip, Sydney, 1900 (*Technical Series No. 1*, Technical College).

Strickland, Ina *The Commonwealth Cookery Book: Recipes of Housekeeping, Dinner Parties, and General Cookery*. William Brooks, Ltd., Sydney, 1904.

Sugg, Marie Jenny *The Art of Cooking by Gas*. Cassell, London, Paris & Melbourne, 1890.

Symons, Michael *One Continuous Picnic: A history of eating in Australia*. Duck Press, Adelaide, 1982.

Technical Education Branch, NSW *A Quarter Century of Technical Education in New South Wales*. Government Printer, Sydney, 1909.

Teale, Ruth (editor) *Colonial Eve: Sources on Women in Australia 1788-1914*. Oxford University Press, Melbourne, 1978.

Twopenny, Richard *Town Life in Australia*. First published by Elliot Stock, 1883. Facsimile edition by Penguin Books, Melbourne, 1973.

Tyrrell, James R. *Old Books, Old Friends, Old Sydney*. Angus and Robertson, Sydney, 1952.

War Chest Fund *War Chest Cookery Book*. Websdale Shoosmith Ltd, Sydney, 1917. Later revised and republished by Motor Press, Sydney as the *Kindergarten Cookery Book* in aid of the Kindergarten Union, New South Wales (second edition 1924):

West Redfern Cookery School *The Public School Girls' Book of Recipes*. William Brooks, Sydney, 1908.

Wicken, H F *The Kingswood Cookery Book*. First edition Chapman and Hall, London, 1885; second edition George Robertson, Melbourne and Sydney, 1888; third edition Edwards, Dunlop, Sydney, 1891; fourth edition, Angus & Robertson, Sydney, 1898; sixth edition Whitcome and Tombs, Melbourne, nd.

Wilkinson, Alfred J *The Australian Cook: a Complete Manual of Cookery suitable for the Australian colonies with especial reference to the gas cooking stove*. George Robertson, Melbourne, Sydney & Adelaide, 1876.

William, T J *The Australasian Butchers Manual. A book of reference for butchers, bacon curers, small-goodsmen, and other industries associated with the meat and provision trades*. Nd (post 1923).

Index

Recipes
Adelaide sausage 141
Almonds, devilled 205
Angels on horseback 150
Barley water 182
Barrier goose 90
Beef olives 94
Beef tea 181
Beef fillet, braised 151
Biscuits, lemon 71
Brisbane puffs 140
Cabbage, savoury 47
Cake, Gidleigh 91
Cake, good plain 165
Cake, Irish 70
Cake, railway 143
Caramel for colouring 169
Cauliflower au gratin 204
Chicken casserole 106
Curry of cold meat 173
Eggs preserved 168
Fat clarified 168
Fish à la Tasmania 140
Fish pie 94
Fish pudding 128
Fish stew, brown (Jewish) 118
Fish, baked 203
Fowl, roast 203
Fritters, lemon 110
Hodge-podge 90
Jelly moulded with fruit 109
Kangaroo or wallaby steamer 105
Little pigs in blankets 93
Maids of honour 108
Meat pie (1660 recipe) 27
Meat pudding (bush recipe) 153
Milk, baked 182
Mutton and rice 176
Mutton and rice, steamed 104
Mutton, roast saddle 204

Olive custards 93
Orange sponge 205
Ox eyes 144
Oysters, curried 174
Pastry, suet 151
Pilaff 94
Potato gems 138
Pudding, Aunt Nellie's 167
Pudding, bread and butter 53
Pudding, cabinet 68
Pudding, Federation 43
Pudding, hasty 175
Pudding, Kingswood 36
Pudding, Kirkcudbright 65
Pudding, Louise 178
Pudding, Melbourne 141
Pudding, paradise 95
Pudding, poor woman's 166
Pudding, queen 95
Pudding, rice (with eggs) 204
Pudding, rice (without eggs) 205
Pudding, shearers' 78
Pudding, surprise 149
Pudding, treacle 67
Pudding, Victoria 142
Rabbit stew (camp cooking) 79
Rissoles (1730 recipe) 131
Rissoles of chicken 131
Rissoles, jam 130
Roly poly, jam 151
Sago jelly 176
Salad, Australian 75
Sauce for steamed puddings 176
Sauce, almond 95
Sauce, bread 203
Sauce, melted butter 53
Sauce, oyster 164
Scones, Quong Tart 63
Soup, mulligatawny 203

Soup, ox-tail 93
Soup, Sydney 140
Sprats (a nice way of cooking) 117
Trifle, Australian 141
Vermicelli porridge 177
Yeast 77

General
Abbott, Edward 26f, 105, 191ff
Aboriginal influence 85, 210
Acton, Eliza 88
adaptation of recipes 210f
adulteration of food 113f, 134
Aronson, Zara 99ff
Art of Living in Australia 28ff, 45
artistic presentation 100, 146f
Australian dishes 139ff
Australian Enquiry Book 81ff
Australian Etiquette 97
bachelor women 170
baked meat 57
Beeton, Isabella 14, 22, 184ff
blancmange 158
braised meat 58
bread 77f
breakfast menus 185f, 189f
buffet 194
bush and station cookery 77ff, 82, 85ff, 90, 153, 160
cakes and biscuits 38, 69ff, 74, 91, 110
Cambridge, Ada (Mrs George Cross) 13
camping and weekend cookery 170
Carter, Charles *Complete Practical Cook* 22
celebration in food 137
Chinese in Australia 62

247

Church Hill 113ff
Civil Service Stores 106
class distinctions 17, 96f, 189, 211f
Colcord, Anna *A Friend in the Kitchen* 21, 23
colour in food presentation 148f
cooked meat 91, 156f
cookery books 19ff, Appendix 1
cookery books (first Australian) 26
Cookery Class Recipes 125ff
cookery lessons 41, 44
Cookery Recipes for the People 52
cookery teaching 33, 40, 52f
Corrie, Sophie 162f
curry 173ff
damper 217f
diet 29f
dinner menus 51ff, 92ff, 192f, 198ff, 201ff
Dutch oven 57
economy 36f, 48, 79, 103, 163ff
English influence 45f, 206ff
entrée 101, 127
etiquette 97, 195ff
fantasy in food 144f
fast food 154
Federation food, description 213ff
fish and seafood 49f, 57, 89, 117f, 127f
foreign dishes 142, 158f
Fort Street Model School 39
French cookery 158
fritters 109f
fruit 12ff, 110, 119
fruit preserving 92, 161ff
game 27, 59, 86, 118f
garnishes 147f
gas cooking 123ff, 125
German influence 206ff
Gilmore, Dame Mary 76f
ginger 120
Goulburn Cookery Book 86ff, 92ff
Gould, Nat 13
hash 157
health 30ff
housekeeping 11, 81, 100
houses and furnishings 97ff, 110ff
imitation in cookery 155f
Indian influence 207

invalid cookery 126f, 180ff
Irish influence 206ff
Italian cookery 158f
jam 92, 161f, 163
jellies and creams 69, 108f
johnny cake 143
kangaroo 86, 105
Keeyuga Cookery Book 169ff
killing day on a station 84f, 159f
Kinglake, Edward 179
Kingswood Cookery Book 45, 49, 51
kitchen 18, 35, 82ff, 167ff, 171f
Kitchen Companion 84ff
Lamington 218
Liebig, his meat extract 120ff
lunch menus 31, 186f, 190
MacInnes, Mrs George 64
Maclurcan, Hannah 114ff, 190, 199ff
May, Robert *The Accomplisht Cook* 22
McGowan, Henrietta 169ff
meat 37, 50, 57f, 89f, 103ff, 128f
meat carving 101ff
meat consumption 12, 14ff, 103
meat cookery 57f, 89ff, 121f
meat pickled or cured 85, 159f
meat pie 218
meat tinned 43
menus 185ff (also individual entries)
mock dishes 79, 155f
Monro, Amie 44f
Morison, Rev. James 12
Mrs Maclurcan's Cookery Book 115ff
Muskett, Dr Philip 28ff, 33, 38ff
'muttonwool' 97, 110ff
naming dishes 137ff
National Training School, London 42, 43, 52, 125
origin of Australian cookery 206ff
oysters 34
Pearson, Margaret 52
pigeon 59
places in dish names 139ff
plain cookery 41, 44, 164ff
Presbyterian Church 61ff
Presbyterian cookery book 64ff, 73ff
prices 36
puddings 38, 66ff, 107ff

Quong Tart 62f
Rawson, Mina 11, 18, 80ff, 190
recipes, copied 166f
recipes, multiple 152f
remains, using up 156ff
rissoles 129ff, 184
roast meat 57
roly-poly 150
romance in food 145f, 212f
Ross, Isabel 125f
royalty, dishes named for 142
Rutledge, Jean 86ff, 189f
salad 31, 38
sauces 52, 89, 127
savouries 55f, 128
Schauer Cookery Book 53ff, 60, 150
Schauer, Amy 53ff, 60, 198
Scottish cookery 65, 206ff
seafood, see fish
service à la française 191f
service à la russe 193f
short cuts 154
sickroom cookery 126f, 180ff
soup 37, 46, 56, 127, 160
station cookery (see bush and station)
steamed meat 104f
stock 56, 84
Story, Annie Fawcett 40, 42
Story, Fanny Fawcett 43
supper menu 188
'surprise' dishes 149f
'survival' cookery 208f
sweetbreads 128
sweetness index 72f
Sydney Technical College 42
tea 16, 133, 218
tea menu 187f, 190, 197f
travel food 143
turtle soup 118
Twentieth Century Cookery 99ff
Twopenny, Richard 15, 96f
vegetables 37f, 48, 50, 106f, 119, 129, 160f
Walker gas cookers 123f
wallaby (see kangaroo)
Wentworth Hotel 113ff
Whiteside, Ramsay 40
Wicken, Harriet 43, 45, 198f
Wilkinson, Alfred 123f
wine 34
Women's Missionary Association 61ff, 64
Worker Cookbook 76ff
yeast 78
yin and yang 137